Praise for *Life Is Here, and*

"In *Life Is Here, and I Have Been A*
together two compelling narratives into a
a memoir of a young boy struggling to survive in the hostile environment of an all-boys boarding school and an intimate portrait of a loving mother climbing her way out of deep depression to be reunited with her sons, *Life Is Here, and I Have Been Away* begins with Bessie's mother, Mary Burnett, as she stands on the brink of suicide. She realizes she needs help and, for the sake of her sons, signs herself into a psychiatric clinic. There, with the help of her journals, she sifts through her life, searching for the root causes of her illness, so she can come to terms with and heal her past.

"In the meantime, Dan and his brother, David, are sent to a boarding school, where they encounter strict religious authority and a gang of vicious bullies. The two boys, who do not know where their mother has gone, do their best to protect each other while hoping she will return and bring them home.

"Tender, compassionate, and deeply moving, *Life Is Here, and I Have Been Away* reminds us that the motivating force of love truly can overcome the darkness of emotional trauma and bring healing and light to the future."

—Amber Lea Starfire, editor, writing coach, and award-winning author of *Not the Mother I Remember* (MoonSkye Publishing, 2013) and *Times They Were A-Changing; Women Remember the '60s and '70s* (She Writes Press, 2013)

"A compassionate, considered account of one woman's struggle with mental illness, with suicide's seductive call, and with a heroic reinvention of her life and ambitions. Additionally, as the story interweaves actual documents with empathetic imagining on the author's part, it feels like an honest but loving attempt to understand how people fall apart and put themselves back together again—how the circumstances of our lives, and often the people who are in them and then leave, also shape our emotional perspective, our very core self.

"The story is told with careful deliberation and gentle humor, and, too, doesn't shy away from the difficult, heartbreaking moments—though the language never veers toward overwrought sentimentality or salacious investigation. The characters in this memoir retain their dignity because of its empathetic rendering. This will be an important addition to our understanding of women living through mental illness, despite a culture that generally offers little support."

—Kerry Beth Neville, short story writer, creative writing teacher, and author of *Necessary Lies* (BkMK Press, 2006) and *Remember to Forget Me* (Braddock Avenue Books, 2017); stories and essays included in *Best American Essays* and *Best American Short Stories*; coordinator of the MFA program and faculty member at Georgia College and State University

"As Mary Burnett struggles with depression and self-doubt through her thirties and forties and finally expels her demons, *Life is Here, and I Have Been Away* makes visible the power of women to shape their own lives. By weaving together much of the material from her journals and other writing, Dan Bessie augments his mother's strength in a loving and respectful manner, one that makes the events of her life, and those of his brother and himself (then nine and six), accessible without becoming maudlin. Mary's journey from the depths of despair to achieve the goal she's long sought—'to be of some use in this world'—resolves in a strong, affirmative conclusion. I highly recommend *Life Is Here, and I Have Been Away*, a story that will move and inspire its readers."

—Yetta Goodman, Regents Professor Emeritus, University of Arizona; credited with popularizing the concept of "kidwatching" (i.e., encouraging teachers to be professional observers of the language and learning development of their students)

"I read *Life Is Here, and I Have Been Away* in a sitting. So much of Mary Burnett's struggle with mental illness resonated with me, as someone who has also suffered bouts of serious depression. Mary's story is told partly in her own words, collated from the eloquent and moving notebooks of the book's title, as well as in the equally powerful and lyrical voice of her son Dan, both as a boy and as a narrator. At times, the subject matter is harrowing, but Mary finds a way to recovery that can help anyone facing their own demons."

—Rachel Kelly, reporter, health columnist, and author of the *London Sunday Times* top-ten bestseller *Black Rainbow: How Words Healed Me—My Journey through Depression* (Hodder & Stoughton, 2014)

"As a therapist and coach, I've long known the value of diary work. This book humbly, yet powerfully, illustrates the value of reflective journaling.

"Dan Bessie's most excellent book chronicling his mother's troubled journey from mental illness to mental wellness is beautifully written. Mary was a successful and influential woman in her community, championing the enhancement and development of young lives, but very few knew of her earlier life struggles. After Mary's death, Dan Bessie discovered his mother had left diary entries that told of a time of deep heartache, near suicide, and the deep desire to somehow be 'of use to this world.' As he worked his way through the many volumes, he came to the conclusion that her story needed to be told to inspire others and to prove to the world that from the depths of despair can arise great strength.

"This is not a depressing book. It's not a book full of the theory of overcoming depression and finding life's meaning. It is, instead, the story of a real woman finding a real way through harrowing emotions, thoughts, and circumstances. This makes it deeply powerful and life-changing. I read the book in the space of two weeks, and I found Mary walked with me throughout those two weeks. She was a living, breathing woman who was working through her life, and I felt her courage influence mine. It is therefore no surprise that I firmly believe *Life Is Here, and I Have Been Away* is a book that should be shared far and wide."

—Beverly Taylor, coach, counselor, and trainer specializing in stress management, depression, addiction, communication skills, and cognitive behavioral therapy

LIFE IS HERE, AND I HAVE BEEN AWAY

DAN BESSIE

BELLE ISLE BOOKS
www.belleislebooks.com

ISBN: 978-1-951565-85-5
LCCN: 2022901285

Designed by Michael Hardison
Project managed by Grace Ball

Printed in the United States of America

Published by
Belle Isle Books (an imprint of Brandylane Publishers, Inc.)
5 S. 1st Street
Richmond, Virginia 23219

BELLE ISLE BOOKS
www.belleislebooks.com

belleislebooks.com | brandylanepublishers.com

To Mary Burnett, who gifted David and me with her diaries, notebooks, and other writings that detail the sometimes sad but ultimately awe-inspiring story of all she went through on the way to becoming a kind and thoughtful mother and guide to everyone who knew her—especially to countless young children. And to any reader, for the effort to overcome whatever challenges the years may have burdened you with before moving on.

To David Bessie, for his brotherly affection, for standing by me through the good times and those not so good, and for all we've meant to one another.

To my amazingly perceptive and much-loved wife and best friend Jeanne (née Olieff) Johnson. Without her constant encouragement and remarkable insight into what both Mary and I wrote, my struggle to create something Jeanne and I feel is worthwhile would have been akin to the futile effort of Sisyphus pushing his gigantic boulder up the mountain.

FOREWORD

I was bowled over by the close bond I felt with Mary Burnett. What a woman! What a survivor! What an expressive artist and writer she was! It's the kind of book that women will read and say, "Oh my God, that's my story!"

Life Is Here, and I Have Been Away is a beautiful book. It will speak to anyone who has coped with depression or lived with a loved one who has. Single parents will also connect with this tale of a woman struggling to make sense of her relationships: with her children, with the men in her life, and with her place in the world. Although the book is set in the thirties and forties, the deeply felt words in these intimate notebooks speak to today's woman. The pages are filled with universal issues we all face as women in a post-Victorian world. With the pen as her tool, Mary travels through a tangled mass of confusion and despair to find herself. An alchemist, she turns pain and despair into gold as she discovers her path of service to the world.

The ability to write is also passed down. A special gift of this book is her son's side of the story. We see a child's vivid experiences growing up with an extraordinarily courageous mother facing hard, hard times. *Life Is Here, and I Have Been Away* is a present from a son to his mother and is filled with love on every page. Although this is *not* a self-help book, it is an inspiring example of how one person approached the huge problem of depression and overcame the deadly demons that plagued her for so long. In this regard, Mary's story is timely in today's world, where depression and anxiety are skyrocketing.

I was deeply moved by the author's dedication to letting his mother tell her story. The organization of the material truly illuminates and elucidates for the reader the context of her experiences, historically and socially.

—Lucia Capacchione, PhD, art and journal therapist,
author of twenty-three self-help titles, including *The Creative Journal: The Art of Finding Yourself* (Career Press, 2002) and *Recovery of Your Inner Child* (Simon & Shuster, 1991)
http://expressivearts.com/bio.html, http://www.luciac.com

PREFACE

My decision to create this memoir began when I opened a big box of diaries I found in my mother's tiny apartment after she died in March 1982—diaries containing not only notes about everyday events, but also an abundance of meditations on life that revealed the perceptive person she was:

The whirlpool, the human destiny. The running scared. The things we learn about, the way we look and judge, advise, gossip, denounce, put down, condemn until comes the day we discover we've been looking outward (for years then more years) before we begin to know what the mirror is trying to tell us. Either way, whether you're trapped in another's whirlpool or one of your own making it seems more helpful to recognize that you have let yourself get trapped in one. Somewhere along the way we have to learn, to know—without judgment.

—Mary Burnett, August 14, 1978

The box held journals too; journals crammed with her eighty-three years of experience. And other writing: short stories, snatches of poetry, and notes about growing up. Mom's early years were somewhat unworldly and starry-eyed—though basically a happy childhood in spite of an often-frustrating mother, who, steeped in Victorian sensibilities, constantly pushed her children to succeed.

And they did. Mom's oldest brother, Leo Burnett, founded what became one of America's largest advertising agencies and was selected as one of *TIME* magazine's one hundred most influential people of the twentieth century. The middle brother, Verne, achieved success in the corporate world. The youngest brother, Harry, became a celebrated puppeteer. For Mary, her mother envisioned marriage to a "substantial provider, someone quite unlike your father," who she regarded as "too soft."

But Mary's creative mind and romantic sensibilities wanted something more. It would take decades for her to formulate and eventually realize a vision of her own. Despite memorable periods of happiness along the way, until her mid-forties Mom's road was all too often rutted with disappointment and self-doubt, dispiriting detours frequently knocking her off course. As with countless women of every age, anxiety, depression, divorce, and financial hardship were huge factors in holding her back.

How, then, did Mary Burnett become the remarkable person she was: a supportive, warm-hearted, and loyal friend to everyone around her? How did she manage to give so much to my brother David and me? As I delved more deeply into her writing, I began to understand: here was a woman brave enough to look inward, to recognize exactly what the mirror was telling her, and to become fiercely determined to overcome the "slings and arrows of outrageous fortune"[1] she'd had to deal with and move on to fulfill a long-felt need to (as she frequently put it) "be of some use in the world."

This memoir, then, is her story, drawn from her own writing, and augmented by the memory of my own experiences as a young boy. But anyone reading about where my mother found herself at age forty-three might well assume she'd never reach forty-four.

---

1 From Shakespeare's *Hamlet*, Act III, Scene I

PART I: DEAD OF NIGHT

Mind led body to the
edge of the precipice.
They stared in desire
at the naked abyss.
If you love me, said
mind, take that step
into silence
If you love me, said body,
turn and exist.

—Ann Stevenson[2]

2 From her poem "Vertigo"

1.

Danbury, Connecticut. January 1943

Spring rains have swollen Candlewood Lake to the top of its banks, almost to flood stage. Standing by the shore, Mary Burnett is vaguely aware of the distant cackling of Canada geese. But her attention is drawn elsewhere, to beyond a grove of still-naked birches where a windblown swell of waves surging past seems urgent and inviting. She gazes at the cold, comforting water, whose obliterating depth could so easily wash away the past. The tendrils of slimy green lake-weed waving softly back and forth just below the surface look like beckoning hands.

"It would be easy," she mumbles. "So easy . . ."

Go ahead; do it then, urges the chorus of demon voices she'd been struggling to ignore since the painful events of 1941 reached their tragic conclusion in November of that year. Depression and loneliness had been no strangers since even before then, but of late they've moved furtively into her house. And they've lingered, obsessing each waking moment, turning every chance remark into an accusation.

In one of her later journals, my mother would look back on the months leading to that nearly fatal day at Candlewood Lake . . .

2.

Santa Monica, California. August 1962

Depression, loneliness had rarely been strangers to me during the years of striving to discover of what stuff life is made. Brief episodes had assaulted my brain after leaving a failed marriage in 1925, and again in 1938 when the boys and I struggled to get by on relief while their father, my second husband, was absent for a year. Though on both occasions a distraction came along—a cause, the greater needs of a friend—events that helped pull me out of my self-pitying gloom.

In the winter of 1942-43, the demons moved into my house again. Louder and more insistent this time, like uninvited guests who long since should have announced, 'We've had a good time, Mary, and should we ever meet again, we'll always remember your many kindnesses, the feasts you prepared, your untiring efforts to make our stay pleasant."

Instead they lingered, sucking me into their putrid black hole of despondency. Oh, I continued functioning, performing everyday tasks: packing lunch boxes, doing laundry, shopping—but always with a gnawing sorrow. My "Hi, how's everything?" when Danny and David came barging in after school was still voiced, but with the old joy and gladness gone. There was no caring. Day after day dragged by with an increasing sense of guilt over the poor job of mothering I was doing. What was there to do but continue trying to penetrate this monstrous fog, to fight it off with the only weapons I had? Yet with a constant "end of the rope" feeling, what weapons were there? I could mop the floors every day, paint the windowsills, or hang new curtains in the boys' bedroom. None of it worked. When Danny asked why we were rearranging the furniture when we'd done it just days before, I snapped back, "Just help me, will you?"

It had become a repeating pattern. Night after night, I'd sit in the kitchen, feeling little but the hopelessness that invaded every waking moment. Weeks had passed. Birds had long since flown south. Snow had caked the bare branches in the backyard, and I'd barely noticed. Tomorrow, Dan would want money for the movies. Well, why not? It was the only treat I could give him, or afford.

Slowly I climbed the stairs to my room and lay on the floor. There would be awhile yet before the demands of supper would pull me out of my desolation.

Then it happened. How did it come to me? What words flashed through my mind? Instantly, I had the answer. The irrefutable and final answer: I would kill myself. This was not the cavity of loneliness known and lived through long ago; this was the sudden opening of a door into the future. In that frightening moment, I entered the secret world. Little did I know of the journey I was about to take, a journey along the silent shore where the wind is still "and no birds sing."[3]

---

3 From the *poem La Belle Dame sans Mercia*, by John Keats.

◆◆◆◆◆

Time passed. How much? Twenty minutes? An hour? Feeling like a sack of potatoes, I pulled myself from the floor and walked into my son's bedroom. There they were: Davy almost seven, Dan not yet ten, sleeping in their separate beds. All that sustained me in that moment was a profound yet amorphous sense of guilt. I looked down at each of them. *My sons,* I thought. *What will become of you?* Momentarily it seemed I could fight, keep on automatically doing the things of every day, and by the doing, life would come back into focus. But even as the spark flared, it died, for the room, the house itself had become a framework for shoving around meaningless pieces of furniture that could never be rearranged to make a home. My private brand of magic, of somehow muddling through life's major catastrophes, was a rotten apple. The cart I was hauling with its load of fruit had suddenly turned upside down and spilled its load for all to see, a sodden, moldy mess, a symbol of my disintegration. Shame and guilt had settled and taken root. Mind and body were going down together.

◆◆◆◆◆

As I stirred breakfast oatmeal the next morning, both boys came into the kitchen, excited, dressed, and ready to head out for the Saturday movie matinee I'd promised they could attend.

"Don't you undress when you go to bed, Mom?" Danny asked. "Your clothes look like you slept in them."

"Are you sick?" asked David.

I stared at them blankly for several moments, began to feel slightly dizzy, but after a deep breath I answered, "I'm just a bit tired. And I have a little headache." Could I say it, admit what I was feeling? That I was a "dirty mother." What more could a six- and a nine-year-old understand? While Danny stood waiting for the answer to his question, I stared off into space, vaguely aware of his "Mom?" or of David going to the sink to fill a glass of water then bringing it to me, along with an aspirin.

I did my best to smile. "You really know how to look after people, don't you, Davy?" I said. And my little boy betrayed a proud grin.

As they left, I stood in the hall saying goodbye. "I'll probably come by the theater after the show," I said, "and we'll stop by Chew's Café for a Chinese lunch."

Thinking back after they were out the door, I could see that my recent listless attempts at mothering had become increasingly confusing to them. Though I forced myself to inspire a bit of cheer, money was tight, and I knew it would have to be the cheapest plate of chow mein. Turning back into the kitchen, I caught my reflection in the hall mirror. Framed in the glass was a sallow, plain-looking woman of forty-three with an expressionless mouth and soft black hair streaked with gray and pulled into a severe bun. With a face empty of color, and, echoing Danny's accusation, I was wearing the same faded print housedress I'd not considered changing for days. *The mirror doesn't lie,* I thought. *You've let yourself get to looking like some downtrodden migrant from the Oklahoma dust bowl. What the hell happened to you? Where did it all go, Mary? The great joy you felt in Vermont the day Danny was born, David's birth? Getting all dolled up to go into Manhattan to take the boys to Macy's Thanksgiving Day Parade? Laughing with David as he tossed peanuts to the monkeys in the Prospect Park Zoo?*

Overcome by self-pity again, I began to sob, moved into the kitchen, paced back and forth, then stopped to stare out the window at nothing in particular. Tears gradually abating, I scanned the room; the cereal box that hadn't been put away, the unwashed breakfast dishes sitting in the sink, the row of knives in their wooden caddy. My gaze halted at the gas stove. I stared at it, wondering . . .

My mind had become a blank. Without another thought, I stuffed a dishtowel under the kitchen door leading to the backyard.

Then I collapsed into a chair and the tears resumed. *A dirty mother,* said my inner voice. *You're a dirty mother. Useless.* I sat at the table, crying for I don't know how long.

Finally, the sense of shame I felt at being unable to hide from the eyes of my own children pulled me upstairs to grab my frayed mouton coat from a closet and search frantically for a stylish brown felt hat I'd once worn with much panache, to now pull haphazardly down over my ears. I felt in a panic. Confused. I had to do something. Do what? How?

The chorus of demon voices rose again and wouldn't leave me alone. *You know the answer, Mary,* they taunted. Could I ignore them?

Put things in order, I told myself. I started downstairs. After all, I'd burned a bunch of old junk the previous night. That was a start. I'd spent the evening in the basement, sorting through a large battered suitcase I'd lugged around since leaving for college in 1917. Though it originally held clothes, it had long since become a traveling archive of my life. Now, half the contents were gone; decades of accumulated papers and correspondence documenting old regrets, sorrows, and outlived experiences had been consigned to the flames. If I was truly going to end it all, there was to be no suggestion I'd led anything but a circumspect life.

Put things in order, put things in order; the mantra kept repeating.

And now I was downtown at the bank, examining my check stubs to see if there was enough money to cover the two or three small bills that loomed like mountainous debts too long owed, for light, coal, food. These, I knew, couldn't be left for my brothers to find. They must be able to say, "Well, at least she left her affairs in pretty good shape." And I recalled my father's final words before he died: "Take care of yourself, Sis," he told me, "and remember to live within your means."

As I signed the checks, there was a second of wonder at how easily one signs their name. *When, where,* I asked myself, *does a little scribble, accomplished with such ease, have a beginning?* And there was a momentary feeling of having a skill, one small thing emerging from the lived past to give me confidence, make me feel a person again. But it fled on silent wings as quickly as it had come, and, conscious of my inability to return the smile of a woman I knew as I moved across the marble floor, I hurried out.

Concrete now, the sidewalks cold and impersonal. Though alive with cars and Saturday shoppers, to me the streets were empty. I had walked only a block or two before the voices sneaked in again, a reminder that life seemed without purpose: three failed marriages; needing to rely on the occasional small check from my brothers to support myself and the boys; having to give up for lack of funding the little backyard playgroup I'd started for children of mothers working in wartime industries—something that had briefly made me feel of genuine use.

"Oh, sorry, please excuse me," said a passerby after bumping into me. I stopped and looked around. Being seen by people suddenly became insufferable. Strangers seemed to be gathered in little knots, talking.

Talking about me? It has to be. They know me. Me, a despicable, loathsome "thing." I pulled my coat collar up, avoiding their looks. *I must get away quickly, out of sight, up the side streets, through the alleys. But to where?* Making sure my coat was buttoned tightly so no one would notice my shabby dress, I ducked into a small, almost empty café, ordered coffee, and sat composing suicide notes on napkins. But unable to decide where to leave them, I crumpled and stuffed them into a pocket, and, placing two nickels on the bill, got ready to leave. But at the doorway I paused, panic rising once more. An entering customer, annoyed, cleared his throat. I stepped aside.

As I wandered beyond downtown and into a residential area toward . . . toward I didn't know what . . . some aimless destination, the haunting words returned. I was heading to "the silent shore where the wind is still and no birds sing."

And then I stood on that shore—at the edge of Danbury's Candlewood Lake.

◆◆◆◆◆

How long had I been standing there? I had no idea. The morning had become one continuous blur. The only sensation I felt was of the slender thread holding me to life during the past many months, the thread that alternately stretched and threatened to break then tightened, pulling me back from the edge.

As the waving lake weeds continued to beckon, my inner demons kept repeating their lethal invitation: *Do it, Mary. Just do it!*

A chill wind started to kick up. I remember taking a step toward the water, my shoes crunching the thin ice still clinging to the shore.

The demon voices again . . .

"Be still," I mumbled. "Be still."

As my eyes fixed on a dead, floating limb pushed along by the wind, images of Danny and David materialized in the trailing ripples and began to reel through my head like an old black and white movie: Danny at three, his mop of curls bobbing up and down amid a grassy Vermont meadow; a Christmas evening at my brother Verne's New York apartment, with Davy at two, asleep and slumped over like a big rag doll on an ottoman chair; both boys inviting me into the "secret cave" they'd put together with the sofa, the chairs, and an old frayed blanket in our Danbury living room.

The images signaled a resistance, and I cried out, "My boys! My darling boys!"

Suddenly I remembered my promise to take them for Chinese after the show. . . . *They're probably home by now, waiting for me. . . .*

Was the mental fog so thick that I'd completely forgotten?

And once again, the voices: *Time to stop procrastinating, Mary. You've always been so indecisive. . . . Go ahead, just do it!*

"No, I can't! My boys . . ."

Quitter, carped the voices. *Quitter!*

The voices seemed to be coming from the lake itself.

"No! No!" I cried out, shaking my head. "I can't. Not now . . . The boys . . . I have to get home to my boys. . . ." *My God, did I turn the gas on?*

With a sudden mixture of fear and determination, I turned from the lake and started hurrying along the street, winding up the long hill toward the only place there was, the house that could no longer hide my shame.

3.

"What's that smell?" asked my brother, Davy, as I opened the front door of our house in Danbury after we returned from the Saturday matinee.

"It's gas," I told him. "Stay on the porch." And I started along the hall, stopping every few steps before heading into the kitchen, from which I heard a low, hissing sound.

"Where's Mom?" my brother demanded as he came up behind me.

"Just go wait outside!" I insisted.

The stove's oven door was open, and the gas was on. I quickly shut it off. Then I noticed a dishtowel stuffed under the door leading to the back porch, jerked it away, and shouted into the yard. "Mom, are you out there?"

No reply.

"How come there's gas?" Davy asked, following me into the kitchen. "Where's Mom?"

I spun around to face him and yelled, "Go back out front!"

"No, I won't. I—"

"Go wait out front! It's dangerous!"

Davy hesitated, then hurried back up the hall.

Panic! I paused for a moment. Then, covering my mouth with the dishtowel, I rushed around the house opening windows. In Mom's room, Mackie, David's black cocker spaniel, was lying on the bed wagging his tail. I scooped him up, hurried back to the front porch, and set him down next to my brother.

"I gotta find Mom," I announced as I leaped off the porch.

"Where are you going?"

"To find her! I think she said something about taking us for Chinese food. Maybe she decided to meet us at the Palace."

"I'll come too."

"No! Stay here in case she comes home; stay on the porch with Mackie. There's still a lotta gas."

I sprinted off down the block. Moments later I pulled up short with a sudden thought. Mom wouldn't know the movie had let out early. . . . Maybe she'd been planning to buy something to cook and forgot to light the gas? *Yeah, that's it; she's at the A & P. . . . Just a couple blocks* . . . And I was off again.

No, wait. She'd said she'd take us to Chew's café. But she coulda changed her mind. . . . So, I raced into the store and ran up and down the front, scanning the aisles. No Mom.

I ran out again, deciding she'd probably planned to meet us at the theater.

Then why did she turn the gas on?

I headed back toward where I'd started. Running the next mile along a tree-lined street, I relived all that had happened since breakfast. Mom hadn't even smiled when I left. In fact, she hardly smiled at all anymore, and I'd been so annoyed when she insisted I take Davy along to the show. That had immediately killed the plan my pal Kenji Okanishi and I had to sneak into the old Rialto Theater, a decaying wreck that Kenji called "the rat hole." Who knew what we might have found inside?

As I raced toward the Palace, hoping to find Mom there, I thought back about the film.

After the *Green Hornet* serial, a big burning hole like the sun suddenly spread over the screen, and the film, *King of the Zombies*, stopped ten minutes in. A couple minutes later the lights came up, and the little bald-headed manager appeared to announce that the film had caught fire and it might take a couple hours to fix it. All the kids stood up and started booing and hissing and tossing popcorn at each other. Davy wanted to stay but I told him we should leave.

Outside, Rico, the dumbest kid in my school, began to rag Kenji and called me a "Jap lover" when I stood up for him, and shoved me into another couple kids while Rico's two buddies laughed—until the manager showed up and broke it off. Rico shook his fist, cursed me, and said, "This ain't finished yet, you curly-headed jerkoff freak. I'll get you!"

By the time I reached the Palace, I remembered; the show had long since let out. If Mom had been here, she'd know that by now. *Better get home,* I thought, *she's probably there; she never goes off for long without telling us where she'll be.*

My stomach was in knots.

Gotta be calm, gotta get home. But what if she's not there? Davy'll be getting worried. Tears welled up, and even though my legs felt like rubber, I kept on running as fast as I could back though town. *Gotta find Mom. She has to be at home. Have to tell her she left the gas on . . . And ask about that towel under the door . . .*

Out of breath as I turned the corner onto our block, I spotted Rico racing up the sidewalk toward me, his two buddies right behind him. I stopped short, certain I was about to get knocked around.

"Getoutatheway!" he screamed as he roared past, clutching his behind.

I jumped clear. Whirling around, I saw that the seat of his pants had been ripped open. Chasing after Rico and his buddies was Mackie, yapping furiously.

Seconds later, Davy tore past, shouting, "Come back and fight!"

Momentarily stunned, I recovered enough to yell, "Mackie, Davy, stop!"

Davy pulled up short, looked around, then grudgingly returned, angry, teary-eyed, his shirt a torn, grass-stained mess.

"What happened?" I asked. My brother, whose fists were still at the ready, stood glaring down the street.

"Rico and his stupid friends came by," he began. "They . . . they were gonna beat you up, but I told him to get lost. He said our father was no good 'cause he ran away from Mom . . . so I started punching him, and he ripped my shirt. Mackie came down the steps an' started biting his legs . . . and we were wrestling on the lawn, and . . ."

"Hi there," a voice called.

We both turned. Mom was hurrying toward us from around the corner. Trailed by Mackie, still barking like mad, we ran to Mom, our tears of relief flowing.

"Why weren't you at home?" sobbed Davy.

"Where've you been?" I cried.

Where have I been? she wrote, as I discovered years later in another of her journal entries. *What can I tell them? That I've been to the edge and back again?* She put her arms around us and tried her best to sound cheerful: "Oh, I just needed a long walk. I'm so sorry you were worried. I should have left you a note. How was the movie?"

"They stopped it," I told her. "Because of the fire."

"Fire? What fire? At the theater?"

I sniffed back tears. "How come you left the gas on, Mom? I turned it off, and—"

"In the movie," Davy interjected. "And how come—"

"A fire in the movie? I don't—"

Impatient for Mom to hear him out, Davy trailed us as we climbed the steps.

"The film caught on fire," I added.

"Were either of you hurt?" she asked, turning to look us over.

"Jeez, Mom, it was on the screen," I went on. "And there was a dishtowel under the back door, and—"

Jerking at Mom's coat, Davy demanded, "How come Papa doesn't live with us?"

"Shut up, will you!" I hissed.

"No, I won't shut up!"

"I'm talking about the gas."

"I don't care about the gas!" shouted my brother.

Caught between news of the incident and our anxious questions, Mom took a deep, hesitant breath before answering. "Well, let's go in the house, and I'll put on some nice hot soup, and we'll talk about everything, okay? About the fire and—"

"No!" shouted Davy. "About Papa. Tell me now!"

"And about the gas," I demanded.

"Well . . . well, It's kind of complicated . . . but after lunch, I'll—"

Davy's tears welled up again. He turned and bolted down the street, with Mackie bounding after and yapping loudly.

"David . . ." Mom called halfheartedly.

"Come on back, Davy! Mackie! Come back!" I shouted.

"They will. They'll come back," said Mom, exhausted, drained of emotion.

But all we could hear in the gathering twilight was the fading sound of my brother's running feet and the barks of his feisty cocker spaniel.

David's forever faithful Mackie, who he later reluctantly agreed to have adopted by a Danbury friend.

4.

With the sun going down, unable to cope with any more drama, Mom set about making dinner as I, still agitated about the gas and worried about my brother, stood by the kitchen counter tapping a spoon.

"For God's sake, stop that!" Mom snapped. "Just go on and set the table."

"Okay," I grumbled, stunned by her retort. "But what about David?" I added. "Shouldn't I go look for him? It's getting dark."

"He's smart enough to be back before then. But go if you want." Mom shrugged. "Just get back before dinner."

As I grabbed my jacket and headed for the front door, I saw her slump into a chair with her head in her hands.

◆◆◆◆◆

What to do? I thought. *So many questions . . . "Oh God defend me! How am I beset! What kind of—"* I dropped my hands to the table and looked up. *'God defend me?'* Then I remembered; it was a line I'd learned long years before in high school when I played Hero in *Much Ado About Nothing.*

No, Mary! No! I told myself. *You can't wait for God to come to your rescue. You've got to find a way out of this by yourself. For you and the*

Mary's high school photo

boys. Then something clicked: why not explore writing from my past? There must have been a less depressing time; months, years even, when life was positive, cheerful, upbeat. When I didn't feel the need to burn old letters or write suicide notes.

I got up, hurried to open the cellar door, and started down the stairs.

Old letters? Old journals? Maybe there's something in those? And with this glimmer of hope, I pulled my battered suitcase from its dusty shelf, clicked it open, and began scanning the writing I hadn't burned, anything that might help me escape the mental quicksand.

Plenty still here, I thought. I sorted through the contents, snapped the case shut, picked it up, and turned toward the stairs. Fixed across the rafters lay the water pipes from which a week earlier I'd thought to hang myself; that was the day I'd also rummaged frantically through a storage cabinet for a rope as the carping voices assaulted my mind yet again: *Go ahead, Mary, have done with it!*

But I'd never found the rope.

And if I had, would I have done it? Could I do it now? What of its effect on the boys?

"Oh dear God!" I suddenly cried out. *Affect them? How can you even ask that? Don't you see what it's already doing? Danny, always questioning, going into a sulk when I chide him for something trivial, and whose every look tells me he knows something's not right with his mom. And David, dear Davy, whose demand reminded me there would be no father to look after them. No Alvah, with his new life in California now... and no Harold.*

As the tears began to flow, I heard the cellar door open. Danny was back.

◆◆◆◆◆

Standing at the top of the stairs, I called, "Mom, are you down there?"

"Be right up," she called back.

As she reached the stairs, I thought I saw her dabbing her eyes. "What's the suitcase for?" I asked. "Are we going someplace?"

"No, just some old stuff I've been wanting to look at, and—"

"I couldn't find Davy," I sighed. "He musta got lost."

Mom arrived on the landing and closed the cellar door. "Well, Mackie isn't back yet, either, so hows about you turn on the porch light while I put this old suitcase in my room. Then come wait in the kitchen with me while I finish cooking dinner."

I headed back along the hall, clicked on the porch light, and opened the door. Outside, I crossed to the edge of the sidewalk and looked both ways along the deserted street. No sign of my brother.

Back in the kitchen, Mom was cutting up vegetables. I fell into a chair and watched as she mechanically poured carrots and a few small potatoes into the soup pot, then lit a burner.

"Mom," I finally asked, "How come you left the gas on before? It was coming out of the oven when we came home. But it wasn't lit."

She didn't turn around.

"Oh, well . . ." She hesitated, as though searching for a reply. "I guess . . . Well, I thought about baking a cake and was getting ready to melt some butter, some chocolate for a topping, and—"

"There was a dishtowel under the back door."

She turned back to face me but said nothing.

◆◆◆◆◆

How could I tell a boy of ten that his mother had been about to do away with herself? Would it make him angry? Terrify him? One parent was already absent. And not so long ago, to spare the boys a painful and complicated explanation, I'd lied about how my last husband, Harold Frisbie, a gentle and caring man I'd hoped might be a kind of surrogate father, had died. What should I have said?

◆◆◆◆◆

But at the time, she had to offer an explanation. Hoping I was old enough to understand if she just let it come out piece by piece, she decided to let my reactions guide what she'd say. She pulled out a chair, sat down, and took both my hands in hers—something she only did when she had a serious thought to get across.

"This might be hard, sweetie," she began, "but you see, things have been pretty difficult for me lately, and . . . Well, it's not easy to explain, but . . . Do you know how it feels when you get really sad? Like everything and everybody in the world is against you?"

"I guess. Sometimes."

Mom seemed about to choke up, but then she coughed and cleared her throat. "Well," she said. "Well, you see, that's the way I've been feeling for a long time. You see . . ."

But finally, unable to carry on, she broke down crying, pulled her hands away, and covered her face.

I rose from the chair. "Gosh, Mom," I said, "what's the matter? Is it about Davy? Or me? Did we—"

At the sound of barking, we both looked up. The front door banged open, and Mackie, caked in mud, bounded into the kitchen—followed by David, shivering and bedraggled, his shoes sodden, a trouser leg torn, and tears flooding down his face.

As I tried to calm Mackie and sponged him off, Mom did her best to pull herself together. But at a loss for words, she dabbed at her eyes and stared at Davy for several moments before asking, in the same emotionless tone that had become normal of late, "Where were you all this time?"

"Jeez, Davy, I was out looking for you forever," I said, in a mixture of anger and relief.

Breaking into sobs, Davy rushed to Mom.

Unable to offer anything but a tentative hug, her arms fell to her side as Davy blurted out, "I just ran and ran. I got to the mill pond and was gonna go across and find the road around the lake and come back, but Mackie was barking and running along the bank and getting all dirty, and I started to cross the pond on an old log, but it broke and I fell in, and . . ."

"You fell in?" I exclaimed. "You coulda drowned . . . right, Mom?"

She barely nodded, her face still empty of expression.

"Cripes, it wasn't deep!" Davy railed. "And Mackie grabbed my pants with his teeth and pulled me on the bank, and we got out, and it was a long time before I could find the road, but we did, and we cut across through the cemetery and found our street, and . . ."

Breaking off, his sobs finally became huge gasps.

Slowly, Mom stood and in a flat voice said, "Okay, well, you're home now, so go get cleaned up and into dry clothes, and I'll finish making supper."

I looked at Davy, sighed, then mumbled, "Pretty dumb, if you ask me."

◆◆◆◆◆

Later that evening, Mom sat in the wing-back chair in her bedroom with Davy and me on the rug by her feet. I noticed her staring at a water stain that traced a long line down the fading wallpaper. She'd already evaded my brother's renewed question about why our father had left, and had launched instead into a disjointed ramble about the war, trying to get across the idea that bad people were trying to take over the world, and President Roosevelt was working hard to stop them. He was a good and wise man, she said, an honest president, and had helped America through the dark days when thousands of men roamed the country looking for work, and when millions of children went to bed hungry every night.

Her talk, of little interest to me in my muddled state of mind, and, meaning nothing to Davy, had us both feeling confused and miserable. Looking back now, I think Mom was probably trying to find a way to end a stressful day on a calming note.

"Well then, sleepy time," she finally announced, sensing our lack of attention. And after perfunctory goodnight hugs, we headed reluctantly to our room.

"No reading from Mom tonight," I told Davy as he crawled into bed.

"No Windy Willers? Jeez, we're never gonna find out what happened after Mister Toad stole that motor car."

"*Wind in the Willows.*"

"Huh?

"That's the name of the book. *The Wind in the Willows.*"

"I don't care," mumbled my brother as he rolled over in bed.

After several moments I offered a tentative, "Sorry."

No response. So I pulled the covers up, glanced at Davy, who seemed to be sniffling, and drifted back to thinking about Mom. *When's she ever gonna get back to who she was?* I wondered. And now Davy's all upset. *Jeez, what's wrong with her?*

◆◆◆◆◆

Lost for a while in my own dark, foreboding thoughts as I stared at the wallpaper stain, I eventually became aware of an occasional muffled sob from down the hall, then listlessly forced myself from the chair to look in on the boys. Somehow I managed my expected nightly recitation, which, though I didn't know it then, would be almost the last time for months I'd be able to offer a comforting word. "Try not to worry, dears," I said as brightly as I could. "Sleep tight; don't let the bedbugs bite."

Davy was lying face to the wall, and neither of them added their usual, "And if they do, bite 'em back."

As I returned to the chair in my room, a deathly weariness began to permeate my body. Within minutes, I was asleep. In the fog of a half-dream state, I saw myself standing on the damp earth of a deep cave. Above me was a wide, grilled gate.

I'd hold onto these images for many years . . .

My family stood outside: my father, mother, and three brothers, Leo, Verne and Harry. All stood silently, somber, tight-lipped, arms at their sides, like pallbearers at a funeral. Behind me, in the far recesses of the cave, were sounds—yet not sounds, more a knowledge within me of "insanity," and knowledge that somehow there was no other place to go. Still looking at my family outside, I cried, "Help!" but no word emerged. In the dream there was an urgency that they hear me, and again I cried, "Help!" Unmoving they stood, like zombies. They hadn't heard the cry I couldn't voice.

◆◆◆◆◆

Startled from the dream and in a sweat, I remained haunted by the phantoms. Were these to become yet another symbol of hopelessness in my fractured existence? I felt the inner demons beginning to stir and once again feared the thread of life was about to break.

"No!" I whispered. "I won't let you drag me into your miserable hole again."

Rousing myself, I got up, then sat on the rug to open the old suitcase. Instantly, my gaze fell on one of my recent diaries. I opened it and turned a few pages. The first two letters reflected my continuing sense of both hopefulness and despair.

Danbury, Connecticut. June 1942

Friday night. The carnival has come to town. It was a good evening, spending dimes and quarters, laughing, the boys pursuing their own interests. Danny anxious to find a concessionaire who would let him pick up balls behind a curtain or pieces of broken plates that had fallen behind the counter when some lucky man or woman managed to crash some with his allotted three balls for a dime. David hurrying from ride to ride, testing, challenging his own fears and excitement against the upside-down ride, the airplanes, the jumblebee cars, the Ferris wheel. My feet ached after a day with the backyard playgroup, and I only wanted to sit at the bingo counter. When David talked me into riding with him on the Ferris wheel, I froze in my tracks. Fear of getting caught up at the top, as had happened once when I was a girl . . . But I swallowed hard and said, "Sure, why not?" And survived.

I got through that, I thought. *Can I get through this?*

With a forced determination I rose from the floor and walked quietly into the boys' room. By now, both were asleep.

"My poor boys," I whispered, "what will become of you if I can't keep the miseries at bay?" But somehow, looking back on happier times had generated an inkling of hope. I returned to my room and turned a few more pages of my open journal.

Danbury, Connecticut. December 18, 1942

Dear Dave and Dan,

All day Saturday and all day yesterday, the wind has blown a cold gale around the house. You didn't know that there wasn't any coal in the cellar, that corn meal and milk was all the food we had, and that your foolish mother was more worried than perhaps ever before in all the hard times since both of you were born. That is why Mom let you make boats of all the furniture, play you were monkeys in a zoo, play cops and robbers and Lone Rangers all over the house. It was good to see you two, not knowing, getting a kick out of life even in a cold house.

And last night when I went to bed, I too felt the same thing you had felt during the day. The blackness of other nights, the loneliness, the worry—all fled, because just looking at you both asleep in your beds gave me strength and courage and hope to pick up the fight again, to continue it, and it gave me the knowledge that it won't always be this way.

No, it won't always be this way, I told myself. *But can I hang on till then?*

I put down the diary and sighed. Desperate for sleep, yet terrified that if I closed my eyes the always-lurking phantoms would once again assault my unconscious, I stared out the window into the black void, searching for a solution. Minutes passed. Finally, fighting deep fatigue, I got up from the wing chair and crossed into the hall again to look in once more on my now sleeping sons. Then I walked softly down the stairs to the kitchen.

I hesitated for several moments, then steeled myself and picked up the phone.

5.

In our bedroom, Davy was dead to the world.

While my tears had dried, my brain, half asleep since Mom came in to say good night, had become a hodgepodge of the day's events: the hassle with Rico; Davy running away; our mom's rambling talk about President Roosevelt.

Reliving *King of the Zombies*, the horror film Davy and I had seen that morning, I'd begun to associate its images with the look on Mom's face, the look of someone lost in a strange world I didn't understand. Upsetting though it was, I finally managed to fall asleep.

Tossing and turning then briefly half awake, I could hear Mom's footsteps on the stair. Then she was talking on the phone in the kitchen, and soon after, crying softly in her room. After what must have been another fifteen minutes and with no clue about what was going on, I remember covering my head with my soft plaid blanket and falling into a deep, nightmare-troubled sleep.

◆◆◆◆◆

From the murky waters of a dismal swamp, a ghostly vapor crept slowly upward, half-obscuring the trees. Through the mist I could make out figures in tattered clothing, shadowy at first then coming into focus as they drew closer, their faces an ashen gray, their eyes blank and staring. Zombies; the living dead! Closer they came, closer, trudging in my direction, their hands outstretched, seeking, grasping . . .

Even in the dream I recognized the images from the film we'd seen that morning before it caught on fire.

"Danny . . . Danny . . ." came a wailing voice.

I turned—and was face to face with my mom! Her eyes stark and cold, her crumpled dress the one she'd been wearing all week.

"Wake up, Daniel . . ." A firm yet gentle male voice was cutting through the dream. "Rise and shine. Sorry, but you have to wake up . . ."

Eyes barely open, I looked into the friendly round face of my uncle, Mom's brother Verne, who, with my aunt Laura and my two cousins, lived in the country just outside Danbury.

"Uncle Verne?" I asked, puzzled.

"I'm afraid you have to get up, son."

"Is it morning?"

"Not quite. It's three o'clock. We're going to the farm. Here, put this around you."

As I crawled sleepily out of bed, my uncle wrapped me in my plaid blanket, put an arm around me, and led me into the hall.

"How come we're going to the farm?" I asked. "Is it because of the war?"

"We'll talk about it later."

Only half awake and too muddled to think about what was happening, I was aware that my face hurt just below my ears, and that I was being helped down the porch steps and into the back seat of my uncle's 1942 "woody" Ford station wagon. Davy and Mom were in the car too, along with my Aunt Laura with her wavy hair and sympathetic smile. In moments, my head was on Mom's lap, and I was off again to the Land of Nod.

But everything had changed; the swamp was gone, and a spooky mansion Davy and I had seen in *King of the Zombies* was now the White House. A zombie maid from the film came down the wide marble staircase to greet me. "The president needs the secret plans," she announced in a cold, threatening voice. "Unless you can find them, we will never beat the Japs."

"I don't know where they are," I wailed.

"In the gas station, in the gas station!" replied the zombie maid as she disappeared down a long, dimly lit corridor.

"Fill it up please."

At the sound of my uncle's voice, my eyes flickered open. Lifting my head from Mom's lap, I looked out the car's window; high above, I saw a big red Texaco gas station sign.

"I have to find the secret plans," I mumbled. "And my face hurts."

"I think you have a little fever, dear," said Mom, smoothing down my hair that had become soaked with sweat.

But I was already drifting back to sleep. For a while I was dead to the world, but the zombies hadn't quite finished with me. Back in the White House, two of the swamp's living dead were dragging me up a broad staircase.

"Let me go!" I demanded. "I want my mom, I want my mom. Where is she?'

"I'm right here," came her voice. "I'm right here."

Still groggy and in a feverish sweat but relieved to find myself suddenly awake, I realized I was arm in arm between Mom and Aunt

Laura, being helped along the walkway toward the front door of my aunt and uncle's impressive three-story country home. (Why they called it "the farm," I never found out. Weekend gardening was about all that ever went on there.)

"My face hurts," I managed to say. "And I'm cold."

Aunt Laura felt my forehead. "Don't worry, dear. We'll soon have you in a nice cozy bed, and I'll take good care of you." I glanced at her, then looked back at Uncle Verne, who was carrying Davy, sound asleep. "You've been having a bad dream," Aunt Laura went on as she unlocked the front door.

Within minutes, she was turning down the covers on a guest room bed. Uncle Verne laid Davy, still asleep, at one end. I climbed in after him, and soon I too was beginning to drift.

Mom sat on the edge of the bed and stroked my hair. "Just try to sleep now, dear," she said. "I might not be here when you wake up."

"What's the matter? Where are you going?" I asked.

"I just need a long rest," she said, and somehow, even at my age, I could tell she was trying to put on a brave face. Noting my frown, she added, "Well, I might still be here, but if I'm gone, try not to worry. Uncle Verne and Aunt Laura will explain. You just try to be a good boy, okay?"

"Where's Mackie?" I managed to ask.

"Still at home. Mrs. Koocher next door will take care of him. He'll be fine."

I wanted to stay awake, but my body wouldn't cooperate. And my face still hurt. In moments I was asleep again, drifting in and out of another weird dream. I'd become lost among the skyscraper canyons of New York, with everything frozen and colored a sinister gray.

In the distance, buildings were on fire. Alone and helpless, I wanted desperately to go home, but couldn't find the way. Every street I tried seemed to be the wrong one. The fire was crawling closer now. And there were no people anywhere, just the shadow of some huge creature that seemed to follow me everywhere I turned, the shadow of a demon or monster . . . or perhaps a zombie.

6.

With Danny and David now asleep, I walked into the living room to say goodnight to Laura and Verne. Still a bit anxious, I'd been wondering if they saw me as the despicable thing, the useless dirty mother I'd come to believe I was. But as Laura put a comforting arm around my shoulders and ushered me upstairs to the room their housekeeper, Selma, had prepared for me, all I could think of was the oblivion of sleep. Which mercifully came almost as soon as I got into bed.

In what seemed like no time, Selma woke me. Along with a steaming pot of coffee, she brought news that Verne and Laura's doctor would be calling shortly to see Danny. Thankful for the coffee but afraid that Danny had become worse, I dressed hurriedly and went into the boys' room.

The doctor was already there. "Mumps," he announced, looking up as I entered. "Aspirin for the pain, plenty of fluid, and rest. That's the ticket."

I stood silently, tearing myself in half. My poor son—could I leave him like this? And with Davy likely to catch it too? My boys were the only ones who sounded a bell. For them I'd continued to smile, if not to function. I knew they sensed the unreality of my smile, my voice, and would soon discover the terrible things happening to their mother: the defeat, the disintegration.

It's too cruel to subject them to more strain, I told myself. *I have to go.*

I bent down and kissed Danny's hot forehead. "I do have to leave soon, sweetie," I said. "Not sure for how long, but you be good and do what your aunt Laura says, okay? Get lots of sleep and remember, don't let the bedbugs bite."

"And if they do, bite 'em back," said Danny, trying to force a reassuring grin.

Still not quite ten and having been through tonsillitis, chickenpox, and measles, mumps may not have seemed such a big deal to my brave son, but his mom going off to who knows where and for how long certainly was. And just like me, I could see he was doing his best to hold back the tears.

◆◆◆◆◆

Within the hour, mechanically descending the stairs and sick with worry, I noticed Davy peeking up at me through the banisters. *Don't fret about me,* his determined expression seemed to say. *I'll be all right.* For a second, the old fight flared in me, and I stopped. *I can't go*, I thought. *I have to stay with them*. But as quickly as I'd resolved not to leave, I could feel the doubt creeping back in. Suppose it happened again, the irrational impulse to loop a rope over the water pipes, or stuff the cracks and turn on the gas? Or even head back to the lake? When might those strange, terrifying experiences I dared not share even with Verne or Laura return? *Today? Tomorrow? What then?*

If the next time I actually went through with it, my boys would lose me forever. The realization hit me like a thunderclap. Yes, I had to go.

Laura was putting my small valise onto the back seat of the woody as Davy, with his plucky little smile, held my hand and walked with me to the car.

"Now take good care of yourself, Mom," he said.

As the station wagon pulled away, I saw my precious boy wiping his eyes with one hand as he waved with the other. All I could manage was a weak smile.

Overwhelmed by my sense of loss as Laura navigated the car through the countryside then along the elevated West Side Highway into Manhattan that Sunday morning, guilt continued to tug at me. Had I made the right decision? What if it didn't work? In my doubt I could feel the demons of despair creeping back, and I shuddered.

"Are you all right?" asked Laura, sensing my tension.

The ugly voices surfaced once more. *She knows*, they whispered. *Might as well jump from the car into traffic.*

"Oh, shut up!" I growled, compelling myself to focus on the road ahead.

"What?" asked Laura.

"Sorry," I muttered. "Just thinking aloud."

The woody turned into 68th Street amid a gloomy half-mist, and the nine-storied neo-Gothic walls of the Payne Whitney Psychiatric Clinic loomed ahead like some medieval fortress. I felt numb with foreboding as Laura pulled up in front, got out, retrieved the suitcase, and came around to open the passenger door.

Is this it, I wondered, *the end of the line, the place of no return?*

A distressing memory came suddenly to mind; shadowy images and nauseous smells from a long-forgotten past clutched at me and held me riveted to the seat. I remembered the "crazy woman" who had been kept in a barred window attic room over the living quarters of the county jail across from our family home in St. Johns, Michigan. No one then had thought of her as a human being; she was just "the crazy woman." She'd been taken away in the night, and the next day the Feeney children led my brother Harry and me upstairs and showed us the stuffy room and the pot she had peed in and the smelly bed she had slept in. "There aren't any sheets or blankets," explained Annabelle Feeney, "because she'd just tear them to pieces, so she has to sleep on only the mattress."

Then, without a word, we had all climbed back down the steep, narrow stairs.

As a child, it had taken weeks for the memory to dissipate. And now, as I sat in Laura's station wagon in front of Payne Whitney, the shadowy images and nauseating smells from that long-forgotten past once again clutched at me. Was I to become that helpless old woman? I sat riveted to the seat.

"Shall we go in?" Laura suggested.

I looked up. Somehow, even though the pictures inside my head still reeked of decay and desolation, I pushed aside my sense of a place of no return, got out of the car, took my valise from Laura, managed a tenuous smile, and promised, "I'll try."

"That's all we're asking of you," encouraged Laura.

I drew a deep breath, momentarily hesitated, then took my sister-in-law's extended hand and, making every effort to mask the foul, putrid lump I was convinced that she and everyone else saw me as, headed up the steps with as much dignity as I could muster.

7.

My head turned on its pillow as I heard the door opening.

"Stay out," I croaked as Davy stuck his head in. "You'll get the mumps."

"I think I already got 'em," he replied, indicating his face and neck. "It's beginnin' t' hurt here. And I feel all shivery."

Closer to the bed, he noticed my tear-stained cheeks.

"You been crying?"

I sniffled, swallowed, and turned away.

"'Cause o' Mom?"

His question got me crying again.

"She's gonna be okay," said my always compassionate brother, bravely holding back his emotions as he hitched himself up onto the end of the bed. "She'll be back pretty soon; you'll see."

I couldn't stop the tears. And when Davy laid a gentle hand on my blanket-covered legs, I jerked them back to my chest, rolled over to stare at the wall, and growled, "I'm okay, I'm okay." Then, through continuing sniffles, I added, "When she gets home, you better tell Aunt Laura you're coming down with 'em. We need to get better quick so Mom doesn't worry."

Davy thought for a moment then said, "I was downstairs just now, and Uncle Verne was in his office. On the telephone, an' he was talking to someone. A school or a home or something, asking how much it'd cost for two boys for six months."

"Six months?" I gasped as I rolled back over to face him. "They're gonna put us in a home?"

"Maybe it's just a school."

But my anxiety button had already been pressed. "They think Mom's gonna be away for six months?"

"Dunno. But then he made another call to some other place, long distance."

"How come we can't stay here?" I demanded. "Or in Danbury? We don't need anyone to take care of us; we could be okay by ourselves."

"Sure."

"I bet they wouldn't let us, though. I'll bet—" I stopped suddenly, listened intently, then wiped my eyes as Davy whispered, "Shhh . . . He's coming up the stairs."

We both looked to the door as it opened and our uncle came in, beaming. "Well, well, sitting up, I see. You must be feeling better, son, right?"

"I guess," I mumbled.

"Great! You'll be up and about in a few days. But you, Master David, seem a bit peaked," he added with a frown. "Let's have a look."

Sitting in a chair, Uncle Verne motioned my brother to him, felt his neck and lower face, then laid a hand on his temple. "Feeling chilled?"

Davy nodded.

"First sign of a fever. A hundred, I'd say. Let's get you to bed. Soon as your aunt gets back, we'll set up a cot next to your brother. Meanwhile, you come on down to my office and rest on the couch."

As Davy was being steered toward the door, he looked around at me. I had a finger to my lips, indicating not to mention what he'd overheard. He nodded, and as Uncle Verne stopped and turned briefly back, I let my hand fall to the bed.

"And," added our uncle, smiling, "I'll ask your aunt to fetch a couple quarts of Neapolitan ice cream: chocolate, vanilla, and strawberry. Yum, yum! Best thing for the mumps. That ought to keep you boys happy until they're all gone."

"I don't like storeberry," mumbled Davy as they left the room.

Uncle Verne started to close the door. "Strawberry," he corrected, oblivious to the tears welling up in Davy's eyes and mine.

PART II:
THE WEE SMALL HOURS

"Not until we are lost do we begin to understand ourselves."

—Henry David Thoreau[4]

4 From Thoreau's *Walden*, 1854

8.

"Follow me," directed a short, buxom nurse after I'd checked in at Payne Whitney's reception desk. With an air of defeated resignation, I turned to Laura and forced a thin smile.

"You'll be fine," my sister-in-law said, giving me a hug, but then looked on anxiously as the nurse and I disappeared into an elevator.

As we emerged into an anteroom on the clinic's seventh floor psychiatric wing, the floor I'd soon learn was for severely depressed patients, my eyes darted back and forth suspiciously, and I immediately began to feel like a small, whipped child who had nothing to offer the world, and with no one to accept the nothing. *And I'm forty-three!* I sighed. *Why should I feel like this?*

The nurse pressed a button. A buzzer sounded, and a heavy iron door clicked open, leading into the central corridor.

Almost immediately, a thin old woman in a wheelchair rolled toward me and peered over her dirty glasses. "Is that you, Jenny? Did Jenny come to see me?" she asked the nurse as she reached out to clasp my hand.

This was the crazy house, a bad dream coming true. I wanted to run and hide. Dread of being shut up with sick and senile old women vied with my natural empathy for such people. For the sake of Laura and Verne and the boys, I'd managed to hold back the tears this morning. But now, as the nurse gently took my arm and led me to a small bright room off the long institutional corridor, I felt those pent-up tears burning my eyelids.

"Here's your suitcase," said the nurse, indicating my small valise that a janitor had brought to the room. "We'll unpack your things and put them in the bureau drawer. I'll help you." She shook out my skirt, blouse, and underwear, and laid them on the bed. I placed my toothbrush, powder, and comb on the dresser as the nurse put my valise, hat, and coat inside the closet, locked the door, and dropped the key into her apron pocket. Then she turned and, with a smile, left the room.

This is it, I thought. *I'm trapped in here. Undone.*

My eyes flooding with tears, I threw myself onto the bed and sobbed for what seemed like hours, but it was probably only twenty minutes. Slowly, there came an end to sobbing, and the old inner resolve I always somehow seemed to muster pushed through. *What next?* I wondered. *What do I do now?* Slowly, I rose from the bed and tried the door. It was locked, of course. But then, I knew it would be. *Or did I? Why did they have to lock the door? Do they think I'm dangerous? A lunatic?*

I turned to a full-length mirror on the closet door. The reflection appalled me: red, puffy eyes, my hair in disarray, the suit I'd thought so proper when I'd put it on that morning rumpled and hanging on me like an empty laundry bag. Where had I been for the past few weeks to lose so much weight, to so neglect my appearance?

I crossed to a small washbowl on the bureau and doused my face with cold water. Looking in the mirror again, I recognized someone who resembled myself. *What a catastrophe*, I thought. I knew I'd laid my comb on the dresser, but when I looked it wasn't there. About to search for my valise, I remembered that the nurse had locked it in the closet.

I turned at the sound of the door being unlocked.

"Lunch is ready," announced a freshly starched nurse with a pasted-on smile. "The other ladies are all going in."

"But I can't find my comb. And my hair is a dreadful mess."

"I'll get it for you," said the nurse, who unlocked the closet then handed it to me. But I noticed that she stood watching as I ran the comb through my hair, then held out her hand for it. A bizarre thought raced through my head: *Maybe they think I'll use the sharp end to stab myself.* That form of suicide hadn't occurred to me; the lake, a rope, leaping from Laura's car, certainly; but a comb?

"We'll go into the dining room with the ladies now," directed the starched nurse after she locked the comb back in the closet.

The "ladies," perhaps sixteen or twenty of them, were moving slowly and seriously down the corridor. I fell in with the group, forced to walk in the same sluggish gait to where small tables were arranged in a large, square space. It reminded me of some of the rather elegant hotel dining rooms my younger brother Harry and his partners performed in during the summer I'd helped out with his small marionette troupe while touring Michigan's Upper Peninsula. So grateful I was to my brothers for making it possible for me to spend time here instead of being carted off to some state institution like the poor crazy woman in the Feeney's upstairs room must have ended up in.

"We'll sit here," said the nurse, indicating a nicely set table with a basket of rolls, bread and butter plates, ice water, and napkins.

We? Why does she keep saying "we"? Will she be joining us?

I sat. My three companions remained slumped in their chairs, staring at the tablecloth. Long accustomed to being polite and making conversation when thrown in with strangers, and feeling sad they should look so miserable, I picked up the basket of rolls and, offering it to each in turn, asked, "Won't you have a roll?"

No one glanced at the rolls. No one gave an indication they'd even heard me.

"It was so cold this morning, wasn't it?" I continued, trying to make conversation.

Silence.

"Perhaps the sun will come out later."

Continuing silence. It was no use. It felt like I was once more in my childhood home, forced to endure a meal with a hurt and silently petulant mother. I had committed the memory to my journal:

> I was fourteen. We had all sat down for dinner. In spite of Mother's advice, Dad announced he wasn't going to dismiss the new clerk he'd taken on in his dry-goods store, even though business had fallen off.
>
> "What?" Mother fumed.
>
> "Well, they've got a child on the way."
>
> "You're a damn fool! A soft touch, sacrificing your own family's welfare for a stranger."
>
> "There aren't many jobs around, Mother, and—"

> She kept at him until finally folding her arms she retreated into one of her sulks, and the family endured yet another miserable, silent dinner while Mother sat there, refusing to touch a morsel.

I looked around at my companions. One thin-faced young woman, not more than twenty-five, sat through the entire meal with her hands in her lap, her mouth drooping, looking at her plate. Another, about my age, picked at her food, then finally pushed the plate aside and began sobbing into her napkin. The third, a sullen, plumpish woman of thirty or so, made an attempt to eat, then gave up and spent the rest of the meal staring out the window.

It was during this lunch, I think, when the first realization of depression hit me. I tried to place the remote and sullen expressions on the women's faces, to relate them to something I knew. Not just to the memory of the family dinner. Something else was familiar here. What was it?

Sunlight slanted through the windows, and though I could hear the casual chatter of the nurses behind the counters, the entire dining room of "us ladies" felt unreal, like a chamber unearthed from an ancient, long-buried city. As cut off as I was from the world of real people, some life-giving force urged me to look around, to say thank you when the food was served, to pick up a roll and nibble on it. Perhaps it was the habit of pride, of activity, or putting on a front that kept me gnawing on the bun and trying to penetrate the gloom. Gradually, I began to understand what was so familiar. I was looking into a mirror.

That's me, I thought, and I felt like running from the room and hiding from this awful reflection. In the shuttered personalities of my companions I saw myself, and the implications shattered me. I ate the meal with difficulty.

With the luncheon hour finished, we all filed back down the corridor. As I stepped into my room, a sudden frenzy seized me, an urgency to get out, to finish it off. With a secretive cunning to make sure this would be final, I closed the door, hurried to the window, and picked at the screen, only to find it firmly planted with bars just outside. And the steel encasing the small glass panes opened no more than six inches. Impossible.

Looking out over the East River, Manhattan's many bridges came to mind, especially Brooklyn Bridge, which I'd crossed over so often in past years. Quickly, I formed a new plan: to slip out, go down in the elevator, and find my way to the street before anyone could catch me. But then I remembered the nurse with her big ring of keys. All the doors would be locked. I was trapped.

As quickly as it had come on, the frenzy began to dissipate.

I slumped into the cretonne-covered chair and waited for whatever was going to happen next. *Well, this is it. I must be the good girl now; the good girl Mother always wanted. Make every effort to cooperate, do what I'm asked, but try to hold on to some small vestige of the life I've mostly lived until now.*

"A good girl?" I whispered aloud. "My God, how ironic; and with me past forty!"

Within moments, the nurse who had locked up my comb arrived, crossed to the window, pulled down the shade, and said, "It's time for a nap. And be sure to turn down your bedspread so it doesn't get rumpled." Then, about to exit, she turned back and added, "Please leave your door open."

Having obediently folded back the top cover, I stretched out on the bed and lay staring at the ceiling. From somewhere, a gentle but high-pitched voice began to sing "Onward Christian Soldiers." Then another voice ordered, "Be quiet, Mrs. Sullivan; all the ladies are going to sleep now."

The clinic soon became quiet. The stillness itself became the focus of my attention, and gradually I drifted off into a stark, bare dream, a dream that within itself made sense but also broke my heart.

I found myself in an empty, run-down, rambling house, searching for Danny and Davy, whom I'd left hours before. I knew they were there, could hear their laughing voices carrying on as though in play. I was frantic: opening doors, running down corridors, examining closets, but they were nowhere to be found. And the longer I searched, the more desolate the house became, until finally their voices faded completely, and there was only silence.

I woke with a slight headache and slowly sat up. My throat felt tight, and my cheeks had become moist with tears. *They're lost to me, my darling boys,* I sobbed. *They must never see what I've become. I'll never again be able to see them . . .*

Yet through the fog of tears, from somewhere deep inside, a small faint voice struggled to push itself into consciousness. *You have to get out of here, Mary,* it said. *Soon. You have two sons who need you, who you need. Do you want them raised by others? By strangers, even? Yes, yes, there's Laura and Verne? And yes, they're kind . . . but so formal, so stuffy. . . . And will they even want to take them in?*

I put both hands over my ears and did my best to push the images away.

No, no, of course not, the voice insisted. *You can't stay here locked up with all these sad, depressed women. You've got a life to live; you have to get out.*

I fell back against the pillow and mumbled softly, "But how? Tell me how."

9.

Now what was that all about? I wondered as I came out of another upsetting dream—though thank goodness not one involving my boys. The starched nurse had just appeared at the door to tell me something.

"Sorry, what?" I asked.

"I said it's time for our bath."

"Oh. Sorry, but I . . . well, I must have dozed off."

As I got off the bed, she raised the shade, then took my dressing gown from the closet and said I could undress here and walk down the hall. "First door on the left." Then she disappeared.

I changed into my robe and set off toward the bathroom, reliving the troublesome dream: in it, I stood by a river, looking on as a little girl struggled in murky, neck-deep water near a swirling eddy. On my left, beyond hearing, were people, perhaps older children; I couldn't be sure. Though I turned momentarily in their direction, imploring help, I quickly realized it was up to me to get into the river and do my best to pull the little girl to safety. I plunged in and reached down, for the girl was now sinking, and pulled her to the surface. Putting my mouth over hers, I blew into it strongly but gently. Water flowed from the girl's lungs. Then, knowing she'd live, I pulled her to shore. *She's all right,* I told myself. But just as I was about to kindly point out that when she went swimming she should steer clear of the swirling eddies, the girl vanished.

As the images faded, I found myself entering the hospital's large institutional bathroom, the walls flanked with rows of showers and bathtubs.

"Do you want a shower or a tub?" asked a middle-aged attendant in a blue uniform and a long white apron. I chose the tub and stood by as she ran the water. Then, embarrassed to be bathing so publicly with strangers, I removed my robe and climbed in.

"I can wash myself," I said, reaching for the washcloth as she began to soap it, obviously ready to scrub my back.

With a "well, I never" kind of look, the woman relinquished the cloth and stepped aside. As I lathered the pleasant-smelling soap onto the thick washcloth, relaxed comfortably into the warm water, and began to wash, my thoughts returned to my dream.

Drowning. That's what the dream was about. Yes, drowning. That's just the way I feel. But why a child?

Then I recalled that the previous year Alvah had sent money so the boys could go to summer camp. Danny, just learning to swim, had been pulled out of his depth by the river current and was about to be swept away when a counselor plunged into the water and hauled him to safety.

But in my dream, it had been a little girl. . . . Why a girl?

Was I saving myself? Is that what I'm here for?

"You do a good job with washing, now," said the attendant as she headed for the door. "I'm going for fresh towels."

I looked up and nodded. Then, lifting my arms to wash, I was surprised to see my ribs standing out and loose flaccid folds of skin from my armpits to the elbows. Normally I weighed about a hundred and thirty pounds, but I must have lost fifteen or twenty and didn't even know it.

Back in my room, I dressed in the same clothes I'd worn to the hospital, the dress I'd bought six months before and had probably been wearing every day since, for I had no recollection of being interested in clothes. As I sat waiting for whatever was to happen next, my boys came to mind, and I burst into a fresh shower of tears. Even as I sat crying, it occurred to me that a patient might be extended the courtesy of being told what she was waiting for. But as I was soon to learn, everyone just waited for the routine to unfold. Doors were locked. Only doctors and nurses had the keys. Only doctors and nurses decided what was to happen next.

I let out a long sigh of resignation; I was just a patient—and "patient" it seemed I must be. Moments later, the starched nurse appeared, and with her fixed smile she directed me to follow her down the corridor to a small examining room where I was introduced to my doctor, an impersonal, gray-haired woman. The doctor went about tapping my knees with her little hammer. She thumped my chest and back, weighed and measured me, drew blood for a test, then left the room with a matter-of-fact, "I'll be seeing you again later."

"We have an appointment tomorrow at eleven with your psychiatrist," the nurse announced as she escorted me back to my room.

Psychiatrist! I immediately felt cornered, again in a place of no escape.

In that moment of panic, I saw an ancient, dour, bespectacled man taking one look, considering me irredeemably mad, and locking me up here forever; a dirty, useless mother who would never again see her boys.

No! I told myself. *That must never happen!* Clearly, one of my mental demons was still lurking about, up to its old mischief. Thankfully, I was able to push that painful picture away and imagine instead a somber, analytical type who would ask why I was here, wanting to know about my childhood and what sort of family I grew up in.

"My childhood," I muttered aloud. "What was it like?"

I turned that idea over, then got up and crossed to the door, which had been left unlocked. *Maybe they've figured out I won't do myself in,* I mused.

I walked to the nurses' station to ask if I could have paper and a pencil. Back in my room, I chewed briefly on the end of the pencil, thinking. Then, slowly, I began to write, first recalling my father's notation in the family Bible:

> August 3, 1898. To my wife, Rose, there was born this day at 12:03 a.m., a girl, our third child and first daughter, Gladys Mae Burnett; weight 7 lbs. 11 oz.

Gladys, I reflected. I always hated the name; 'glad ass,' the boys at school teased me with, so I decided early on that I'd call myself Mary as soon as I left home. I always loved my favorite aunt, Mary.

Letting my mind wander, I continued to write snatches from early childhood.

The Burnett family of St. Johns, Michigan (about 1903).
Back row: Rose, Leo
Front row: Mary (born Gladys Mae), Verne, Harry, Noble

Aunt Mary

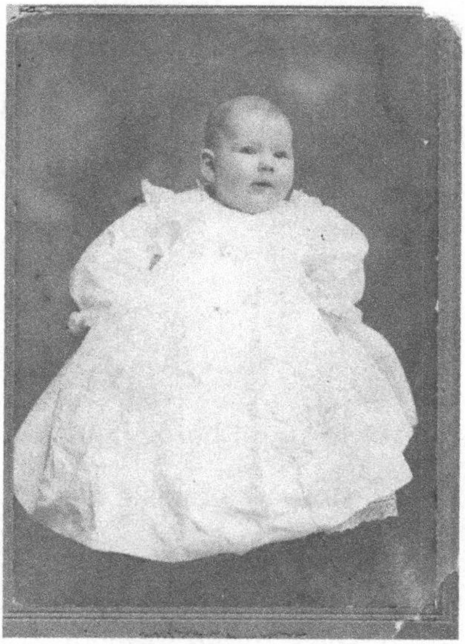

Mary as an infant

> Age 4 . . . pneumonia (they called it "typhoid pneumonia" in those days; I nearly died from it). We lived in the "Taft house" then. Harry was born there, my youngest brother. He came down with it too. Then we moved to the "Dow house". . . . Funny how people assigned names to the houses of those who originally lived in them.
>
> Age 8 . . . Mother was displeased with me because I got grass stains on the new white dress that I got for my birthday, and my big brother Leo didn't feel like selling magazines that afternoon, even though there was no school because it was Saturday. "How do you expect to be successful in this world if you don't work?" Mother chided. So Leo took his bag and went to sell magazines, and I was punished for something I couldn't help, getting grass stains on my dress.

"I recall writing almost exactly that at the time," I whispered. "Except that I didn't spell all the words right. What else? Oh, yes, something like . . ."

> I will pray for light and be as patient as ever I can when Mother is displeased, but oh, it is so hard to understand her sometimes, and I think Dad (forgive me, Mother) feels like that sometimes too.

Was I really that precocious? I asked myself with a hint of a smile. But my next thoughts were more somber. . . .

I remember being in my room and having a tea party with my

teddy bear, and Leo came to tell me about the death in a gas main explosion of Mr. Reynolds, father of two girls in my third-grade class. This immediately engendered in me a terrible fear about losing my own dad.

And I recall Harry and me playing out funerals and creating cemeteries with little graves in the backyard near the grapevines. I wondered if the psychiatrist would want to know about all that. It hardly seemed important. On the other hand, maybe he would. Death, after all, had been so close lately.

I paused for a moment, then took up the pencil again as the memory of that childhood play caused me to think about a cemetery I'd visited as a young woman. It was a small, unkempt cemetery. All the gravestones were small, the largest and tallest no more than four feet, seeming to grow out of the long grass. The place looked as though it was never used anymore. The tallest stone was near the middle of the plot, and as I walked through the uncut grass, almost stumbling on one of the low flat stones (a child's stone) with the name of Ellie, 1891-1893, I remember thinking how very difficult it was to contemplate a tombstone with a child's name engraved upon it. I saw it as a life span, or maybe just part of a life span, and I could identify with this kind of chunk of life being cut off. But a very young child? How terrible. Somehow my sorrow went out to the mother and father who would never forget during their entire lives. And I thought how this happens to other people, people in adolescence, or middle age, or even old people. . . . It wasn't the sorrow for those who have died, of course, but the sorrow and the guilt and the anxiety and the numbness for those left behind.

Would the psychiatrist want to know why I thought about this? I gave a lingering sigh. And I'd probably need to tell him about the dear little dead baby too, Danny's twin, who I never really cried for . . . and the desecration of his grave. . . . I quickly pushed down the lump rising in my throat.

Enough! I decided. *Move on, Mary. . . .*

So I wrote about the time in high school when I desperately wanted a basketball for Christmas but got only a new dress. In a basketball box (one of Mother's spiteful little lessons, I suppose). And the first time I saw myself naked in a mirror. . . . How old was I? Maybe fourteen? I ran into Mother's bedroom to announce, "Look Mama, I'm beautiful," and there came a shocked reprimand, "Pride comes before a fall." Some years later, when she refused to let my eighth-grade graduation date, Charlie Britton, whom she thought not good enough, take me on a sleigh ride, out came, "There are lots of pebbles on the beach."

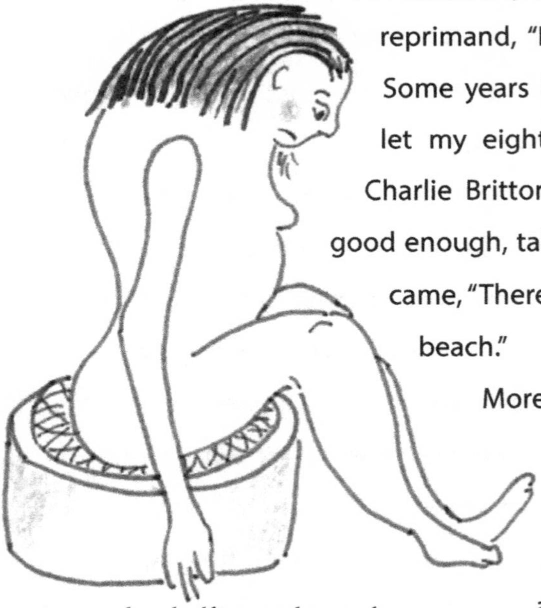

A remembered self image, drawn when Mary was nearly seventy

More of my mother's little homilies came to mind: "A fox smells its own hole," "Pretty is as pretty does," and "Beauty is only skin deep." I recalled her sulks, her drooping mouth, the hurt little girl feelings she'd effect at real or imagined wrongs.

Then another memory popped up, a particular Sunday dinner with everyone seated except Harry, who hadn't shown up. Harry, my youngest brother, had always been different. Nobody in the family seemed to be able to figure him out.

"Harry," my mother called, "we're starting now!"

Then Dad said grace and began cutting the roast. "Mother?" he asked.

"Very little, please."

"Why, you don't eat enough to feed a bird."

"I don't care for much. . . . Harry!" she called again.

Papa cut a thin slice, laid it on her plate, and passed it to her.

"Plenty here!" said Verne.

"And here!" said Harry, who suddenly appeared in the room, wearing a pair of Mother's dress pumps with one of her fringed shawls draped over his head and around his shoulders.

"Take those off!" my mother commanded.

Harry looked down at the floor and mumbled in a low falsetto voice, "Oh Lord forgive me, a poor miz-able sinner."

Papa disguised his chuckle with a cough.

"If you are going to behave like this, you may not join us for dinner," said Mama.

Harry pulled off the shawl

A mystery and a vexation to his mother, Harry was always a cut-up.

and hung his head in pretended shame. Then we all ate without another word spoken—except when Dad looked up to ask, "Aren't you going to eat, Mother?"

"I'm not hungry now," she snapped.

An image of the morose "ladies" at the clinic's lunch table came to mind.

Dinners were frequently like this. There would be no conversation except when my father would ask about our day or about any plans we had. After, we would all move away from the table, and I'd help Mama clear the dishes and go out into the kitchen to help clean up, which was my job. And while we were there, I'd see her eating endlessly as she moved around, putting things away—but I hadn't as yet put much together in my head.

Still, in spite of Mother's moods and prohibitions, I recall a basically happy childhood. What had made it so? I mulled the question for a while, then continued writing:

> My father, Noble Burnett: gentle, hardworking, caring. He loved nature, cultivated a deep respect for every living thing in me, in Leo and Verne. Harry too. He had a genuine kindness, a compassion for not only plants and animals but, it seemed, for every human being; a quality I've found in not too many others.

What else? So many small childhood pleasures . . .

> Bare feet in mud.
>
> Playing tag, blind man's bluff, until we dropped breathless on the grass. Struggling to keep up with my

brothers as we climbed the cherry tree or the crabapple tree, where Leo and Verne had built a tree house. ("That's not ladylike," Mama chided.)

I was five (or was I four?) when I was a flower girl and wore a pretty dress and ribbons in my hair at Aunt Mabe and Uncle Will's wedding.

Daisy, our cow.

The grin on Harry's face when he saw the wagon he got for his sixth birthday.

Dear, funny Harry. His often bizarre but hysterical antics at twelve or fourteen, such as when guests would arrive to discover him standing in the middle of the living room, suddenly shrunken by two feet! He'd removed a furnace grate from the floor, rigged it so he could stand in the hole with everything from floor level down disguised, except for a pair of shoes placed near where his knees were. After the initial gasp, most found this quite amusing. Except for Mother, of course, who didn't appreciate suddenly having Toulouse-Lautrec for a son.

Dad's dry goods store; the feel of muslin, poplin, the gingham print material customers loved, the smell of new wool dresses.

The dog we had; Spot, with his big black patch over one eye.

Piano lessons, elocution lessons.

Sundays at the Congregational church. (I sang in the choir.)

My mother's rare gaiety as she'd burst into a sudden recitation: "Said Briar Rose's mother to the naughty Briar Rose, 'What will become of you my child, the Lord A'mighty knows.'"

Growing up was a theater in the round, a learning garden, with the carefree sights and sounds and sensations of childhood mixed up in my head with confused attempts to understand a petulant and often perplexing mother. Though counterbalanced by a loving father, Dad left too soon, became ill and died just when I'd finally launched myself into a world that, looking back now, I probably wasn't ready for, a world I didn't fully understand. One I might have coped with better if I'd had the benefit of the patient and thoughtful counsel he could have provided.

Noble Burnett

As I lay the pencil aside, the door opened. "Well," chirped the starched nurse, "it looks like they've put off our meeting with the psychiatrist until tomorrow afternoon."

"Oh . . . Do you need to see him too?" I asked.

"I beg your pardon?"

"Well, whenever you remind me about something I've got to do, you say 'we,' or 'our.'"

Her patronizing composure vanished. "It's just an expression," she replied curtly. She looked at my unmade bed, reminded me to do my chores before lunch, then turned and left, closing the door a bit too firmly.

I recall staring after her for several moments. Then, for the first time in months, I chuckled to myself.

10.

My second day at Payne Whitney was crammed with new experiences, with a kaleidoscope of people, events, and impressions.

The first was what I soon discovered would be the morning routine: making the bed, then washing stockings and underwear. Looking back, I can still see my plain pink bloomers hanging on the line next to several pair of lace-trimmed panties of various sizes. What an incongruous contrast between the inward and outward appearances of the patients. It made me wonder if well-meaning relatives brought in the lace-trimmed panties, thinking they would help lift the spirits of hopelessly depressed family members.

The following hour, I think, was probably the worst I experienced while there. As we completed our chores, I saw the nurses laying out coats, jackets, and scarves; we were going for a walk in the garden. Most of the women seemed so cheerful that after the clinic's medicinal atmosphere, I too anticipated the smell of fresh air.

We stood in the corridor for fifteen or twenty minutes, dressed for outdoors. When the nurses were ready, the door to the anteroom was unlocked. As we entered the elevator, I felt that we were like a herd of so many cattle being transported. I don't know how it could have been done differently, but it's certainly the last kind of thing a human being would want to experience. Even my awareness of the tragic suffering endured by millions in wartime Europe didn't alleviate my sense of humiliation. As we moved from one floor to another, doors were locked and unlocked while we stood huddled and waited each time for the nurses. Finally we reached the outdoors, a small, formal garden facing the East River and bordered by a high wire fence. Wind blowing off the river made it bitterly cold.

A picture appeared in my head, a painting by Van Gogh, of prisoners circling within a tiny, high-walled stone courtyard. The monotony and disconnect reflected in Vincent's image tore at me, yet even though we shared the same confinement, I noticed that patients from other floors seemed much more sprightly than the women on mine. In spite of the crowded cold, several even laughed and talked. For a moment, this offered me a tiny spark of hope.

Prisoners' round; Vincent Van Gogh, 1890
(after Gustave Dore)

After a half hour or so, we were herded once more from elevator to elevator back to our assigned floors and into our rooms. The whole procedure, I decided as I shuffled mechanically through the motions like everyone else, seemed a high price to pay for the pleasure of breathing fresh air. Even though I was on the seventh floor, the one with the most serious cases, I was sure there must have been some way it could have been accomplished with greater humanity.

The experience was still too new for total awareness. It had only been twenty-four hours, too close for it to be objective. But I did feel I was beginning to emerge from the fog. Not that I felt in one piece. Far from it, but I don't recall any further impulses for self-destruction and was already developing a strong desire to get out of the place and get back to my boys.

Soon after I returned, a blue-clad attendant arrived in my room to remind me that my appointment with the psychiatrist had been put off until after lunch. "So how's about you come along and join Mrs. Jackson and the ladies in the common room."

Her tone made it clear this was a directive, not simply a suggestion.

I nodded then asked, "Who's Mrs. Jackson?"

"Occupational therapy teacher. Knitting, weaving, that sort of thing," replied the attendant as she held the door open for us both to leave.

In the light, spacious common room I was introduced to a friendly, energetic, sandy-haired woman in her thirties, wearing a green smock over a simple but smartly tailored blouse and skirt. Chatting amiably with the other women, Mrs. Jackson was at the same time unloading skeins of yarn, embroidery frames, and other items from a wheeled cart onto a long table already piled with paints and brushes, pads of paper, and clay. That completed, she wiped her hands on her apron, shook hands with me, enquired how I was getting on, then asked, "What do you think you'd like to do today, Mrs. Burnett?"

I wasn't really sure, so she prodded: "Have you done much knitting? Or sewing?"

A stream of images flooded my brain:

Thread the needle! First step. Sew, sew, sew. Sew doll clothes before you know how to sew. Mend your brother's socks ("because you do it so well"). Ha! Weave a pillow top by pulling those red, green, yellow, and blue strands through that heavy ecru netting. Embroider! With the round wooden hoops. Prick your finger. Blood spots.

Grandma Acheson sits in the rocker, watching.

Hem your large white flannel squares for approaching womanhood. With pattern and pinstripe flannel of blue and white, learn to cut and baste; stitching a blouse in seventh grade.

Sensing my hesitation, Mrs. Jackson added encouragingly, "I'll bet you have." Inconceivable I could accomplish anything remotely creative just then. Nevertheless, I agreed to give it a try. I sat down and quickly found my fingers knitting and purling away. The years during World War I came to mind; years when I'd plowed my way through pounds of navy wool as a volunteer, creating sweaters and socks for the men fighting in France.

Before I realized it, class time was over.

"That's fine, just fine," smiled Mrs. Jackson, patting my shoulder as she checked my work. "You're a real whiz."

I liked this woman, someone who treated the others on the ward, as well as me, like intelligent, self-respecting human beings.

Next on the schedule was lunch, followed by my appointment with the psychiatrist.

Any preconceived cartoon notion of Dr. Thomas as a bearded ancient wearing pince-nez glasses who would probe my unconscious, my childhood, my sexual history, and try to discover if I'd had romantic dreams about my father, quickly vanished. Dr. Thomas was about my age, clean-shaven, soft-spoken, and concerned. Quickly realizing that I was a seriously depressed and anxious but self-aware woman of considerable intelligence, he simply talked to me in an open, friendly way about what I felt were my problems, and suggested a number of ways I might begin to examine aspects of my past to try to put them into some kind of logical framework. Encouraged by his practical, matter-of-fact but respectful and understanding approach, I left his office far more reassured than when I'd entered.

In spite of the "herding" of the patients into the garden that morning, I thought about how fortunate I was to have landed in an institution with such a progressive approach to mental health, and as I headed toward my room I whispered, "Thank you Verne, thank you Leo, thank you dear Harry, for your generosity in funding my treatment."

Of one thing I was certain: no matter what our differences in lifestyles, tastes, or political views, the Burnett siblings were always there for one another.

Passing the nursing station, one of the nurses noticed me and said, "Your sister-in-law's here, Mrs. Burnett. She's waiting in your room." I hadn't expected a visit so soon. Eager (and not a little anxious) to find out how Davy and Danny were, I hurried along the corridor.

After a cursory hug, Laura unloaded a barrage of questions: How are you getting on? Are they feeding you well? Do you have enough to occupy yourself? Is there anything you need? And on and on. What could I do but nod? When I finally managed to slip a word in edgewise, I asked, "How are the boys? Is Dan over the mumps yet?"

"Oh, well, they're fine. My neighbor Mrs. Jacobi is with them right now; she makes a marvelous chicken soup. Little David came down with it too, of course. . . . Uh, not the chicken soup." She let loose a giggle. "The mumps, I mean. But they're both doing well, resting mostly. And eating buckets of ice cream! It's only been two or three days, of course, but they've been playing Chinese checkers on their beds. Monopoly too, and . . ."

Laura put her hand on my arm and hesitated before asking, "What do you want me to do with them?"

Do with them? I thought.

"Well, it's your decision," she went on. They could stay with her and Verne, she said—though his office was in New York and he was frequently away on business trips. Then she added, "They might be better off at a private school. We'd pay, of course."

I nearly collapsed. My eyes became moist. "I don't know," I replied. Confronted with a decision I didn't know how to make, the tears began to flow. "I can't say what's best for them," I answered.

"You'll have to decide. I just don't know."

Although the sense that Laura and Verne had already made the decision was a mild relief, it also left me overcome with helpless anxiety.

◆◆◆◆◆

After Laura left, I sat on the bed, staring out the window across the East River and into the void beyond. *Here it is,* I told myself, *handed to me on a silver platter, the purest gold in the world: my children. But because of what I've become, I have to leave their future to somebody else.*

The sudden emotion set my insides churning.

The childhood impressions I'd written about, which Dr. Thomas hadn't seemed too interested in, flooded my brain again. It had been the kind of childhood Danny and David should be having—though one without a moping and depressed mother. They deserved better. They deserved a strong, healthy head start. What would happen to them now? What kind of school would Laura find? Or would they live with their aunt, with Verne there but off and on? Would they be treated well? With respect?

I sat looking out the window. Once again, the guilt became too much. I collapsed on the bed and buried my face in the pillow, sobbing.

11.

Within two weeks, my mumps (Davy's too) had run their course. On this brisk morning in early March, Uncle Verne had taken the commuter train into Manhattan, and with our aunt at the wheel of the woody, my brother and I left the farm for our new school.

While Aunt Laura kept up a steady stream of chatter, I brooded about what lay ahead and remained tight-lipped with just an occasional "Uh-huh" in response to her comments.

That is, until I cried out, "Danbury! We're in Danbury, Aunt Laura. Can we stop?"

"I'm afraid we don't have time, dear."

"Just for a few minutes?" Davy pleaded. "I want to see Mackie. We had to leave him behind."

"Yes dear, I know, but we have an appointment. Mr. and Mrs. Musgrove are expecting us at the school by noon. We'll all have lunch there. Won't that be fun?"

I slumped against the leather seat and held my tongue.

In the back, Davy sat grim-faced, his arms crossed. But instead of continuing to fret about what the school might be like, and to take my mind off Mom's sudden departure—which upset me every time I thought about what might be wrong with her—I drifted back to a day in Danbury I'd spent with my pal Kenji, a day when we'd dug a deep trench into a backyard snow bank. Dead branches served as

Tommy guns as we held off a desperate charge of German infantry. Leaping from the trench, we charged across the frozen field, blasting away as the crunchy snow became littered with enemy dead. Until a bleeding soldier rose on one arm, pulled a Luger from his jacket, aimed at me, and snarled, "You die, Yankee *schweinhund!*"

I got so deep into the fantasy, it must have been an hour more when I heard, "Birchfield Center! The school's just up this drive."

As my daydream evaporated, I looked through the car's windshield. Shaded by a row of giant trees stood a huge, weathered three-story frame house with gable windows indicating a fourth floor or attic. Boys of varying ages were moving toward the building from several directions.

"Most of 'em are wearing knickers!" I grumbled.

"Yes, knickerbockers, that's the dress code," said Aunt Laura, smiling.

"But I wear long pants now! Mom lets me wear long pants."

"Well, that's the rule. I'll give Mrs. Musgrove a check, and she'll see you get a couple pairs. David too, of course."

"Me too, what?" came Davy's voice. "You woke me up," he whined as he gave the back of my head a shove.

I turned to take a swipe at him, but he ducked.

"Now then, boys," chirped our aunt as the car pulled up next to steps leading to a long veranda where the gathering schoolboys had begun to form a line. "High noon," she added, glancing at her watch. "Looks like we're just in time for lunch. Let's go."

We hesitated.

"Come along, boys," she urged. "You can leave your suitcases; we'll collect them later."

Davy and I grimaced, then climbed out and followed her up the steps to where a gray-haired couple with syrupy smiles had appeared at the door. To me, they seemed ancient. The man, scarecrow thin, his hair combed right and left, wore a starched collar and thick glasses, and clutched a Bible.

"Well, hello there," he said pleasantly, greeting Aunt Laura. "You must be Mrs. Verne Burnett."

"That's right, the boys' aunt. The boys' mother is, well, ah—she's also a Mrs. Burnett, of course." Then, in whispered confidence, she added, "She and the boys' father are divorced, you see. So now she uses her maiden name. She's poorly at the moment, but she'll be up and about soon," she added, glancing at Davy and me.

"Ah, I see, I see. Well, delighted to meet you. I'm Abner Musgrove. And this is Mrs. Musgrove."

I eyed the couple suspiciously. Mrs. Musgrove, stout and dressed in tweed, seemed to appraise Davy and me as though we were some species of noxious insect.

"Mousegrave?" Davy whispered to me, much too loudly.

"Musgrove, son!" corrected Abner with a condescending smile. "It's an old English name."

"Well, they seem like first-rate young fellows," chimed in Mrs. Musgrove, changing the subject but not her expression while she stared at us. "I'm sure they'll fit right in."

"Do I have to wear knickers?" I asked.

"Now, Daniel . . ." chided our aunt.

"I'm afraid that's the rule," added Mr. Musgrove. "All our fellows under fifteen wear 'em. It's how we tell the boys from the men," he chuckled.

With his strange stare, Abner Musgrove reminded me of Eddie Cantor, the pop-eyed comedian. Mrs. Musgrove, I decided, could have been a model for the plump ladies drawn by Helen Hokinson I'd seen in *The New Yorker* at the dentist's office a few weeks earlier. Imagining I might decide to become a cartoonist myself, I'd been paying close attention to the expressions on people's faces.

"Come right on in, won't you?" said Mr. Musgrove. Then, indicating his Bible, he added, "I always like to start off meals with a short passage from the good book, don't you know."

"How nice," smiled Aunt Laura as she followed the Musgroves.

As I was about to enter, I felt a hand clamp onto my shoulder. I looked up. An older boy towered over me. "Some mop ya got, curly," sneered the boy. "What's your name? Shirley Temple?"

Nearby, two of his buddies snickered. I glanced at Davy.

"This your brother?" the tall boy asked, rubbing his knuckles over my brother's very short hair.

"Hey!" Davy protested.

"Cute kid. I like his crew cut. Let's call him Little Bit, yeah?" said the boy, turning to his buddies, who nodded in agreement. "Okay, go gobble your lunch . . . Shirley." He sneered, dismissing me with a sharp poke in the back.

"Curly Shirley," chimed in another boy.

"Curly girly Shirley," snickered a third.

As I turned and followed Davy through the doorway, my thoughts drifted back to Danbury, to the run-in with Rico and his cronies. I didn't need to guess; I was already convinced we'd be in for a rough time at the Musgrove School for Boys.

After our earlier school, a place like this seemed quite grim to both David and me.

12.

Day followed endless day on the seventh floor, with dream-filled nights too often haunted with the sense of an ever-widening gulf between the boys and myself. True, it had only been two weeks, though I felt I was beginning to emerge from the fog. But I was also aware that in order to recover, and more importantly to carry on a successful life outside, especially for Davy and Dan, I'd have to undertake some kind of journey of self-discovery—months-long, perhaps, but how to proceed, I had no clue. While the twice-weekly sessions with Dr. Thomas threw up an occasional insight, I quickly realized that the answers would be up to me.

The dreary morning walks in the windblown garden with the high wire fence continued, and at meals, most of my tablemates continued to eat in silence.

Still, recognition that I'd as yet only dipped my toe into the murky waters leading to my recurring depression somehow gave me courage. At least I'd never reached the stage of the young woman who, in a frenzy of screaming, had to be restrained by several nurses. Nor suffered delusions of the kind that found a woman in her late fifties rocking and talking about Jesus for hours. Or endured the fate of the hysterical patient brought in one morning who was rumored to be getting the "bath" treatment. (Although I wasn't sure such dire remedies were used here.)

Fortunately, the shadows were softened each morning with the cheery arrival of Mrs. Jackson, wheeling in her cart of boxes stuffed with wool, clay, paints, and craft materials. "Is there anything else you'd like to try your hand at, Mrs. Burnett?" she asked, noting that I'd knitted half a dozen identical scarves over the past weeks. "I mean, you're likely to exhaust my supply of wool."

I'd glanced at her anxiously.

"Sorry, I'm just kidding," she added with a disarming laugh.

"Oh . . . Well, it keeps my hands busy."

"And I don't mean to discourage you. Your knitting is superb. But, well, variety is the spice of life as they say. Right?"

I sat quietly, just thinking.

"Maybe some drawing?" Mrs. Jackson went on. "Or writing?"

This brought back a memory: "My father always said I would be a writer."

"He sounds like a perceptive fellow."

"He was."

"And so . . . ?"

Another memory. "Well . . . I had a summer job once, during college, painting paper boxes for Tony Sarg, the puppeteer. In fact, seeing Sarg's production of *The Rose and the Ring* inspired my brother Harry to get into puppetry. And later I worked with him, touring Michigan with his marionettes. I sewed the costumes."

"Really! How splendid. When was that?"

"Let's see. . . . 1920, I believe. Then again in '28, up through New England."

"How marvelous. Wish I'd had a chance to experience something like that. Sounds like it would make a fascinating story. I'd love to hear more if you ever feel like writing about it."

While intrigued with the idea, I felt far from ready just then to share whatever I might write with anyone. "Well, perhaps just some painting for now, okay?" I replied.

"That's fine," said Mrs. Jackson. She turned to her cart, dug into one of her big cardboard boxes, and handed me a small, plain gift box. "Try this," she suggested.

I looked at the box, turning it over slowly in my hands, thinking, reflecting. Within minutes I set to, painting red and green strokes in a simple design on its top. As I worked something gradually began to stir, something deep inside, the idea that if I could begin all over from the bottom, almost like a child, and learn to do one thing at a time, carefully and well, then continue to do more things, one by one, I might discover the courage to just go on living; simply, from day to day, being useful in some capacity. That seemed important—to find a way to be useful.

Coincident with this inside stirring my hands began to tremble, and I smeared the design. Immediately unnerved, I spent the rest of the session mixing red and green paints into a deep brown and covered the entire box with it, until Mrs. Jackson's calming suggestion that I set it aside and try a new pattern tomorrow, after it had dried.

Was it fear, I wondered, that caused me to smear the design, fear of even the simplest assignment? One thing was certain: I had to find out.

◆◆◆◆◆

In the common room's social hour following dinner, I watched the depressed older woman who'd broken down sobbing during my first lunch suddenly become animated. Free of depression for short periods, she set about entertaining everyone with hilariously clever imitations of ballet dancers, clowning in much the way I recalled Harry doing back home in Michigan—to the delight of Dad and my older brothers, but with disapproving looks from mother—who'd then betray a surreptitious smile when she thought none of us would notice.

Tonight, however, though enjoying the comic ballet, something held me back from joining in this lighter mood. Even one of the young student nurses who showed up to ask with a cheerful laugh, "What will it be this evening, ladies? Gin Rummy? Russian Bank? Bridge?" failed to entice me.

As I rose from the chair and headed toward my room, intending to go to bed, I reflected again on what I'd decided was my deepest need: to begin a journey of self-discovery. *What business,* I asked myself, *do I have to be loafing around here, eating three regular meals a day that I didn't even prepare, sleeping eight or nine hours a night, playing Ping-Pong and Chinese checkers, when there's the business of living going on outside?*

The self-questioning became persistent as I changed into my nightgown, pulled back the covers, and settled in. An hour of wakefulness stretched into two. Thoughts of the boys raced through my head; thoughts of my own childhood, of Mother, who had been dead less than three years; of Harry, the brother I was closest to.

Then I came back to my father. Dear Dad. Though gone since 1928, I often talked to him, especially when I was feeling down. Now seemed the right time.

"I know you can hear me, Dad," I whispered. "Should I review my life, do you think? Consciously? Write it down, and with as much kindness for myself as I have for those I think I know? Yes, I remember; you said I should be a writer. Mrs. Jackson seemed encouraging too, so maybe . . ."

Echoes from my previous life came and went as I sifted images and impressions, shadows from the past as I shared them with my father:

"My last husband, Harold, used to spin the most far-fetched yarns, Dad . . . for Danny and David as they followed him around at his chores on the Pennsylvania farm. . . . Let's see now. . . . The polliwog story; how did that go? Oh yes . . . 'Why then that polliwog that didn' have no tail, he looks at them other polliwogs an' says, "You guys don't need t' think y'r so smart 'cause you got tails an' I ain't got no tail."'"

The memory brought back a few tears.

"Harold . . . He barely finished third grade, but he had so many stories to tell. What attracted me to him, Dad? His simplicity, his uncomplicated and childlike way of looking at life, I suppose; his gentleness with the boys? My need to be with someone? Important to think about that."

To be with someone? Was it always like that? Hmm . . .

"Maybe not. Why didn't I bring my old journals along?"

Then I remembered. I'd stuffed a couple I'd been reading into my valise before leaving Danbury. Quickly getting out of bed, I opened the closet (which for the last week had thankfully been left unlocked), retrieved the small suitcase, and found what I was looking for in an inside pocket. Settling back under the covers, I began to read.

"I'll tell you more later, Dad. Okay?"

Landgrove, Vermont. July 23, 1932

This afternoon, still waiting for the baby to be born. I so desperately feel the need to be alone, and Alvah keeps moving around the house, smoking and getting ready to post a book to his brother in New York. I sit there, a newspaper on my lap, trying to draw my thoughts away from themselves, to pocket them for an hour or so, while all the time staring at the mountains dimly outlined in the morning haze.

I'm trying to be there in the room, all of me, so I snatch out a phrase. "You know," I say, "for an old man, Henry How is pretty quick."

So we talk of old Henry who lives in a tumbledown shack in the village, and I escape from my earlier mood for a few minutes, but all the time wishing Alvah would go out to chop kindling so I can be alone for a while.

But I say nothing. Just sit there waiting until he asks, "What's the matter?

"Nothing," I say.

> Sure?"
>
> "Positive."
>
> So he wraps the books and puts a few letters in his file folder, then lights another cigarette and walks around the room while I sit there, my head getting more congested every second until it seems that if I could only scream, "For God's sake, get out!" I would feel better, but knowing if I said it he'd be hurt and wouldn't understand that my wanting to be alone has nothing to do with my feelings for him. Then, because the congestion has to break, I jump up and throw the paper down none too gently and go into the kitchen, thinking, *Oh hell, if I were alone I'd want it otherwise. Better stir around, wash the dishes, do something with my hands, and soon the nerves will quiet.* Then he comes into the kitchen. "I'm going to chop wood now," he says, "so you can be alone."
>
> And I feel ashamed.

Reading this made me think about the marriages I'd had. To good men, kind and decent men. But each flawed in some way: Alvah, Harold . . . and Matt—poor, kind, sensitive Matthew; lying in bed with him in Detroit the night of our wedding, and wondering what to do, and—

"Oh, shit!" I exclaimed. "That's unfair, Mary. Admit it: you were flawed too. Was it my overriding sense of empathy that dictated those choices? Where did that come from? That compassion for men who seemed like lost souls, men like Harold, or not quite grown up, like Matthew and Alvah?"

As I lay quietly again, sifting through the years, it came to me. Much of long ago began to unfold as I tried to penetrate the mists of early childhood. I thought of my mother, a woman with energy to burn but who never matured emotionally in any way. *Not unusual for her day,* I decided. *Let her go.*

Dad. Dear Dad. "You will be a writer," he said to me more than once. "You have such human feelings."

Did I want to write? I'd momentarily balked at Mrs. Jackson's suggestion, but now, seized by a sudden urge, I got out of bed, hurriedly put on my robe, and sat at the small table opposite. Opening the single drawer, I took out the lined writing pad Laura had brought on her previous visit. *I won't have to show anybody. Perhaps just setting down images from the past will help sort out the present. Can't be any more difficult than trying to paint a small, plain box, can it? I've written before, all through high school and college, and even a little after that: my diaries, poems too—one was even published in a New York newspaper,* The Village Voice. *What was that poem? I can't recall. . . . Maybe I should write about Dad. . . . We were so close. . . . So much I remember; his patience, his kindness . . .*

I sat there, staring into space. Then, registering a memory, I gradually smiled and whispered, "Of course!" I picked up a pencil and began to write . . .

> It was the day of my grandmother's funeral. Uncle Milt, my soldier uncle who had fought in the Civil War, hadn't arrived, and everyone assumed he wouldn't show up for his mother's burial. Some thought he didn't know she had died. Some thought he didn't care.

> The day was cold. February. Snow covered the ground. Tiny icicles hung from the leafless branches, and long icicles hung from the eaves of our house.

I paused, thinking, continuing to smile. *What waves of peace come,* I thought, *when the pencil once more gets to the paper. . . .*

> Mother wore a black dress that day. She never normally wore black, but that day she wore black. I didn't like the dress, but I liked the pretty row of small pearl buttons that started at the neck and ran down the front. Her long sleeves ended in cuffs, each closed with a pearl button.
>
> Grandma's body was brought to the house in a black casket and laid across two sawhorses. She had died at seventy-five. The casket was open. Grandma lay there in her black dress. There were no pearl buttons on the dress, only little black buttons. Her hands were folded across her stomach. There was a large gray mole on her chin. A long white hair grew from the mole, and I remembered that she cut it whenever it got too long.

Caught up in the memory of that frozen wintry day, I quickly became lost in the process, recording every detail—from the big beaver hat with the red ribbon around the crown that she wore, to the minister reading from the Bible, to the family and other mourners singing "Rock of Ages," and on to the pallbearers lifting the casket, maneuvering it through the door and down the front steps to the waiting hearse.

I wrote nonstop, my pencil flying across the pages.

At the top of the long hill, the carriage pulled into the cemetery. My aunts and uncles stood together, talking quietly. The pallbearers lowered the casket into the big hole that had been dug in the frozen ground.

The minister told us to gather around. Everyone moved in close to the grave as the minister opened his Bible and said, "We commit your soul to God." All of a sudden, there was an excitement in the air. My aunts and uncles began talking to one another and pointing. Someone was coming over the side of the hill. I looked up. A man was coming, a man dressed in the uniform of an old soldier. He wore a long, thick coat and bent over as he walked. I could see his breath. I could hear him breathing. He had a red beard with ice on it. His eyes were red.

It was my Uncle Milt.

Uncle Milt stumbled to the lowering casket. Two of the pallbearers leaned down and opened it. I could see Grandma. I could see the gray mole on her chin with the long white hair sticking out. Uncle Milt knelt and kissed Grandma. He started to cry, then began sobbing. The pallbearers closed the casket. I shivered. The air was cold, the sky overhead a solid gray.

We all crowded back into the carriage, Uncle Milt too. My mother was crying. My father looked sad. He took off his mittens and gave them to Uncle Milt, telling him to put them on.

And then we were home.

My eyes became moist. Dear, kind Dad, I thought, always taking care of others. What a contrast to Mother.

"Come into the kitchen, Milt," said my father when we got home. He opened the oven door and pulled a chair up next to it. "Put your feet in there," he said.

"His shoes are wet," said Mother. Uncle Milt took off his shoes. Gray wool socks stuck to his feet. Dirty socks. I knew the smell of dirty socks.

Mother made a face, but Uncle Milt didn't see her.

"I'll get you some dry socks," said Dad. Uncle Milt took off his socks. His feet were red. Big veins stuck out on them. His toenails were dirty. My father returned with a pair of socks and gave them to Uncle Milt. "Here," he said. "Put them on. Put your feet up on the oven door. Get yourself thawed out."

Uncle Milt rested his feet on the oven door and smiled. Then my father said, "Mother, get him something hot to drink, won't you?"

Laying down the pencil, I slowly reread the pages. *It's written in the voice of a child,* I realized. *Just the way I remember it, just the way I wanted it to be.* With a satisfied smile I rose from the table, took off my robe, hung it in the closet, then climbed into bed. "Thanks, Dad," I whispered, "Thanks for the inspiration."

Within five minutes, I was sound asleep.

13.

"Way to go, Little Bit!" barked Gordon Arbuckle. From my position at shortstop, I saw him thump Davy on the back. Arbuckle was the pack leader of the trio who'd greeted us on our first day at Musgrove. And though Davy hated the irksome name he'd been dubbed with, I noticed him grinning as he returned to the bench after driving in two runs for their team on the school's scruffy baseball diamond.

"Yeah, we're gonna skunk those wieners," chimed in Arbuckle's buddy Morris, the freckle-faced joker of the gang. His loud banter echoed across the diamond.

"Right you are," laughed Arbuckle. "Did you see the way Shirley let that ball bounce clean off his glove and roll into left field?"

Davy's reply was deliberately loud enough for me to hear.

"My brother's name is Dan!"

Taunts continued from Arbuckle's pack; insults I was sure were supposed to provoke me.

"Yeah, yeah," replied Arbuckle with a dismissive pat on Davy's head. "But he still missed by a country mile when he finally picked up the ball and tried to throw to first."

"Too bad he's such a pansy," guffawed Charlie, the roly-poly third member of Arbuckle's clique—a bunch who saw themselves as the Grand Poobahs of anything that went on among the boys when they were out of sight of the Musgroves.

I could see Davy mumbling something. Later, he let me know he'd told them I didn't really like baseball that much. I couldn't hear anything else, so he more or less gave me a rundown of it after dinner that night.

"Charlie got pissed off at you because you read better than the other guys," said Davy. "He said that you, uh . . . 'breezed through a couple pages o' *Treasure Island*' like you was 'cutting butter.' And another guy called you 'a damn wisenheimer,' and some other jerk told everyone you were 'a real snotnose.'"

I wasn't too surprised that they talked about me like that, but the next thing Davy told me was what they had in store. Morris had leaned over and whispered to Arbuckle that they should get a two-by-four, or something like an old railroad tie, and bounce me around the school on it.

"And Arbuckle said they were gonna . . ." Davy's voice dropped to a whisper. ". . . bust your balls. Most everyone thought that was really funny; they were all laughing."

Convinced at the time their talk was all bluff, what I didn't know was that Davy, terrified, decided that in order to keep up to date with their plans he'd better stay on their good side, play up to them, and go on pretending to be their "Little Bit" mascot. Since our mom had gone away—to exactly where, neither of us had a clue—I was all he had in the way of family, so he had to do what he could to protect me. No use both of us worrying, he'd decided; he'd just tough it out until school finished for the summer or until Mom showed up to take us home.

◆◆◆◆◆

To both Davy's and my irritation, Musgrove rules consisted of two pages of closely spaced type on school stationary that was handed to each new student. Most involved prohibitions: no running in the halls, no spitting, no playing with matches (you'd get expelled for that), no talking back to instructors, no long pants for boys under fifteen, no socks with holes in them, no visitors in rooms without permission, no food taken outside the dining room, and, oddly enough, no frogs allowed in the school—rumor had it that an enormous bullfrog smuggled in by a former student had escaped and terrified the school's cook when she removed the lid from a big pot of day-old spaghetti and discovered the slimy creature staring up at her. The no frogs prohibition worried me, since we'd just had a letter from our Pop in California to let Davy and me know he'd captured a horned toad in the Mojave Desert and it was on its way to us, packed in a small box with air holes.

Another rule, though unwritten and most often enforced with a penetrating scowl was, as we learned on arrival, never to make fun of Mr. Musgrove's name. A rule frequently ignored when no adults were within earshot, especially by Arbuckle and his buddies, who flouted the dictum with half a dozen variations.

Two more, Wilma Musgrove's favorites, echoed across the dining hall at every meal: "Finish whatever is on your plate, boys; we must always remember the starving children in India." And finally, "Never take the Lord's name in vain."

◆◆◆◆◆

Following dinner each night, and before lights out at 8:30, all the boys gathered in the Musgrove living room, a space crammed to excess with dark mahogany furniture placed just so on a fading oriental carpet. It reminded me of the Murdstone residence I'd seen in the movie version of David Copperfield, with W.C. Fields as Wilkins Micawber.

Wearing the much-hated knickerbockers, the obligatory necktie under V-neck sweaters or cardigans, along with slippers, the boys in the assembly feigned attention as our sanctimoniously dour headmaster read from a book of Bible stories he felt sure would inspire his young charges: Noah and the flood, Sodom and Gomorrah (with child-appropriate wickedness), or perhaps Daniel in the lion's den. Following these homilies, each boy lined up to receive the expected brightly wrapped piece of hard candy doled out by a smiling Wilma Musgrove. A bribe, as we all thought of it, for listening to her husband's oration. Had any perceptive outsider witnessed Musgrove's weekly pontifications, they could well have been reminded of a group of down-at-the-heels vagrants (as they were sometimes politely called) enduring a Gospel lecture at a skid row mission, waiting for their reward of a hot meal.

Tonight's moral instruction (for such it was) related the tale of the infant Moses, saved from Pharaoh's order to kill all newborn male Israelites. Abner Musgrove set to his task with a measured oratorical tone, matching that of the kind of small-town preacher he'd once aspired to be.

"'He was such a lovely child that his mother kept him hid so that Pharaoh's soldiers would not find him. But when she could no longer hide him, she formed a plan to save his life, sure that God would help her to protect her beautiful little boy.'"

Davy and I, sitting cross-legged on the rug, eyed one another, for prior to arrival at the school, our religious indoctrination—except for a Bible Aunt Laura presented me with one Christmas—had been as remote as a lecture on alchemy.

"'She made a little basket out of reeds,'" Musgrove went on, "'weaving them tight so that water could not get in. She knew that at certain times the daughter of the Pharaoh—'" He looked around at all the seemingly attentive young faces. "All the kings of Egypt were called Pharaoh, for Pharaoh means king— '. . . would come down to the river to have a bath, and . . .'"

Davy yawned. Wilma Musgrove's frown told me she'd noticed. I nudged Davy. He looked at me quizzically.

Abner Musgrove's eyes became moist as he went on to describe the tender scene among the bulrushes, with the Nile rising to near flood stage. (It almost seemed as though he'd been witness to the event.) "'. . . she placed her baby boy in the basket of reeds and let it float down the river to where—'"

At that moment, a long, sonorous fart punctuated the sermon.

Instantly, Abner Musgrove slammed his book shut, swept the room with an accusatory scowl, and loudly demanded, "Who broke wind?"

Dead silence. Every boy knew that the wrath of God was about to descend. Except Davy and me, who would quickly discover the school's final taboo, a transgression whispered in secret but never spoken aloud; one that Abner Musgrove considered a grave offence against common decency. And he would have none of it. "Will the boy who broke wind so indicate," Musgrove enunciated slowly, clearly, and with grim determination.

Every boy sat frozen. Mrs. Musgrove eyed her husband with anguished sympathy.

Davy was sure the fart had come from near where we were sitting. He turned to me. I stared back with an open-mouthed and wide-eyed "not me" expression.

Davy wasn't convinced. He knew that even if I'd been the offender, I wouldn't own up.

"One final chance," exclaimed Abner, his Eddie Cantor eyes bulging. "Everyone is aware of my rule: if the vulgar boy who flatulated fails to confess, there will be no treat of candy tonight for anyone!"

Flatulated? I'd never heard the term. My cheeks puffed into a wide, suppressed grin. Davy caught on. Would the big kids blame me if they didn't get their treat?

Abner Musgrove spotted me and leaned forward in his chair, knitting his brows.

Davy noticed. His hand shot into the air. I stared at him.

Musgrove sat back in his chair, surprised. Then a schoolmasterly finger beckoned and indicated a spot on the floor in front of his chair.

Davy looked anxiously at me.

I swallowed hard as Davy got up and with eyes downcast made his way through the sitting boys to accept his punishment. All across the room, little knots of students began mumbling to one another.

"There will be no talking!" commanded Mrs. Musgrove.

My jaw tightened. What would happen to my brother? Would he be sent home? Well, we had no real home. We were kind of like orphans. Would Mom find out? She didn't need more worries. My eyes caught a few of the boys smirking as they looked at Davy. He wasn't the farter. Why didn't whoever did it own up?

I watched apprehensively as Musgrove lectured Davy. Then Davy nodded several times and slogged back across the floor to join me as Abner announced, "That will be all for tonight, boys. We'll find out what happened to the baby Moses tomorrow. Line up for your candy."

As the boys did so, Davy hung back. Then, as everyone filed out and headed up the stairs to their separate rooms, I whispered, "How come you put your hand up? You didn't fart."

"I thought maybe you did."

"No! Why'd you think that?"

"It was close by. And if you got blamed, the big guys would beat you up."

As we mounted the stairs, I said nothing more until we reached the second-floor landing. Then I asked, "You gonna get whipped or what?"

"Uh-uh. They don't hit kids here. Just no candy."

As he was about to head down the corridor, I reached into a pocket and pulled out my treat. "Here," I said, "You can have mine."

Davy shook his head.

I stared at the confection in my hand, then looked at him and mumbled, "You're sure?"

Halfway along the corridor now, he hadn't heard.

I took a few steps up the stairs leading to my third-floor room.

Then I stopped, leaned over the banister and called, "I can take care o' myself, you know. Those big guys don't scare me."

Davy opened his door, glanced back up at me, and nodded. . . . Though I wasn't sure he agreed.

14.

When the clinic's bell woke me at 7 a.m., I'd been dreaming again. No earthshaking revelations, just a jumble of unrelated images. But reflecting on these often helped me sort out dormant anxieties from those of the here and now. So I lay quietly for several minutes piecing together the fragments, then retrieved my pad and pencil to commit this particular dream to paper:

> Two orange birds, one with a broken wing. I'm trying to help the injured bird. Then two little boys appear. They're searching for a home, but how am I to persuade the people who run a small and already overcrowded home for boys that they can take two more? I'm desperate to persuade them, because somehow the boys are as injured as the orange bird, which is trying to flutter away—while at the same time it calls out to be caught and cared for.

But instead of waking me, this dream merges into another:

> Now I'm wearing an old tweed coat, and I seem to have been paying no attention to what's on my feet, a sandal on one foot and a pump on the other. Then I'm

> climbing a rickety staircase toward a dusty attic. A torn carpet and some kind of metal obstruction make every step a torture. Behind me, at the bottom of the stairs, are lights from a theater. A show is about to begin. Then Laura is at the top of the stairs, expressing cranky displeasure with my disheveled appearance, with my rumpled dress in particular.

Well, I thought as I climbed out of bed, slipped on my robe, and headed for the bathroom, *some of the dream isn't so hard to understand.*

The stairs? Having asked permission, I'd been allowed to leave the clinic with Laura for a brief shopping expedition where I'd bought stockings, underwear, and a smart blouse. On our return, elevators between the fourth and seventh floors were on the blink, and we'd been obliged to trudge wearily up three flights.

The theater lights? Laura had brought a letter from Harry conveying excited news of nightly full houses at his recently opened marionette cabaret in Hollywood.

And her disapproving look? No mystery; I'd all too often seen myself in the mirror, a bony wild-eyed scarecrow. My shabby dress didn't meet Laura's high standards? Well, so what? I was certainly capable of looking presentable. After all, hadn't I picked out that smart new blouse?

As for the orange birds, I knew only too well who they were. "Dear Davy," I whispered as my eyes began to tear. "Dear Dan." But what more could I do at that moment than write encouraging letters and trust my beloved sons were being well cared for?

One day at a time, I decided. I looked in the bathroom mirror and, forcing a smile and clenching my fist into a kind of "you can do it" gesture, committed myself to the long healing journey that lay ahead. Suddenly, some of what I'd fed to the furnace now seemed like precious gems that might have provided fresh insight.

Why in God's name did I get rid of most of the stuff in that box? I shook off the question. Water over the damn dam, that's what it was.

◆◆◆◆◆

March slipped into April, and I was still on the seventh floor. The routine remained the same: a morning shower, my mainly silent breakfast companions, and being herded from floor to floor (thankfully the elevators had been repaired). The agonizing fog of my first few days had lifted, and even the plodding circular walk in the soulless garden was made bearable as the springtime air signaled new possibilities.

I still had two hours until lunch, time to dig into the remaining box of old letters and notebooks I'd asked Laura to bring the previous day. Removing the tie from the first bundle, I opened a file and unfolded the first item, a yellowed sheet of paper:

The blossoms have gone from the tall pear tree,
The hyacinth is dead,
But you have come home to comfort me
And summer is here instead
The quivering leaves on the tree will die,
And you'll be going too,
And I will wish in my heart that I
Am summer or part of you.

I wrote that for you, my dear cousin Forman, in 1926, as I recall, the month I spent with you in New York before you left for France. That's the poem some Greenwich Village newspaper published. The remembrance led me to an old notebook. Leafing through it, I found the page I had in mind:

Forman Brown, Mary's cousin once removed, in his early twenties

> Forman Brown, dear Forman. Who are you, and what are you? How can I know you? Deep set eyes, wide forehead, dark hair, with your mouth full of poetry and your heart of song. Somehow, whenever I hear or read one of your verses, Lord Byron comes to mind.

And there were others before Forman. Once more, not having access to discarded writing nagged at me, and I cursed myself. As though to make amends, I took my pencil and started recreating remembered images:

> Round Lake, Michigan. Summer vacation 1914. Charlie Britton, my first date. The day after 8th grade graduation. First date? Was it really a date? The whole class went to Round Lake for a picnic. Our teacher took us, Mr. Huckabee. You asked me to "take a row," Charlie. There was the little dinghy, a bottle of strawberry pop, a great shyness between us, a fumble for words to say to each other as the water slipped by.
>
> Later, when winter came, the first year of high school, my first telephone call from a boy (it was you), mumbling on the phone, still as shy as I (a Sunday evening it was). You asked me if I would go on the sleigh ride. "The whole class is going."
>
> I asked Mama.
>
> "No, you can't go."
>
> So back to the telephone to tell you I was sorry, but I wouldn't be able to.

Before continuing to write, I hesitated a moment, recalling the anger and disappointment: I pounded our green velvet piano bench in frustrated rage, then knelt on the floor and buried my head in my arms, sobbing.

Was anyone there? My mother, Dad, Harry . . . Verne, maybe? But no one heard me.

Then of course, there was Warren Atterbury. Sixteen I was that

August. He, what? Nineteen? Twenty? Anyhow, romance bloomed again, and there was the canoe ride, but there were no kisses, and there was war across the ocean.

Yes, there were many and there were good, glorious, and happy times; walking home in stocking feet from a dance, tossing snowballs at one another after a basketball game, silly fun. But I knew so little then, not even what that old "joke" meant, the one my girlfriends told before anyone had indoor plumbing and we'd use only a basin to bathe in: "Wash up as far as possible, then down as far as possible. And then wash 'possible.'"

My God, how blocked off a girl can get from her center.

My thoughts began to drift to Matthew Parker (Matt), my first real boyfriend. I laid the pencil down and thought it all out before committing to paper. But as I started writing again, the pieces fell quickly into place:

> We'd been to the skating rink the night before, you in a white turtleneck and knitted cap. Sure on the ice, learned from childhood on the lakes of northern Michigan. Me in a long green sweater, scotch plaid skirt, and knitted tam. My weak ankles turning. You laughed at me in a joyful mood and caught me by the arm whenever it seemed that I might fall. So we walked the mile home on snow-packed sidewalks, swinging our skates and laughing at such foolish things.
>
> Then we reached the door. "Come in," I said, "and I'll make us hot chocolate."
>
> My mother: asleep? Awake? Her bedroom door

closed. Harry, surely sound asleep by now in his narrow cot in the tiny bedroom off the kitchen; the other bedrooms, except Mother's, being occupied by university students she rented to—including Forman, now lodging in what had been my little space at the top of the back stairs.

We tiptoed through the dark dining room where my cot stood by the wall; with my teaching job, I was just a weekend border then, from Friday night to Sunday night, and still nineteen. In the kitchen, the silly talk had stopped, and we whispered as I made the chocolate, and we raised the cups to our lips, smiling over the rims at one another as we drank. Then into the living room, and you came to sit beside me on the sofa. You put your arm around my waist and kissed me gently.

He has such thick lips, I thought, and (forgive me) I thought somehow of fish, and I thought of other images I care not to unearth right now but might have to sometime. You stood, then pulled me up and held me close. I had been kissed before, with passion; I had felt a penis (clothed of course) against me.

Then you reached down to pull up my plaid skirt. I felt you against me for a moment, whirled away, and said, "Perhaps you'd better go now." Once more you put your arms about my waist, gentle but sure.

"How," you said quietly, "will we ever know what we feel for each other unless we try?"

That moment, I think, was my first conscious awareness and recognition of the furnace within, burning a fury. Way down deep, there was urgency, a knowing that this was sex. It frightened me that the burning was so big, so close to overwhelming me. I had no defense except a half-baked knowledge that this was not the time or place for whatever might happen, and I said (I think), "Please go now." So you kissed me hard on the lips then turned and left, quietly closing the door. . . .

"I saw you kissing him!" said Mother.

I whirled around, hadn't heard her come down the stairs. "I . . . I think I might be in love with him."

"Just put a love affair out of your mind, dear."

"But Mother, you don't understand. That's all life is . . . a love affair."

"You're crazy. Life is full of misery and hard work, and you may as well make up your mind to it."

Crazy, perhaps. But if the world weren't here for love, I'd not care to be part of it any longer, I thought. "What do you mean by love, Mother?" I asked.

She stared hard at me for several moments, then shook her head, and with what seemed like a disgusted sigh turned and padded back up the stairs.

The luncheon bell rang, and I was almost glad for the interruption because memories had been tumbling forth like an emotional Niagara, and I couldn't keep up. *Got to approach it methodically,* I decided, *sort out all those years like I would the shapes and colors in a jigsaw puzzle, then fit them together piece by piece.*

A pinch of hope was added to the lunch menu when the woman who had sat most days with drooping mouth and hands in her lap and staring at her plate suddenly asked, "Would you please pass me the rolls?" *Such a simple thing,* I thought, *but a huge victory;* not only for the woman but for me too, for it meant that even though the request had been flat and unsmiling, my own persistent attempts at conversation during the stony silences during most meals had perhaps born a little fruit.

I'd also discovered things about my table companions from an especially chatty attendant who encouraged patients to talk during the social hour following lunch. This woman who asked me to pass the rolls had, before marrying, cared for thirty children in an orphanage. Then, following the birth of her first baby, she'd become depressed and unable to do the simplest things, until finally she'd found it impossible to even prepare his formula.

"She's been on the floor for eight months," the attendant had confided. "Husband comes in once or twice a week, takes her out on Sundays now and again, but it doesn't seem to make any difference."

Her first baby, I reflected, recalling Danny's early months, the joy I felt, and how much the poor woman had missed.

◆◆◆◆◆

"Aren't you joining the other ladies?" asked Mrs. Jackson, smiling, as she looked in at my door after lunch.

"Oh, not today, but thank you. I'm in the middle of looking over some things." Unwittingly, Forman had tiptoed into my thoughts again. "Perhaps tomorrow. Is that all right?"

"Of course. You do what you must. I'll just leave you to it."

I returned her friendly smile and turned back to my old diary.

> Mid-May. The dogtooth violets are gone. Spring carpeting the countryside with daisies, and at night the hooting of a lonely owl over on the hillside. Why does sadness invade the heart in the midst of all this beauty, sweet melancholy that colors happiness with sorrow? Oh, sentimental fool . . . Yearn for the moon and be quiet in your heart.

Why the melancholy? What was going on then? Forman, of course, mysterious Forman; such a singular melding of minds. My memory drifted back to lazy summer afternoons picnicking by the river, with Forman quoting from memory long passages by Keats, Shelly, and Walt Whitman, and me reciting Hero's lines from *Much Ado About Nothing*. The way he courted me, hinting at a future together. And how though tied by blood it was so exhausting at times to understand him, his moods and sudden silences, trying to fathom his eyes that held secrets.

It took so long to unlock the riddle, and what a shock when I finally did.

I'm not so sure I'm quite ready to deal with that yet. . . .

"Oh, pisspot! Enough for now. Time to switch this train to another track." I turned to another notebook. In moments I was back to the year of teaching in Manchester, Michigan. The short piece I'd written about one remembered day certainly seemed innocent enough to have been held back from the Danbury furnace's hungry flames:

THE SPITBALL YEAR

It was after four, the hour when I dismissed the thirteen pupils enrolled. Three Kappler children lingered on the stoop of the one-room schoolhouse, waiting for Alvin, their brother.

Alvin, chubby cheeked and freckled, sat at his desk, the third row back from the raised platform where I sat at my desk pretended to be busy correcting papers. It was the first time I had kept anyone after school since I'd taken the job two months before.

It had started during the noon hour lunch break. The thrill of the October sunshine, the autumn leaves that sparkled and danced over the countryside, the thought of tomorrow being Friday churned and swirled as I sat on the stoop and took the last bite of an apple. The children were playing in the gravel, selecting pretty leaves to wax, and it seemed to me all at once that it was silly to go inside.

I was still a big kid at nineteen, with two years of college behind me and memories of my own school days still close. Teachers' frowns and pencils tapping, flies buzzing and sunlight beckoning blended with the urgency of my body to move, high, wide, and deep. I dashed into the schoolroom and saw by the wall clock it was only twelve-thirty; a half-hour yet before I must ring the hand bell ending the lunch break.

There was a game we all knew, Lay-Lo, a glorified hide-and-seek where you chose sides and hid. But hiding could be almost anywhere within range of the human voice. This, I thought, was the perfect day for Lay-Lo.

We chose sides, girls and boys. The five girls and I held our hands over our eyes and giggled as the eight boys ran off to hide. We heard their feet crunching quickly across the gravel, a shout or two, and waited for the far off cry of "Lay-Lo," which should come to us soon from over the low hill behind the schoolhouse, beyond the bushes along a bend in the road, or even from up in the trees down by the creek. We waited. Minutes passed and no sound came. It seemed longer than usual; still, it didn't seem important, really. It was such a beautiful day, and the boys were probably playing some kind of trick on us.

Finally, I called, and could hear my voice echo, "Lay-Lo . . . Lay-Lo . . . Where are you?"

"Come on, girls," I said. "We can't wait any longer; we'll have to find them." The girls followed.

We searched behind the outhouse; we ran down the road to the bend and searched the bushes, expecting at any moment the boys would jump out with screams and laughter and chase us all the way back to home base at the schoolhouse.

Again I called. Again no answer. We went down to the creek and looked up into the trees. Once we thought we heard a snicker, but a careful survey turned up nothing. By this time, I was beginning to feel some small agitation over my responsibility to the sixty-dollar-a-month job. It was highly unlikely that any school board member was on the road today, but you could never be sure.

My agitation increased. It was less what anyone would think, than the fact that the boys were disobedient. They'd played silly tricks before and bombarded the room with spitballs when they were sure nobody was looking, but they genuinely liked me and nearly always obeyed the rules, or came when I called. But now the authority I felt was mine had begun to evaporate—and without it, what would I have?

Finally, a bit desperate, I said, "Come on, girls. Let's go back, and I'll ring the bell."

They ran with me up the hill and into the schoolhouse, where I took the handle of the large brass bell and flew back into the yard and rang it. I rang it and rang it. Still, no response from the brigands. I rang it again and again. Nothing. I was still ringing it when Alvin's little sister tugged at my skirt.

"Someone's comin'," she said, and I looked down the

road. Appearing around a bend over the hill was a black Ford. Before I had time to consider whom it might be the Ford had made the hill and a small, plump, ruddy man in his sixties had set his brake and stepped out. He frowned at me over his glasses, took a gold watch from his vest pocket, and looked at it. Then he walked over to me.

"You don't remember me, do you?" he said with a smile that reminded me of an old cat we had when I was a child.

"No." I hesitated. "Oh, you're Mr. Halloran, the county superintendent," I said, and felt the ground give way under my feet.

"Are you aware that it is well after one o'clock?"

"Yes, I know. But we can't find the boys."

Mr. Halloran glanced around, then looked at me again over his glasses; suspiciously, I thought. As I stood there awkwardly, trying to decide what to say next, the boys suddenly appeared, Alvin bringing up the rear. Somehow, they sensed the visitor's position of authority, and without a word they tromped into the school and took their seats. I followed with the girls. Mr. Halloran entered and immediately began lecturing the children.

They don't need your lecture, I thought. *I'm strong. I can handle this myself. Besides, I like these children. Play is good for them.*

But instead of speaking my mind, as soon as Mr. Halloran finished, I began oral arithmetic, recalling a wonderful lesson my own grade-school teacher had taught: One plus two times three divided by three equals three; ten minus four plus one times two divided by two equals seven; four plus three—

Mr. Halloran interrupted to give me a lecture on teaching to meet the realities of today. These were rural children, he said. What they needed was practical mathematics drawn from the daily cycle of farming life: how many yards in an acre; how many pigs were in an average litter; how many quarts of milk a typical dairy cow gave, and so on. Finished with the speech, he wiped his glasses, smiled at me with his little cat smile, and walked out the door.

I stood at the desk, towering over the children. None of us moved a muscle until the Ford started up, chugged off down the road and disappeared around a bend. The children's eyes were glued to me; looking for what? My reaction? My relief? I scanned the class. Alvin grinned mischievously and raised his hand, a signal for wanting to go to the outhouse.

I stiffly granted permission, and as he got up and started for the door, I added, in a tirade, "And also, Alvin Kappler, you will stay after school and write fifty times, 'I will come when I am called.'"

Subdued then, we took up our schoolwork. I looked

at the clock. *One forty-five; two hours and a quarter to go before dismissal.* The clatter of dinner pails being tucked under desks. Chalk on slates. The beautiful outdoors.

"And," I announced finally, "There will be no afternoon recess!"

"Now why in blazes did I cancel the recess?" I asked myself as I lay aside the story. The children had been having such fun, and play was as important as letters and numbers. I thought for a long moment, then let out a guffaw of realization. It could only have been fear for my own reputation in the eyes of the school superintendent.

Wonder where I got that from?

I didn't really have to guess. It went back to Mama's prohibitions, always squelching our fun: "No, Mary, you cannot go on a sleigh ride with that young man. It's not proper." Or, "Harry, you look ridiculous. Take off that shawl this instant!" when he'd be clowning around as an old woman.

Not the kind of negativity I want to pass on to Danny or Davy or to any other children. Though I suppose that's how I've been acting of late. . . . Sorry, boys. You deserve better.

"So the hell with you, Mr. School Superintendent Halloran!" I exclaimed, snapping the notebook shut.

15.

During Laura's next visit, we got into a bit of a tiff. It began with a letter from Davy she'd brought. Davy had written about a "horny toad" their father had sent from California, and I'd laughed, pointing out that he meant *horned* toad. The word "horny" elicited a prudish cough from Laura (which I ignored). I went right on to explain the "secret code" the boys and I had established: the little sun that Davy had drawn at the top of his letter indicated that he and Danny were doing okay; a dark rain cloud would indicate if they were unhappy.

"I'm sure the boys are doing just fine," said Laura. "The school is a lovely place with a grand old house on pleasant grounds, with lots of activities, two boys to a room. And the Musgroves are good Christian people. There are Bible classes every Sunday, and—"

At that I got a bit miffed, pointed out that the dark cloud on Danny's letter indicated he was upset about something, that the boys had never had any religious training, that Alvah was an agnostic, perhaps even an atheist, and that although he and I had not always seen eye to eye, we felt it important to expose the boys to all kinds of different ideas and trust that in their own good time they'd decide for themselves what was right or wrong.

This got Laura on her high horse about the importance of moral values, explaining that she and Verne had chosen Musgrove precisely because of the religious training the boys would receive. "After all, your first marriage was in a Congregational church."

So on and on we went, with me finally telling Laura that whether the boys became Catholics or Buddhists or atheists or whatever, it should be up to them. They didn't need the Bible rammed down their throats, and I felt what children needed most to become decent people were tolerant, understanding parents.

By now I was in tears.

"Here, take this," said Laura, handing me a handkerchief.

"It's the boys I worry about most," I sobbed. "So I'll stand a chance of becoming the mom I need to be."

"Come now, dear, you've always been good to the boys.

"Oh. I've tried. Goodness knows I've tried. Though it hasn't been easy."

Laura nodded.

"I . . . I miss reading to them at night." I went on, forcing a tiny laugh. "Still, I suppose they'll survive a few months of Bible lessons."

Laura opened her mouth to say something . . . then decided she'd better not.

◆◆◆◆◆

That night found me restless. Concerns about Davy and Danny triggered by the letters Laura brought had kept me awake until near dawn. When sleep did come, it arrived with a parade of unsettling fragmentary images, dreams that finally gave way to a few hours of merciful oblivion.

After an early shower, I stood by the mirror, combing my hair. While noting the circles remaining under my eyes, my general appearance seemed better. "Perking up, aren't you, Eagle Beak?" I remarked with a nod. The joking name Alvah had dubbed me with because of my aquiline nose didn't seem disparaging this morning. Actually, I felt honored to have it; *me and old Abe Lincoln,* I thought, chuckling.

But returning to my room, the concerns about the boys came rushing back. I slumped onto the bed. As depression once more began seeping in, I sat there like a bump on a log—until a knock sounded at the door.

"It's time for breakfast, Mrs. Burnett," said a thin, uncertain female voice.

Too deeply into myself, I didn't look up or even respond.

"Mrs. Burnett?"

I slowly raised my eyes. Standing in the doorway was a thin, pale, sad-faced young woman with stringy blonde hair; one of the student nurses who came in from time to time to help out with patients' activities.

"Sorry," I said, sitting up. "I've been preoccupied. Martha, aren't you?" I asked.

The nurse nodded, took a handkerchief from a pocket, and blew into it.

"It seems you've caught a cold, dear," I commented.

She shook her head, then wiped her eyes.

As always when encountering someone whose troubles possibly outweighed my own, my sympathies were immediately aroused.

I got up, moved toward the young woman, and asked what the problem was. As she burst into tears, I put an arm around her, led her to sit on the bed, and sat beside her. With a little encouragement, I urged her to talk.

"Well, you see," Martha went on between sobs, "my fiancé . . . Peter's a pilot in the navy and, well . . . we got word that he's been missing . . . a telegram, it was. His plane didn't return from a reconnaissance mission in the South Pacific, and—"

As she continued, I flashed back to World War I, with one of my brothers overseas, and the family's deep concern about him. Then I asked Martha if she should be here at work.

"I had to do something," she replied, still sobbing. "I was going crazy at home waiting for news."

Other than suggesting she not give up hope, I could only listen and interject an occasional supportive thought as she described how she and her young man had known one another since grade school, had been talking of marriage even then, and had begun to save small sums toward buying a modest home. "Somewhere across the river, in New Jersey, in the country, away from all the traffic and such," Martha explained sadly.

Just my listening seemed to buoy her, allow her to finally dry her tears, offer a thin smile, and say, "Thank you so much, Mrs. Burnett, I think I can get through the day now."

While joining the other women at breakfast, I realized that as tragic as might be the outcome of the young nurse's news, being able to offer a bit of comfort to someone snapped me out of my doldrums. *No more self-pity,* I vowed. *Concentrate on the journey, unravel the shambles and horrors of my yesterdays, and get ready for whatever tomorrow brings.*

Easier said than done, of course, but if I could maintain a positive frame of mind, I knew I'd be ahead of the game.

Though continuing attempts at conversation weren't forthcoming, I felt my efforts were beginning to pay off when the young woman who a few days earlier had asked for the rolls to be passed said "Thank you" again when I handed her the basket—and then added, "You're very kind, Mrs. Burnett."

"Please, just call me Mary," I replied

"Mary," she repeated with a slow nod.

◆◆◆◆◆

While traces of snow no longer lingered in the garden's shadows and greenery was sprouting here and there, a stiff wind blowing off the river made me glad I'd bundled up for the morning exercise. I'd hoped the student nurse would be among those accompanying us so we could talk further, but she hadn't shown up, so, sitting alone with my thoughts and an early diary, my anguish over the possible death in action of Martha's fiancé brought me back to memories of my first long ago husband-to-be.

I opened the diary and began to leaf through it.

> *January 10, 1918*
>
> Matt. Sweet, precious Matthew. Serious, thin, and earnest, so childishly disappointed because they would not let you play at soldier, but whose image, whose

presence makes my blood run sweet and hot and my knees tremble. Can we make a life together, one that will be deeper, richer, and fuller than the rest? Why can't I say these things to you? Because they would embarrass you, and you would close yourself away.

Reflecting on the words, I could almost hear his voice . . .

"I was rejected by the army; you know that."

I had known.

"But I never said why. I just told you I didn't pass the physical."

I'd listened.

"But . . . Well, the reason . . . It was because my lungs are none too good."

I'd said I was happy for him, but this just got his dander up.

"You're happy?"

Of course I was happy, because he wouldn't have to serve, maybe get killed. And what were they fighting for anyway? I'd wondered.

In Flanders fields the poppies blow,
between the crosses, row on row . . .

Now, in this Second World War, so many boys from my hometown of St. Johns had already died. Thirty-two, I'd read. And from Ann Arbor, where I was then living? I didn't know, but whatever the number, it was certainly another terrible waste.

Matt's voice returned, cutting into my thoughts: "You women are strange," he'd said; that much I recall. Then he went on to maintain that if he'd been fit and been shipped off to France I'd be proud of him, but if he'd refused or "been a milksop like that fellow Forman," I'd be ashamed. But now that he was not fit for the army, I was happy. "It's insane!" he carped.

Milksop? Forman? I hadn't been surprised. Matthew was so jealous the year before when Forman and I toured the Upper Peninsula with Harry's little marionette show.

The argument went on, with Matt grumbling about me traveling "unescorted," and with me retorting, "With my brother and my cousin?"

Even as I recalled that quarrel, another voice bulled its way into my ruminations. "I don't care for Matthew Parker," it said.

"Why ever not, Mother?"

"He's soft, like your father."

I'd dismissed the remark. What Mother had described as Dad's softness, I had always regarded as his sensitivity.

As for Matthew—rejected by the army, with barely adequate grades at university and a long way from being established as the lawyer he hoped to become, he had, in Mother's eyes, poor prospects. She'd been frank about that. Her own damn precious reputation was what mattered! Judgments were formed on that basis, formed then kept under lock and key in an emotionally pigheaded strongbox.

Thank God I've let that go, I thought, recalling the years it had taken me to shuck the smug, self-satisfied posturing Mother had clung to.

"Who gives a fig what the neighbors think?"

I looked briefly around the garden to check if anyone had noticed me talking to myself, and had just turned back to my diary when the yard's genial, rotund nurse reminded me in her strong Irish brogue that in this cold weather what I needed was "brisk walkin' because, to be sure, it keeps the blood movin'."

Agreeing it was a good idea, I obediently got up to join other patients circling the path. But even as I walked, I reopened the diary to a page that had just caught my eye:

> Matthew came out to Marshall to drive me home every afternoon when my day's teaching ended. Soft kisses before we'd part, his ardor ever more insistent. Then there was the Saturday he picked me up at the rooming house soon after he'd told me about the army rejecting him. Then his, "God, I want you, girl" as he ran a hand up under my skirt. The long drive through wooded hills, and the sun setting as a cool mist rose from the river. I put on my sweater, and soon he turned off onto a side road and parked near a grove of birches. We walked hand in hand into the wood and sat on a log. He kissed me again, long and hard, and . . . *It's going to happen now,* I thought. He helped me to the ground and asked if I was afraid. "I belong to you," I said, and he reminded me it could be four years until he finished law school. I told him I could wait. Then he lay me gently back against the leaves and we held each other close, face to face. . . . *It's going to happen now.* . . . He slipped his hand under

my sweater, and his hand was on my breast, and even though I felt the strength leave my body, something held me back. "Not now," I said. "Not yet . . ."

What was it Mother always said? "Marry in haste; repent at leisure." (What didn't Mother always say?) And what else had run through my mind way back then? Self-doubts, wanting to get away from home? Was marriage the way? Was Matt the man? Or Forman? What was it my new sister-in-law Laura had said? The next diary entry gave me the answer:

"Sis, I think your cousin Forman is sweet on you."

"Fiddlesticks," I scoffed—even as I thought of Forman's searching eyes, his velvet lips spouting lines from Shelly or Shakespeare, or from Harry's play as we rehearsed backstage in little theaters along last summer's tour; his introducing me to the poetry of Michael Drayton, with whose fifteenth-century sonnet he tried to convey a message that remained a mystery to me for so long, and is so burned in memory that I can recite it still:

Since there's no help, come, let us kiss and part
Nay, I have done, you get no more of me,
And I am glad, yea, glad with all my heart,
That thus so cleanly I myself can free.
Shake hands forever, cancel all our vows,
And when we meet at any time again
Be it not even in either of our brows
That we one jot of former love retain.

Now at the last gasp of Love's latest breath,
When, his pulse failing, Passion speechless lies,
When Faith is kneeling by his bed of death,
And innocence is closing up his eyes.
Now, if thou wouldst, when all have given him over,
From death to life though might'st him yet recover.

With a sigh, I tried to bring my attention back to Matthew, but my memory continued straying to Forman. How well my diary recalled my confusion at the time:

> I'll marry Matt. I love him, don't I? In a way, we're strangers. Do I love him? But then, how much more a stranger Forman is, even though we're bound by family ties; seeing him only on weekends, hearing him and Harry through the ceiling, giggling over shared secrets no one else is privy to. Even me. His rapping out, "I love you," in Morse code on the floorboards in his room above. Knowing him for only a couple of summer months but having known Matt three years now, since our second year at university.
>
> For Christ's sake, Mary, make a decision. Shit or get off the pot!

16.

Back in my room again, a long-ago conversation came to mind, one so distressing that even now I recall my mother's anger, her accusatory words:

"Married? You're getting married?" she said when I announced that Matt Parker and I were tying the knot. At that, Mother put down the kettle of boiling water she'd been pouring into the teapot. "What have you done?" she shouted. "Answer me, Mary," she demanded. "Have you . . . Did he . . . Oh my God!"

My face red with embarrassment, I assured her nothing had happened (nothing had, but almost).

She wouldn't listen. "You are ruined!" she screamed. "He's ruined you! Don't speak to me again, don't ever speak to me again!"

As I looked on in stunned silence, she impulsively picked up the pot holding the freshly made tea, and with a fury I'd never seen before, hurled it wildly, just missing me and crashing against the wall behind. The scalding water ran down the kitchen wallpaper in tiny brown rivulets. Sinking to the floor, Mother lay there stiffly, arms and legs stretched out, as from her mouth came sobs and screams loud enough to wake the dead.

Harry came rushing into the room, realized that Mother had succumbed to another of her tantrums, saw my gesture of exasperation, rolled his eyes, and beat a hasty retreat.

If only we could have spoken together calmly, sensibly, I thought. But that was 1920, and Mother still bore the "men are beasts" scars inherited from her own mother, her great fear of sex. *My God! How on earth did she have four children?* I wondered. *Laid back and thought of England, I suppose!* I had to chuckle.

Focusing then on everything that followed Mother's bitter diatribe let me continue to explore my old diary, let the next years, even with their uncertainty and confusion, unfold in a kaleidoscopic montage of images and snatches of conversation:

> So Matt and I married. The stiff dress, the tight corset, the lilies of the valley, the entire phony thing, the dress, "white for purity."
>
> "This will be a sad occasion for my boy," said Forman's mother, Marion.
>
> She noticed my quizzical frown.
>
> "Well, you must know how he feels about you, dear. I'm sure he'll feel badly about it for a while. Young people have hearts, don't they?"
>
> I bit my lip. "Oh dear God, am I making a mistake?"
>
> "For goodness sake!" Marion whispered. "Don't you breathe a word of what I said. Don't you dare!"
>
> I turned away and walked down the stairs, my face a deadpan mask distorted by a stupid grin. A few steps from the bottom I paused and saw Mother, resigned now, wipe tears from her eyes. Dad, his head held high, beamed up at me.

Piss-pot! I thought. *Isn't this some kettle of fish I've got myself into?*

Mary and Forman, the man she was most attracted to; about 1923

Mary in her wedding dress, when she married her first husband, Matt Parker

The Burnett Family around the time of Mary's wedding

Harry, Rose, and Mary visiting Forman's home in Otsego, Michigan

Looking out my window onto the East River, I thought back on how it had been only weeks since I'd wanted to throw myself into it. Then shadows of my three years with Matthew filtered past: tin cans rattling behind Harry's old Ford that carried us to the Ann Arbor station for the six-hour train ride to Chicago.

"We're staying at the Blackstone, girl," said Matt. "Nothing is too good for the wife of Matthew Parker."

I'd known he was joking, that he'd already rented an apartment.

My own home; would we live in Chicago permanently? Would we travel to Europe? Was it another joke when Matt announced he'd taken a job selling Hoover vacuums door to door? A personal sales representative, he told me. He said nothing could stop him and that he'd be top salesman within a year, that we'd put money away and he'd finish his law degree.

The apartment on 67th street consisted of one room; a tiny kitchenette, even tinier bathroom, and a too-narrow bed stuffed into a curtained alcove. While Matthew trudged the meltingly hot summer streets with the bulky Hoover and a case of attachments, I stayed home to dust, sweep, and polish the apartment.

> *How long does it take to clean one room, for God's sake?* I asked myself. *Even without a vacuum?* Dying of boredom, I ironed and folded Matt's white shirts so he'd look respectable when a housewife in the market for a vacuum opened a door. *Please buy a Hoover today!* The plea came into my head every morning he set out.
>
> We ate dinners in little cafés or an occasional Chi-

> nese restaurant, because the one-ring gas burner took forever to cook a decent meal. Evenings. Matt sat reading *The Count of Monte Cristo* or *Les Miserable*, answering me only briefly when I spoke, or he'd offer a comment now and then without taking his eyes off the page. Set in his ways, as though we'd been twenty years married, not two months, Matt was a pipe and slippers man whose main topic of conversation—when he made any—was his work. Collapsing into the Morris chair after a day of cold calling, he'd disparage his customers.
>
> "An old Jew dame got me to clean her whole damn place then said the machine 'Vas tu damn heaffy fur me, zo I couldn't buy hit.' The old cow!"

Trying to remain sympathetic, I had stifled a laugh.

Whenever I received a letter from Forman, Matthew's resentment became obvious, though there was nothing in them to hurt him:

> Dear Mary,
>
> Harry, I am afraid, is somewhat hurt because I'm not going with his company this summer, but that can't be helped, for if I am to continue to teach the young southern belles I must certainly be conscientious enough to learn more than they already know (which is not much, to be sure, but can be embarrassing!).

Sometimes all Forman sent was a poem. I'd learned them all by heart:

You say, my dear, that I am strange and cold;
But can I say—how can I say the words;
Your sweet reproach would make me swiftly bold
If my faint heart were strong; if, like the birds
I could take wing from my swaying bough,
And were not ever chained beside a wall.

A wall? What wall? What on earth is he talking about? I'd puzzled.

There were occasional letters from Dad, who was looking for work in Detroit. And letters from Mother, newly into real estate:

> *I get into the homes to sign up sellers before other agents and so I can sniff out and scoop up antiques at bargain prices that I can resell. If you come across any old fiddle-back chairs, or hobnail or cathedral bottles, price them for me as there is a vogue for such things just now.*

Nothing in any of her letters asked about me or about Matthew.

A year dragged by. Two. Matt, exhausted from his job, developed a persistent cough. "Possibly a touch of consumption," said the doctor. He advised saying home and getting lots of rest.

So I took a job, three jobs: reading to a half-blind old lady; long, late hours selling toiletries at Marshall Field's until Christmas; typing and filing at the University of Chicago's administration office—then a fourth job, tutoring a not very bright young girl. "And if my teaching position comes through," I promised Matt, "we'll be rolling in money."

As so often, his self-pity and resentment came to the fore. "That's the ticket," he grumped. "I'll just lie here like a sack of potatoes and be supported." Then he produced a letter from Forman that had arrived in the morning mail. "Maybe you should have married him," he went on. "His family's loaded."

His jealousy never let up. Tears of frustration burned my eyes. How could I get Matthew to understand that though I loved him and would do anything for him, the letters from Forman were precious and conveyed ideas and understandings about a world that Matt and I seemed incapable of sharing?

His cough got worse. A "spot" was discovered, so Matthew was hospitalized. "For a month," said the doctor, "perhaps two." I continued to work, stayed home on nights when I wasn't visiting Matt on the ward; reading Dickens, Browning, Emily Dickinson, Whitman, the more recent American poets: Sandburg, Dunbar, Robert Frost.

Later, I took a bus to Detroit to see Dad, who had found work in the rug department of a large store. I loved the smell of rugs, remembering them from when he owned Noble Burnett Mercantile in St. Johns. *Perhaps he can help settle my confusion,* I thought. After confiding my feeling that Matt and I wouldn't be together much longer, he'd become distressed. Was Matthew that ill?

"No," I assured him. "He's out of the hospital, and the spot on his lung has healed well."

"That's good news," said Dad.

After adding that Matt was back at work in a non-stressful job investigating insurance claims, I somehow couldn't explain my attitude toward the marriage any further; it was just a feeling.

"I wish I could help you, Sis," Dad had replied, "but I can't. You'll have to work it out for yourself. . . . After all, I didn't make such a success of my own marriage."

I started to assure him he was the best father a girl could have, the best husband Mother could have—before he suddenly became red in the face and confessed to having had a short-term lady friend, but "Forman's mother saw us together on the street and . . . well, what would your mother have thought?" His gaze fell to the floor, and he mumbled, "I dropped her."

Dad's revelation stunned me; not because of any illicit relationship—he had left Mother several years before anyway, though they'd never divorced—but because of the sorrow I felt for his not grabbing a little happiness.

Soon after, I had an attorney file papers on Matt. My guilt was enormous. *He'll think it's because of his lungs.* I felt his sadness, endured his attempts to talk me out of it. We got back together for a month, two months, but with no real communication except polite talk. At times I hesitated. . . . *Do I stay or do I go?* At times I stood firm. . . . *I can't give in to his constant pleading; we have so little in common.*

I went home for Christmas without him. Which of course aroused his jealousy. "Will that fellow Brown be there?" he asked. I lied. Though Forman had indeed been in Michigan visiting Harry during the holidays, I knew I couldn't mention it to Matt. Even so, on my return to Chicago there were shouting matches, sleepless nights. Then the final break, and more of Matt's misery as I left for Ann Arbor, and him showing up at the family home one day to plead for my return.

And yes, I had misgivings . . .

Now that we have parted
Perhaps I shall never see you again.
The past, our little past
Is almost dead for me.
But whenever I walk on a street
And see men
Growing old and sad
My heart nearly breaks,
For I had always wondered
How you would look
As you grew old.

Somehow, the spring buds in the garden that morning, the mood among even the most disconnected patients who seemed brighter than usual, even more cheerful for some, had lifted my mood. Then, too, I'd spent several hours sifting through the cavalcade of impressions racing through my brain. So perhaps I'd started to find my way back to the light through the long tunnel of hopelessness?

Gradually, that first marriage with all its aching uncertainty was beginning to piece itself together. I'd never given Matthew an adequate explanation for the breakup. How could I have? At the time, there didn't seem to be one. I simply knew the marriage had been a mistake. And it hadn't been Matt's fault. Nor was it Forman's. I knew that now, though the thing that had originally kept two such obviously like-minded people as my cousin and I apart had been, for so very long, beyond my understanding.

And poor Matthew; if only I'd known how to deal with my feelings before plunging in to marry you. . . .

Okay, enough! I couldn't suddenly show up on his doorstep with a big helping of humble pie, could I? He'd married again, had a family now, and had long since broken off all contact. *Let it go,* I told myself. It was what it was.

◆◆◆◆◆

On the way back to my room following lunch, I stopped to have a few words with Martha, the student nurse whose fiancé was missing. After I asked how she was getting on, she admitted that it had been hard holding herself together, but that our previous talk had been helpful.

And with Forman again filling my thoughts, I opened the door.

First, I looked over more of the correspondence I hadn't burned—the letters, snatches of poetry (my own and Forman's), old writing—to see if anything useful remained that might add to the cascade of thoughts these past hours had set in motion; letters or notes that might help me continue writing out my feelings. I sat on the bed and removed the rubber band from a thick packet.

Older, long letters from Mother complained about the meager financial support she was getting from Leo and Verne, and from Harry, "who cares a good deal more for his silly wooden puppets than he does for his flesh-and-blood family." Postcards from Harry updated me on touring plans and ideas he had for shows, and he wondered when I might be available to sew costumes. More poignantly, I found brief notes from Dad, who'd been living for seven years in a Detroit rooming house, a place I had visited soon after he'd found the job selling rugs. I recalled the apple pie order of his tiny room, the washbasin, the fading wallpaper, the photo of the family on the bureau.

"Your father is the finest gentleman I've ever had here," the landlady had told me. Sighing, I remembered the terrible sadness I'd felt while visiting the store, and seen him, more than sixty then, struggling under the heavy carpet roll on his shoulder as I came into the department.

A fading envelope with a twenty-year-old letter from Forman was next. He'd returned to the family home in Otsego and would be taking summer courses at the university before returning to his teaching job at a North Carolina school for the girls of well-to-do parents. And he'd expressed a need for travel when the term ended, perhaps to Europe. Then another letter of his, regretting the wall he felt he'd built between us, his inability to understand why, and concluding with:

> *Do not hold against me, I pray you, this added mystery, this seemingly perverse behavior. It has a reason that I will have to disentangle in solitude and quietness, and then I will offer the reason, and may you understand! Until that day, which I hope is not too far over the horizon, my dear, I am your friend (I know no better word).*
>
> *—Forman*

Now I could see it. The wall, that enigmatic barricade he'd insisted on hiding behind—the meaning of which at the time I had no clue. I recalled being puzzled, mulling it over for days before finally accepting it for what it was: simply another piece of the unsolvable paradox that was Forman.

Before turning in that night, I slipped the letters from David and Dan out of their envelopes and read them one more time. Danny's little black thunderhead drawing still worried me. But with the day's reflection and getting down on paper what I felt, I had a strong sense I was moving toward a place where I'd be able to do something about it. I *had* to do something about it. I'd already been permitted to leave the hospital for a few hours at a time with Laura. Perhaps they'd allow me to visit my boys?

Once in bed, I thought about our times together; the good times, especially the good times. And after turning off the light, I whispered softly into the dark, "Good night, dear ones. Sleep tight. Don't let the bedbugs bite."

How I longed to hear, "And if they do, bite 'em back."

17.

"*King of the Zombies,* huh? Really scary, yeah? I'll bet that flick had you pissin' in your pants, huh, Shirley?" said Gordon Arbuckle as he eyed Charlie and Morris for approval.

His flunkies provided the expected guffaw.

As I was walking along a dirt pathway behind the school with my roommate, Henry Smith, a quiet, reclusive boy, we passed the Arbuckle crew (assisted by Davy) in the midst of reinforcing a high fieldstone wall. Built, fallen apart, then rebuilt again by generations of Musgrove boys, the wall served as a defensive fortification behind which older boys traditionally held secret meetings, barred younger students, and waged snowball fights against them during winter. About thirty feet long, the fort ran below a thick outcropping of schist protruding from a low hill. At one end, a deep and mysterious cave tunneled into the hill; mysterious because, according to rumors spread by the Arbuckle bunch, "anybody going in there never comes out again."

As my brother later confided, he'd regretted mentioning the zombie film, and decided he'd better keep his mouth shut after that; who knew what kind of stupid game Gordon and his buddies might cook up to use against me? Though I'd shrugged off their boast, Davy was still worried about their plan to bounce me around on a splintered railroad tie.

"What do you think they're up to?" I asked Henry as we stood looking on.

"I don't care."

"They're probably planning some dirty tricks."

"Could be."

"I heard the big kids used to throw rocks from behind that wall," I continued. "Not just snowballs. But Musgrove made 'em stop. Maybe they're going to start doing that again, you think?"

As Henry shrugged and started off again along the path, Arbuckle shouted out, "Heil Heinrich!" In quick succession Charlie shouted, "Heil Heinie," and with Morris's "Heil Hitler!" all three cracked up.

I could see that Davy was puzzled. Catching up with Henry, I glanced back at the rowdies, then asked, "What's that all about?"

"Just some stupid stuff," Henry replied. "It's because I'm German." Noting my puzzled expression he added, "My real name's Heinrich. Heinrich Schmidt."

"Heinrich? But . . . Well, you don't sound German."

"My father thought 'Henry' would be better in America; Smith too, instead of Schmidt. We left Berlin when I was a baby, about a year old."

"Well . . . But how come they know your German name?"

"Arbuckle is Mrs. Musgrove's nephew; he can find out most anything he wants."

I thought for a moment, then asked, "How come it doesn't bother you? When they call you those names, I mean."

Henry shrugged again.

"You know," I went on, "I didn't do a thing to Gordon. I never said a word to him, but he just doesn't seem to like me. . . . You've heard how he calls me Shirley."

"He doesn't like anyone except Charlie and Morris, because they drool all over him. . . . And how come your brother hangs out with that bunch?"

"Well, I asked him, but all he says is it's because they do fun stuff. Like building that fort by the cave, I guess. He always liked that kinda thing. And I suppose it's because they've made him some sort of mascot. They call him Little Bit because he's small."

"He should stay away from them."

"He pretty much does what he wants."

"You're the older one; you should tell him."

"Well, yeah, but he's got a mind of his own."

All I could think about was Henry being a German. But when I heard Arbuckle call out to my brother, "Hey, Little Bit, see that empty space up there?" I turned around.

"Yeah, I see it," Davy replied.

"Go get a half-dozen good sized rocks and hoist 'em up to fill the hole," Arbuckle directed.

As Henry continued walking, I stood watching as Davy picked up a large rock and strained to fit it into a cavity in the wall high above him. As he did, Arbuckle and his crew, chatting back and forth excitedly, had just started into the cave at one end of the wall; the cave they claimed that which "anybody who goes in never comes out again."

I had no sense of what they had in mind, but from what little my brother told me, I was sure they were up to no good.

18.

What are my precious boys going through? I thought as Laura steered the station wagon through a rainy green countryside toward Musgrove School on this "visiting Sunday." *They must feel so lost, so confused.*

Of course: Dan, asking if I slept in my clothes; David, angrily running off then returning late and covered in mud, both crying themselves to sleep that last night in Danbury, the night I'd finally reached out for help. *And now, here I am about to face them. Am I ready to deal with their questions, their certain pleas to come home, their need for reassurance that they'll soon have their happy, optimistic mom back again?*

If I owe them anything it's that, a mother they can curl up next to while I read The Wind in the Willows, *who'll play tag with them in the backyard, take them for Chinese when I have a few extra dollars; a mother with an upbeat slant on life. Can I pull it off?*

Probably not quite yet, I sighed, *but I've got to offer them hope.*

"Well, here we are!" Laura announced as the woody passed the Musgrove School sign next to the gravel entry.

"So we are," I echoed, and quickly dug into my purse for a small mirror and a lipstick.

As I entered the front hall, an immediate familiarity overpowered me. It was as though I'd been there before, yet all I'd heard until now was Laura's vague description. I looked around. A dark oak staircase ascended between cracking paneled walls. Ancient polished tongue and groove flooring peeked out from beneath thick and faded oriental rugs. An oppressive formality permeated the place. In moments, I recognized the feeling: I'd traveled back in time, a hundred years into the past, to Salem House, the boarding school David Copperfield had been shipped off to by Mr. Murdstone, his callous stepfather. . . . *Murdstone? Hmm . . . Musgrove School. How similar.* Davy and Dan must have felt it too; I'd read them the novel. I immediately disliked the place, and my anticipation at seeing my boys turned into apprehension.

In the adjacent long dining hall, the custodian, a stoop-shouldered black man in his sixties, the stub of a fat, unlit cigar stuck in his mouth, was mopping the floor. He didn't seem to notice us, so I cleared my throat. No response. "Hello there," I said. Still no response.

"Boy!" an impatient Laura shouted.

I eyed her and sighed.

The man looked up, took the cigar from his mouth, laid aside his mop, and came toward us, smiling. He apologized, said he was hard of hearing, then asked, "Can I help you, missus?"

I explained that we'd come to visit my sons. The man headed off to summon Wilma Musgrove—who shortly arrived in a flutter of apologies that we'd been greeted by "the help." Explaining that the boys were just finishing Sunday school but would be along shortly, she then checked the ancient watch pinned to her blouse before directing the custodian to, "Finish up here quickly, George."

Mrs. Musgrove escorted us to a large and gloomy room across the hall and asked if we'd be joining her for lunch.

"That's most kind," I replied. "But we'd hoped to take David and Daniel out to a restaurant."

"And when we return, perhaps the boys could show us around the school?" Laura added.

"That will be fine," replied Mrs. Musgrove. "Little David's become quite popular here, you know, and I'm sure he's familiar with the grounds by now."

And Daniel, what about him? I pondered.

As Laura continued to chat, I suddenly felt a need for fresh air. After excusing myself, I walked out onto the long front porch and arrived just as students were coming out of a small, churchlike building opposite a broad lawn and moving toward the main house.

For a moment, I saw myself back in St. Johns. I was twelve, school had let out, and though ours was coed and here there were only boys, the loud chatter and joshing banter seemed exactly the same:

"You're so dumb. That was an easy question Mr. Winslow asked."

"You tell on me again, you'll sure be sorry," warned another voice.

"I'll bet it's macaroni and cheese again today," grumbled another boy.

As the voices faded, I heard, "Mom! It's Mom!" as Danny and David came pushing through the group of students and raced toward the porch. An instant later, they were both in my arms, receiving hugs, and demanding as one to know—as I felt certain they would—"Are we going home? Is it gonna be today?"

Their questions tore at me. Their eyes were searching mine for an answer. Just responding, "I'm afraid not," I'd already decided, would upset them both. So I offered a broad smile and enthusiastically told them we were all going out to lunch at a nice restaurant. "We'll talk about it then," I added. "And when we come back, you can show Aunt Laura and me around the school, okay?"

"Sure," Danny replied. "But then we're gonna go home, right?"

What could I say? I put a comforting arm around him and gently replied, "I'm afraid not right away, honey, so for now let's just enjoy the day, shall we?"

Danny bit his lip.

"Where's Mackie? Is he in the car?" Davy asked Laura as she appeared on the porch.

"Well, no, you see—"

"We weren't able to bring him, honey," I interrupted. "And that's something else we need to talk about."

◆◆◆◆◆

The Tavern in the Park was a more upscale restaurant than I would have selected, but since Laura had announced this would be her treat and the boys could order anything they'd like, I didn't object.

My slow and patient explanation that I was feeling better but probably had a while yet before I could leave the rest home (as I described it) seemed to allay their fears, if not their disappointment. Slowly drawing Davy and Dan out on what they'd been doing at Musgrove, expressing pleasure at what they liked and commiserating over what they didn't—and mixing this with talk of my need to find a job and a new place where we'd all live together, which might take a bit more time—had them both excited.

"But what about Mackie?" Davy asked again.

"Well," I began, choosing my words carefully, "do you remember Clint Jenkins, your friend over on Stevens Street in Danbury?"

"Uh-huh."

"You see, he's been watching Mackie for the last several weeks while you boys are here, and until I find us a new place to live, it's going to be quite difficult for me to look after him."

"Maybe he could come and stay here," said Davy.

"They don't allow pets," Dan reminded, a bit too sharply.

"Actually," I replied, trying to sound positive, "Clint has told Aunt Laura that his family would love to have him as their own dog . . . if that would be all right with you, of course. Is that something you're willing to think about? Because I really don't know if any place I find to rent is going to allow animals."

Dan remained silent. After a deep frown, Davy opened his mouth to say something, but then, clearly fighting the answer, drew his lips tightly together. He looked up at me and, I think, understanding that I had nothing better to offer, muttered a reluctant, "I suppose" before he went on to announce, "Papa sent us a horny toad, and—"

"Horned toad," corrected Laura.

"Uh-huh. Can we bring him home when we come?"

"I don't see why not," I said with a smile.

"He eats ants," added Davy.

Laura shuddered.

By the time the meal was over (the somewhat aloof waiter had grudgingly agreed that the Tavern in the Park could supply hamburgers), the boys had begun to loosen up, laugh, and poke fun at the Musgrove formalities, with Dan complaining about having to wear knickerbockers and Davy admitting (while Laura kept her peace) that he hated Sunday morning Bible lessons.

◆◆◆◆◆

Leaving the restaurant hand in hand with the boys, I felt as though a new ray of hope was breaking after a long, dark winter. Though I had a hunch their grins were provoked more by the enormous ice cream sundaes they'd ordered for dessert than by anything specific I could offer right now.

"Will we get home by Christmastime?" asked Danny.

"I'd like to think so," I replied cheerfully. "Let's shoot for that, okay?"

While he'd clearly hoped for something more definite, it seemed as though a slight squeeze of my hand before we all climbed into the station wagon helped reassure him that I knew he and Davy would do their best to tough it out.

The rather unenthusiastic school tour led by Davy was necessarily brief; lunch had lasted two hours, and it would be a long drive back to Manhattan for Laura and me.

As we said our goodbyes, we noticed three rambunctious boys hanging around by one of the huge elms near the dining hall. Crossing the nearby lawn was a thin, blond-haired boy about Danny's age. Abruptly, one of the trio called out, "Heil Hitler!" A second one added, "The Fuhrer wants to see you; he has a special assignment."

Except this was uttered in a guttural German accent.

As the trio laughed and the blond boy, ignoring them, continued toward the main building, I asked Dan what this name calling was all about, and if he knew the blond boy.

"Sure. He's my roommate. Henry."

"Do you really think it's funny to tease another boy in that way, Danny?"

"Well, maybe not. But . . ."

"But what?" I asked.

"Those guys think he's a Nazi."

"It's because he's German," added Davy.

"Oh come now, it's hardly likely that Henry's a Nazi."

"Well, those older guys say he is," Dan replied.

"Do you like Henry? Is he a good roommate?"

Danny shrugged. Then, "Yeah, he's okay, but . . . "

"But what?" I asked after his long silence.

"Well, what if he *is* a Nazi?"

Catching my quizzical look, Danny went on to explain Henry's birth in Germany. Following that, he added, "We play Monopoly. He wins most of the time."

"I see. . . . Do you know why his family left Germany?"

Another shrug, then another long pause before he added, "Maybe I could find out?"

"Maybe you could," I replied with a smile. "No doubt they had a very good reason."

◆◆◆◆◆

All too soon there were lingering hugs for my dear sons, along with assurances of my love, and a brief admonition from Laura to "be good boys." Then she and I were into the station wagon and off. I fought back tears as I waved goodbye through the car's rear window. David and Danny became tiny figures in the distance, my face finally went slack, and I sagged back against the seat.

"Well, that was certainly a fine visit," chirped Laura as we headed for New York.

"I suppose. But you know, I can't shake off how sad I feel that I can't bring the boys home right away."

"Well, four years of boarding school certainly hasn't done our Verne Junior any harm," was Laura's evasive response.

"He's certainly a fine young man" was the best I could offer.

Then, needing to review the day on my own, I closed my eyes and gradually tuned out Laura's continuing chatter extolling Musgrove's virtues, how healthy the boys looked, how lucky we'd been with the weather, and her hope that it wouldn't rain.

Yes, it had been good to spend this brief time with Davy and Danny, a relief to see them looking well, and though initially downcast at not coming home right away, able to have accepted my explanations. I knew they were strong. They'd already survived so much: the hardscrabble years in Vermont; their father, Alvah, leaving the family, then going off to the war in Spain when Dan was six and Davy just three; the horror of Pennsylvania—an episode I'd decided they were still too young to be told about; events hidden away in my big mental trunk of secrets, the repercussions of which I still needed to make my peace with. Much as I'd loved to have scooped them into Laura's car and said, "We're going home, darlings, we'll be together," I knew I wasn't ready.

In my last session with Payne Whitney's friendly Dr. Thomas, he'd told me, "You're making remarkable progress, Mrs. Burnett; a couple more months should see you back in the real world." It felt so good to hear that, of course, but deep down lay a lingering fear it might be some time after that I would be completely out of the woods; before I could become the kind of mother my boys deserved. There seemed to be so much about myself I still needed to understand.

Just then, I heard another voice—thankfully no longer one urging self-destruction. By now I'd chased the nagging demons back into their putrid hole. This one offered a brighter and reassuring path: *Just remember that you're on a journey,* it said; *a journey toward the day when you've proven yourself worthy of heading your little family again. That day will come. You're going to make it come!*

Then Laura's voice cut into my thoughts: "We're here, Sis."

"Yes. Yes, I hope so," I replied a bit blearily.

She looked at me, puzzled.

"Sorry, I was miles away." I straightened up in the seat and gazed out the window, surprised to see we were turning onto East 68th Street. Payne Whitney loomed just ahead.

19.

At Payne Whitney

After a heavy sleep, I woke from a version of the same agonizing dream I'd had before: Dan and David lost in a ramshackle house; me searching high and low, opening doors, and in each room their laughing voices seeming to echo from someplace else. After much searching, I'd given up looking, stood alone and frustrated, and somehow knew they were irrevocably lost. I would never see them again.

At Musgrove School

Weird dreams seemed to run in our family. It wasn't until years later that my brother, Davy, told me about waking that morning from a terrifying nightmare. He'd been watching helplessly as Gordon Arbuckle and his goons raced about the grounds bouncing me up and down on a long, rough-hewn timber. While ignoring Davy's plea for help, other students, along with teachers and the Musgroves themselves, looked on, seeming to relish my torment. No matter how loud he yelled, no one paid attention.

On the third floor, my sleeping mind had also been busy. Marching in an eerie torchlight procession and dressed in an ill-fitting Nazi uniform, I wore a helmet several sizes too big, a swastika armband that kept slipping. And instead of straight-legged trousers tucked into jackboots like the others, my legs were covered with embarrassing tweed knickerbockers and knitted socks. Looking around, I realized that every soldier in the parade was my age, each a carbon copy of my roommate, Henry Smith. Panicked, I turned to the soldier next to me and whispered, "Henry, these are Nazis! We have to get out of here."

"Heinrich!" came the reply. "Heinrich Schmidt."

"Heinrich Schmidt," echoed a thousand voices. Then, "Eyes front, or you'll go on report to the Führer for wearing knickerbockers!" snapped a platoon leader looking decidedly like Abner Musgrove.

At Payne Whitney

Working at the craft table later that morning, I'd all but shaken off last night's disturbing dream; creative activity frequently had that effect. In the midst of sewing up a puppet out of a holey sock I'd found in the bits box, Mrs. Jackson stopped to ask what I was doing.

"Well, it's something I learned from my brother Harry," I replied.

"Your brother wears holey socks, does he?"

"Often," I replied with a chuckle. "But he also makes amazing puppets for the marionette theater he opened in Los Angeles just last year."

Mrs. Jackson nodded, then said, "You know, Mrs. Burnett, it's really great to hear you laugh."

Her encouragement further helped me dispel my memory of the dream. Then she added, "By the way, my husband's got a drawer full of socks I've never found the mates for. I'll bring them in. Also, I've a box of buttons that would make great eyes."

"Sounds like you're trying to keep me busy."

"Well, how's about you teach the ladies to make these puppets?"

I smiled agreement. *Something else I can do,* I told myself, delighted that this skill I'd picked up from Harry would keep me usefully occupied.

Harry . . . my adored youngest brother, I thought, remembering the day he'd appeared in Brooklyn during one of my blackest periods. He'd brought along the original sketches for marionettes he'd talked a famous Broadway designer into creating; sketches I was to use as a guide to fabricate the puppet costumes.

"Did I really make all those?" I recalled asking.

"Yep, you sure did."

"I can't believe it."

"You were very bright in those days," he chuckled.

Was it bright and able? I asked myself, *or was it being loved and loving that made it all possible?* The question brought me back to 1927. After bumping around Europe in third class railroad cars to visit famous marionette theaters in Salzburg, Munich, Naples, Palermo, and Lyon, Harry had returned with a trunk full of puppets and show posters—and with an idea that, he told me and anyone else who would listen, was sure to set the puppet world on fire.

Then the spring of 1928, the New England tour; Harry's huge loan from Verne and a few hundred dollars from brother Leo. The Dodge truck Harry bought, along with the Model T Depot Hack, an ancestor of the station wagon, and so off we went, Harry and Roddy—they'd met while studying theater at Yale—plus Forman and me.

Days into the trip, we ran into a tree-splitting nor'easter. Downpours drenched both vehicles and leaked through onto our still optimistic little group. "Land o' Goshen, we is saved!" exclaimed Harry, trying to calm everyone's fright as lightning shattered glass insulators atop a nearby utility pole.

Drying out at that hotel in Vermont; White River Junction it was. The small audiences, the meager pickings . . . Rain turning the beautiful sets in the back of the truck into a sodden mess. The Dodge (Forman called it Camille) finally sputtering consumptively then giving out . . . The four of us down in the dumps and limping back to New York in the Depot Hack; nothing to eat along the way but peanut butter sandwiches.

And yet, the freedom I felt, the camaraderie, the love . . .

"So much for the life of a theatrical," I chuckled as I began to stitch a smiling red mouth onto the sock puppet.

Roddy Brandon, Forman Brown, Harry Burnett; on the running board of their Model T Ford Depot Hack during their 1928 tour through New England

Mary accompanied the puppeteers on this tour

Was there ever really such another time in life?

Returning to my room with the memory of the 1928 tour still fresh, after a brief search through correspondence, I discovered an envelope crammed with old snapshots. After spreading them out on the bed, I selected one: a shot of myself standing by the Depot Hack somewhere in New England, grinning broadly. *What a marvelous spring,* I reflected. *Pure joy, in spite of the downpours, the mud, the catastrophes.*

I'd have done it again in a minute.

It had been a lovely April morning the day we started off. Looking down from the loft of Harry's New York workshop where I'd been sewing puppet costumes, I saw Forman and Harry below, tinkering with the Depot Hack. Forman spotted me watching, went down on one knee, and declaimed, "What light through yonder window breaks? 'Tis the east, and Juliet is the sun."

I'd laughed, opened the window and called out, "Get thee to a nunnery, sir!"

Another photo: Forman and me in a canoe, he in front wearing a sleeveless sweater-vest, myself behind, both of us paddling. Turning the photo over, an inscription: Sunday, April 11, 1926, two years before the New England tour; Forman and me on the Huron River outside of Ann Arbor.

Dear Forman, my poetry-spouting cousin; I knew so many of your lines by heart; even those that on my first reading seemed a mystery. I had no concept then of what you were trying to express:

What struggle has a tree to be a tree?
What dare expands a flower to be a flower?
Yet I through every whirling perilous hour
Must battle all my fellows to be me.
There is no answer to this mystery.
That men must point and laugh, or frown and glower
While I fight back, or, failing, crouch and cower;
No answer but to battle, or to flee.
There is no answer, but there is ruse—
Whose fruit is silence and much suffering;
The wall invisible, which feigns a truce;
Yet it confines me in so close a ring
I tremble lest it burst, and set me loose.
A stark, terrific soul, some spring.

The photo and Forman's poem led me to explore my diary for that year:

April 1926

Forman is going to Europe. England, France. Where

else? He's wiring ahead for reservations tonight. How easily he presented this news, as though announcing, "I'm going to the store for a loaf of bread." Well good for him; his family has money, after all. What was it Dad said? "People of independent means can go anywhere they want, any time they want." When Forman took my hands and said he wanted me to go with him, my throat immediately felt parched and dry. What excitement! But he didn't mean Europe, just New York, from where his ship will leave in June. Well, all right then, New York; a place I've dreamed of for years. Actually, since I've told Harry I won't be going on the road with the troupe this summer, and since I desperately want to get away from Mother (yes, again; the first time was when I married Matthew), New York would be perfect.

"We'll have time together," Forman said, "I'll show you the town; Broadway, Harlem, the Village. . . ." He's going to Europe, he says, to "straighten things out with myself," and when he returns, "I'll be able to handle you, young lady."

Handle me? I didn't realize I needed to be handled; have to ask him about that.

And there it ended. I'd torn several pages from the diary, pages I'd impulsively discarded on that desperate Danbury morning just a few weeks earlier, when I'd fed anything Leo and Verne might find unseemly to the hungry flames.

Still, I recall the lingering hope I had in 1926: *Could this be a beginning for us?*

New York! The memories; the weeks we'd spent together before he left; my heart felt as though it was going to leap out of my chest. Manhattan, an "isle of joy." Even now, I couldn't get those wonderful lyrics out of my head:

> *East Side, West Side, all around the town*
> *The tots sang, "Ring around Rosie,"*
> *London Bridge is falling down.*
> *Boys and girls together, me and Mamie O'Rourke,*
> *We tripped the light fantastic on the sidewalks of New York.*

The song, along with wistful reminiscences of the weeks I'd spent painting the town red with Forman—and thoughts of the previous day I'd spent with Dan and David—gradually found me dozing off. . . . *Boys and girls together . . .*

20.

After a positive session with Dr. Thomas and a long refreshing sleep, I spent much of the next morning with Forman and "Sidewalks of New York" still on my mind. A heavy April rain had kept the seventh floor from our scheduled garden exercise, so I eagerly began working with several of the women to create hand puppets from the box of socks Mrs. Jackson brought in.

Increasingly upbeat as I headed for my room after lunch, another song floated through my head. I quickly glanced both ways along the corridor, then, while softly singing the lyrics, danced a few awkwardly remembered kick-steps of the Charleston.

Come and hear those dancing feet,
On the avenue I'm taking you to, Forty-Second Street.
Hear the beat of dancing feet,
It's the melody of Forty-Second Street . . .

Written years after my New York month with Forman, it somehow still fit with those long-ago wonderful weeks, and with my more optimistic mood. Back in my room, I pulled my chair to the window. A steady rain pelted the river.

Got to look back at that period as honestly as I can, I told myself; *on the pain as well as the joy . . .*

Remembering June 1926

I'd telegraphed ahead to Forman, who'd been in New York for a few weeks.

Even before arriving at Grand Central, the city assaulted my senses: the train roaring past square black factory buildings with soot-covered windows like those in Detroit and Chicago; immense skyscrapers visible in the distance ahead; great steel bridges spanning a broad river (the Hudson? the East?); laundry flapping on lines between tenements as the train cut through the northern outskirts before diving underground, its roar and the hiss of steam as it slowly glided to a stop next to a long platform where porters in red caps stood ready to carry baggage or load heavy trunks onto handcarts.

Then Forman meeting me, his hair carelessly tousled (I loved that), a paisley ascot at his neck. In minutes, we were among the commuters crowding out of the station and onto Park Avenue, and Forman thrust an arm into the air and called, "Taxi!"

Moments later, we were driving along Forty-Second Street. *"Tell all the gang on Forty-Second Street that I will soon be there. . . ."* I couldn't get the lyrics out of my head.

"We're on Fifth Avenue now," announced an excited Forman, "greatest street in the world. Can't compare it to anything in Ann Arbor, even Chicago."

We'd be together almost a month before he sailed. Yet the time sped by faster than I'd thought possible. The city was just as Larry Hart had described it in his lyrics, "a wondrous toy, just made for a girl and boy . . ."

Oh, piss pot! I thought. *Why did I have to burn my notes from back then? Why did I stupidly let what my brothers might have thought obsess me so?*

But even without those diary fragments, my time with Forman was so vivid (and so revealing) that most of the words themselves are sealed in memory.

"Where are we going?" I'd asked Forman.

"Washington Square. There's a cute little hotel I've checked out. I'll put you up there, and we'll leave our things. It's only a twenty-minute walk from my place, which is a couple blocks from a great Italian restaurant."

We'd pushed in among subway passengers, amazingly found seats, and sat shouting frivolities at one another above the train's rackety din as the cars rocketed through the tunnel. An old man across the aisle smiled at us and nodded; as Forman squeezed my arm, we looked into one another's eyes and laughed.

In the small but clean and plainly furnished room he'd rented, I took off my hat and the perky red scarf I'd bought before leaving Ann Arbor, then brushed out my hair and sat on the bed. Now that we were alone, I felt a brief awkward silence fill the space between us. But Forman quickly bridged the gap with talk of his forthcoming trip.

"Less than a month," he said.

Smiling, I said, "I really do know how much this means to you, darling."

"I knew you would."

Did he wince a bit at my endearing word? I wasn't sure.

"And Harry's decided to descend on New York and take the town by storm," Forman went on, "by opening a small marionette theater!"

That was a surprise. "Really!" I exclaimed.

"He and Roddy promised to get here in time to give me a proper sendoff before I take ship," he added.

The news buoyed me. With Forman leaving, I had feared I'd be totally alone in New York. *Maybe,* I thought, *I'll be able to help Harry with his theater.*

"Won't Mother have kittens?" I recall saying, laughing. "I can just see her, storming around the kitchen, banging pots as Harry stands in the doorway pretending to listen while his mind is planning his next show. 'Your sister could be doing exactly the same work right here in Ann Arbor,' she's probably saying, 'and get more money for it and have no expense, instead of—' and on and on. But I can't tell you how liberating it is to be away," I told Forman, "to be really free."

He nodded, his mouth a tight line and his brows furrowed, an expression I had always recognized as his "serious listening" mode.

I went on to explain how I'd always felt a captive, first with Mother then with Matthew. "Oh, he tried," I continued, "but most folks leave their families behind when they go off to college, don't they? Break away, you know. But Harry and I, well . . . we just stayed. Nothing really changed, even when I married Matt. I see it all so much more clearly now. Mother growing cold and hard inside, Harry and I reaching out, changing, and soaking up a world we knew so little about. Mother and I getting farther and farther apart, she fighting all the time and never really understanding why she did."

After lunch, I sat reflecting on that long-ago conversation. Even with all that went on between Forman and myself later that month,

I knew he had understood. He was someone I could talk to far more deeply than with Harry. Though we'd always been close, some mysterious invisible barrier between us never seemed to allow for deep communication. With Forman I'd sensed the beginning of a companionship I'd longed for since before high school, and an intimacy that for so many years seemed as though it might never come.

Still recalling that long past summer, I could feel approaching tears. I wiped my eyes, smiled, shook off the emotion, and continued drifting back in time. . . .

"Perhaps the *signora* would first like the minestrone?" suggested the short jovial man with a black toupée who stood by our table in the little Italian place Forman had mentioned. His name was Giovanni, and he knew Forman by name.

Forman questioned me with a smile. With no idea what minestrone was, I shrugged and returned his smile. Forman turned to Giovanni. "By all means, the minestrone. And scaloppini, *prego*."

Giovanni bowed slightly, then headed for the kitchen.

I looked around at the narrow cellar restaurant, the checkered tablecloths, Chianti bottles with candles stuck in them, and the faded brick walls adorned with posters of Venice, Rome, and Pisa. "It's charming," I said. "Totally charming."

Before we'd exchanged more than a few sentences, Giovanni reappeared with a steaming pewter tureen. Forman ladled the minestrone into our bowls, and we ate, stuffing ourselves with great hunks of bread, all while laughing and reminding one another how fine it was to be together.

Later, we strolled arm-in-arm to Fourth Avenue, to the recently opened Strand Bookstore, where Forman bought me a compilation of the poems of Rupert Brooke, along with *Love's Coming of Age* by Edward Carpenter. *A tender choice,* I thought, though at the time I had no idea what it was about.

As we continued through the Village, Forman pointed out several popular Bohemian nightspots. We took in Sheridan Square, passed the Greenwich Village Playhouse, crossed under the "EL" as a train rattled by—then to Eighth Avenue, over to Fifth, and back up to Fourteenth Street, circling Union Square. "That's Klein's," he said. "Great department store; good stuff, cheap."

We finally made it back to my hotel. With a gentle hug and a kiss on my cheek, he promised to meet me again the next morning to help me look for permanent quarters. I wanted to ask Forman to come in, but somehow I sensed it wasn't something he was ready for. There would be another time, another night. We had a whole month.

Meanwhile, here I was, Mary in New York; May time for Mary. How appropriate; a month I'd never forget. We dined in quaint out-of-the-way eateries offering foods I'd never even heard of: chop suey, moussaka, borscht, goulash—and pastrami on rye, at Katz's on the lower East Side. "A deli," Forman called it. He knew so much, had such sophistication for someone four years younger than me. So much fun, so many new experiences.

But when, I wondered, would we consummate the growing love I felt, that I was sure we both felt? No, I couldn't let that preoccupy me! The time would come soon enough. Right then, I needed work, and based on my experience in Ann Arbor, I quickly found a temporary job at the registrar's office at Columbia University; rent money and expense worries solved for a time.

There were symphony concerts, theater, and art exhibits. After, we'd stroll the Village or streets bordering the Hudson River, or take coffee in some artsy café or in the sparse two-room basement apartment we'd located for me on Christopher Street, and spend hours analyzing and discussing and reliving every line and shape in the paintings, every musical note, every theatrical moment; the acting style of major Broadway stars like Lynn Fontanne or Eva Le Gallienne, or Walter Hampden in *Cyrano*. We took in the *Garrick Gaieties*, Roger's and Hart's musical revue, laughed uproariously together one night as we attempted the Charleston after watching several flappers in an impromptu café performance, took the ferry to Liberty Island and climbed the statue's arm into the torch. One Sunday, we spent the afternoon walking all the way downtown and across the bridge to Brooklyn, where we stood wondering at the Manhattan skyline until after dark, when its reflected lights mingled with that of the moon as it played across the East River.

For both of us, the days flew by much too quickly.

And now we were descending the steps to Giovanni's again, for what we'd both decided was to be a farewell dinner; Forman's ship, the *Leviathan*, would sail for Southampton in two days.

"Let's not spare the wine," he suggested as he asked Giovanni to bring a bottle of the best house red.

◆◆◆◆◆

For me, the past month had been precious; a torrent of loving words from Forman, warm goodnight embraces, gentle kisses—always on the cheek—but with a physical tension I felt building in him; in us both, if I was being honest.

"I'm so sorry we have such little time," said Forman, "I'd like to—"

I reached across the table and pressed my fingers against his lips. I told him we still had tonight . . . and tomorrow.

"I'll have to pack tomorrow, write some letters to Mother, to Harry. . . . He says he won't be getting to New York for a month yet," he answered evasively. "You never thought you'd get here, did you? To the big city."

I shook my head.

Forman said he'd half a mind to cancel the trip; he'd been enjoying our time together so much. I protested, told him he had to go, and that he'd talked about sorting himself out. "Time to do that, don't you think?" I added. "One of us certainly has to."

"Aren't you feeling sorted?" he asked.

"Well, I suppose so. Maybe. Guess I'll know better tomorrow," I replied, giggling, "after my head clears from all this booze."

Forman rested his elbow on the table with his chin in his cupped hands and said, "You're beautiful, you know."

"Big nose." And I blushed.

"Substantial nose! Sculpted with character, a noble schnozzolla. None of your drab, pasty-faced, Pekingese-nosed girls for Signore Forman!" And he began to recite, making the words up on the spot: "She is like a cameo done in some strange and disturbing medium . . . the curved throat, the strong chin, the full expressive lips, the Roman nose . . . the low forehead, the sleek lacquer of black hair pulled smoothly over the head to a knot low in the neck. She is like the portrait on a Messina coin . . ." Then he added, "I rather like that. Maybe I'll include it in a book someday or turn it into a poem."

Still blushing, I was grateful for Giovanni's nick-of-time arrival with his broad smile and plates of scaloppini—which I'd decided by then was my favorite dish.

Dinner eventually finished, and after lingering over glasses of Amaretto, Forman paid the bill. Then, after much bowing and many *arrivedercis* and *tante grazies* between him and Giovanni, and "Thank you so much" from me, we were out onto Fifteenth Street again with the evening's low, threatening clouds releasing a sudden downpour. Running the few blocks to Forman's room, we arrived laughing, breathless, and soaked to the skin.

Will it be now? I wondered as I slipped out of my wet clothes, lay them across the radiator, and then, my back to him (*Is he watching?*), put on Forman's robe and lay back against the pillows.

◆◆◆◆◆

Sifting back through the years as I sat gazing out the window at Payne Whitney, I recalled Forman saying how delighted he was that I'd let him take care of me now and then, that it made him feel grown up and responsible. I called him a silly boy; said he was certainly quite grown up, already had a lot more going for him than he gave himself credit for. "You're wise beyond your years, my dear."

"Oh posh!" he replied. "I'm nothing but a poor, misguided creature who will most likely go to his grave convinced that he was some kind of artistic genius when he was never more than a mediocre versifier."

I shook my head again. Self-deprecation had always annoyed me.

He went on: "Really, to know oneself is the essence of wisdom. Still, I'm afraid I've got decades of experience to accumulate before I can claim to have learned half of what I really ought to know."

I had no immediate reply. Looking at him curiously, I wondered what was really going on in that (to me) brilliant but often so confused brain. After several moments, I quietly asked, "And . . . do you think that my having been married has given me a perspective, a breadth of knowledge that you haven't had? That you perhaps need?"

I sensed an immediate unease from Forman at my question, almost a fear; like that in the eyes of a deer I recalled, the one we'd seen while driving through northern Michigan years before, the deer Harry had mercifully been able to swerve around and avoid when it was caught suddenly in the headlights of his Model T.

"Perhaps so," answered Forman softly after a long, tentative pause.

"I'm afraid it didn't take me long to realize that I never loved Matthew," I admitted. "Oh, I told myself I did. Pretended for too long. But really, the whole thing was an excuse to get away from home, from Mother."

"The old battle ax," replied Forman, forcing a laugh.

"You couldn't have put it better."

Forman seemed frozen in place. I held my arms out toward him, my hands beckoning. "Come to me," I invited.

He crossed to the bed and stood beside it, taking my hands in his as I looked up into his inscrutable face. I patted the bed next to me. He sat. Placing my hands behind his head, I drew him down atop me, my breasts rising to meet his strong young body. Our lips touched; mine, hot and moist. I pulled him closer, my lips parting, inviting his tongue. There was no response. His lips felt cold, almost harsh, dry, and flat. I began to unbutton his shirt. . . .

Something was wrong; I could feel him shrinking away, growing rigid, frightened. The deer in the headlights again. I rolled aside, looking at him, wondering. He managed a weak smile. *This isn't going to work,* I thought. *Not now, at any rate.* I hugged him. As he seemed to not know what to say or how to respond, I got off the bed, crossed to the radiator, slipped on my not-quite-dry shoes and dress, squeezed Forman's hand, and said, "Let's talk tomorrow. Can you be free for an hour or so?"

"Sure," he said. "Let's meet in Central Park along by the pond, off Fifth Avenue and Fifty-Ninth. Do you know where—"

"I'll find it. How's about 3 p.m.?"

"Fine. That'll be fine, it'll give me time to pack, wind up a few other things." A pause, then he added, "Look, I . . . I don't exactly know what happened just then. I suppose—"

I put a finger to his lips. "Not now," I said. "Tomorrow, okay? We'll talk about it tomorrow." And I was out the door.

21.

A threatening rainstorm over Manhattan had passed on. Outside Payne Whitney's dining room, fluffy white clouds hung in a sun-drenched morning sky. Two birds perched on a window ledge. Sparrows, perhaps? Or maybe finches—I couldn't quite tell. "Seems we've got a lovely day," I said. Maybe it was my tablemates' shared awareness of the weather or just my own cheery remark, but most of the other women smiled back.

Breakfast finished, and then it was time for the exercise hour. I was eager for a warming outside day. I hurried to my room for a light sweater, a writing pad, and pencils.

Though one of the elevators was on the blink again, even the cattle-drive-like shuffle from floor to floor didn't seem oppressive this morning. Maybe it was the anticipation of fresh air and a soft breeze blowing off the river. *Perfect day to continue looking back on my time with Forman,* I thought. *What was it he said? Oh, right. . . .* "To know oneself is the essence of wisdom." I sighed.

Hmm . . . Am I even halfway there? How long to go before I can pretend a modicum of self-understanding?

By the time I reached the ground floor, any desire I'd had to spend time circling the yard with other patients had vanished. And Martha, the young nurse whose boyfriend had been reported missing, was absent again. Was this a sign that she'd received final and tragic news? I worried as I crossed to a bench and sat, gazing out through the mesh fence at the river.

Better not fret about Martha right now. Get on with where you left off last night, finish closing the circle of time in your month with Forman, I decided as I watched a gang of raucous seagulls swoop low, diving for garbage dumped overboard from a passing tug.

I brought the writing pad to my lap, pondered a moment, then began to write:

> We had agreed to meet at three o'clock. I was early, having overestimated the time it would take to walk uptown from Christopher Street, where I'd spent the morning in a coffee shop chewing over the previous night. And now there I was, sitting on a bench, wondering what he'd say, what thoughts he had. Would he make an effort to—

"Won't you be walking with us today, dear?" interrupted Mrs. Kelly, the supervising yard nurse. When she added that I needed to keep up my strength, I asked if she'd be upset if I just continued to write.

Responding in her delightful Irish brogue, she confessed, "Never penned a line myself, except in school when they made us do it. Didn't that get me peevish! I suppose it's all right, long as you don't forget it's the whole person needs attention; the body and soul together."

As Mrs. Kelly walked off, I continued dwelling on the river and the seagulls. Then finally returning to the pad and scanning what I'd written, I decided it wasn't right. I needed to write it as it happened. So having made my peace with 1926, and with a hint of summer in the air this morning, it needed the distance of time. Perspective. So I decided to write it as a kind of short story:

AN AFTERNOON IN CENTRAL PARK

What will he say? she asked herself. Will he try to explain away last night's awkward encounter, brush off his fumbling, half-hearted attempt at playing the lover? Should she mention the frustration she'd felt, her aching desire? Her longing? The urge to help, and his inability to respond? She shook off the notion. *That's no good; it would probably upset him. But perhaps not; he's so understanding, so tender. Even though he's younger than me and clearly inexperienced.*

That's it, youth and inexperience!

Well, what did you expect? Time; just give it time. And patience. That's probably all that's needed here, a big fat helping of patience. Then again, she thought, *we're cousins. Maybe that's what put him off. No, couldn't be, we're cousins twice removed, so—*

All at once she felt a presence. She looked up from the bench, and there he was.

"Let's walk," he said.

And so they did, strolling the graveled path that circled the pond, passing other couples lost in thought like them, arguing, laughing.

A middle-aged man, unshaven, dressed in a rumpled suit he'd clearly slept in with a stained tie at his collar, sat half-crumpled on a bench, swilling wine from a bottle he'd tried to conceal in a paper bag. Two fashionably dressed uptown children ran by, each rolling a colorful hoop, and followed by a nursemaid. A small boy in a sailor suit was being rudely pulled from the pond after having stepped in up to his waist trying to retrieve a sailboat.

They found another bench, partially secluded by bushes. They sat in silence for several minutes. Then, mustering courage and with no clue how it might be received, she slid her hand into his. It felt cold, uncertain. But then his other hand covered both of theirs, protectively. A sign? Was this a sign? She laid her head on his shoulder. Her throat felt tense, hollow. But she finally forced the words out. "Forman," she said. "Very dear Forman . . . I'm afraid I love you."

He bolted to his feet. She could feel him stiffen. He turned and walked away a few paces, his back to her as she sat there, frozen.

"You mustn't say that," he said. "You mustn't say that."

His words were straightforward, direct, without anger. Without any particular emotion she could detect.

"Look at me, Forman," she said.

He turned back.

"Are you saying . . . Are you saying you don't love me?"

Now his emotions became a flood. Crestfallen, he moved quickly to the bench, sat, and took both her hands. "No, no," he said, "I don't mean that. Of course I love you, Mary. I've always loved you, it's just that . . ." His face became a kaleidoscope: a frown changing to fear, changing to puzzled uncertainty. Biting his lip, he withdrew his hands and sat staring at her with an embarrassed half smile.

"Well, what is it then? You can talk to me, Forman. We've always been able to talk, haven't we?" She wanted so desperately to hold him, to take him in her arms like the frightened little boy he seemed just then, tell him everything would be all right. Instead, she didn't say a word.

Finally, he spoke. "I . . . I can't love you, Mary. I mean, not in the way you seem to hope; not as a man loves a woman."

He was unnerving her. She could feel the pain racing through her body, her heart throbbing. Still, she waited. He seemed to be gathering his words. Finally he said, "Remember the book I bought you that first night, after we had dinner at Giovanni's?"

"Yes, of course. I read it. Well, most of it. I'm afraid I was confused by it now and then; some of it was rather strange."

He looked off into the distance for a moment, then turned back and said, "I imagine most people would find it so. Do you recall a chapter about . . . well, I think it was called 'The Intermediate Sex.'"

"Yes, of course," she answered. "But . . . well, that's about people who . . . people loving others of the same sex, isn't it? I mean—"

The realization hit. Her throat felt dry and constricted again. Her mouth silently formed the words, *Oh, my God*. Then aloud, "Oh, my God!" She moistened both lips with her tongue and swallowed hard. She took a long, deep breath, then asked, "Are . . . you . . . saying . . . that's what you are, Forman? Is this what you've been trying to get at all along—all these years? That you're . . . someone who can only love men?"

It had been there all the time, she suddenly realized. Even in his poems.

He reached for her hands again. She let him take them, but they remained slack.

"I'm afraid that's what I am, dear. At least I think so."

"Think so?"

"I suppose I know so. I just haven't been able to admit it. I'd thought that perhaps since we've known one another for so long, I might make an effort to—"

She withdrew her hands and pressed her fingers against his lips. Tears welled up and began to flow. "Don't say anything more, Forman," she pleaded,

"Please don't."

But he couldn't hold back his feelings. "Please listen, dearest," he began. "Do you remember once telling me I was the best friend you had in the world?"

She nodded, her tears streaming.

"It's the same with me," he went on. "You're the best friend I have, absolutely the best. That's something we share, something we'll always share. Maybe it's even better than the other thing; what passes for romantic love, I mean. So much of it seems so ordinary. Restricted, artificial even, like some crazy game that men and women play for thirty, fifty years, with little real understanding of what they're doing. That's not the kind of friendship we share—that we've always shared. Isn't it possible that ours is perhaps stronger and more lasting than the other thing?"

He stood again and looked off across the pond.

"Oh, I don't know," he continued. "It's all mixed, a strange kind of three-sided love affair . . ."

"Three-sided? I don't understand."

"You love me. I've loved Harry for years, and—"

"Harry?" she exclaimed. "Harry too?"

"You didn't know, did you? Well, how could you? It's something we don't talk about. Even rarely to one another. It just is."

She almost had to laugh. "How sheltered I've been," she exclaimed. "A babe in the woods; the deep, dark

Michigan woods. Harry. Imagine that! You and he whispering, giggling; I could hear you through the ceiling . . ."

"I didn't know . . ."

Mary waved off the apology. "He's always been different," she went on, "odd, of course, but I just thought, 'Well, that's Harry,' and—"

"He's never returned my love. Not in any deep or meaningful way, that is. Maybe I'll find it with someone someday."

She stared at her hands. Then finally, taking out a handkerchief and dabbing her eyes, she looked up and whispered in a thin, strained voice, "I hope you will."

"I know how hard this must be for you, dear," he said, the regret in his voice spilling over, "and I'm so sorry not to have been able to just come out and express it long ago. But try to understand how hard it's been for me too. For a long time, you see, I just didn't know, I wasn't sure. It was a secret locked in my head for years. And now it's out. I'm sorry I told you so bluntly, but I didn't know how else to. I knew that you had your heart set on us being together, and I know how much you had hoped . . . especially after you left Matthew . . ."

He sat and took her hands again.

"I suppose I was hoping too, hoping these feelings I've had for so long were something I'd get over; that I could force them out of me, come to you, be with you as a man is with a woman, but . . ." He took a long deep breath, then added, "I'm afraid it's not something one does get over. It's just who we are."

She lowered her head once more and could only nod.

"I care for you so much," he went on, "and . . . well, this doesn't need to mean unhappiness for either of us, does it? Please say it doesn't."

She sat quietly gazing out across the park for a minute or more.

Forman watched her, anxiously waiting for an answer.

Then, raising her head again, she managed a weak smile as she looked into his eyes and replied, "It's all right, Forman. It's fine. It's just as you said, we've always been best friends. We'll keep on being best friends. I can't say I quite understand it all yet, but . . ."

She laid her head on his shoulder once more and whispered, "It's all right."

Forman cleared his throat.

She could tell he was feeling awkward. "Let's walk," she said. "Get a little exercise."

As they stood, he kissed her forehead tenderly.

She took his arm and clung to it, and though strangers looking on might assume they were lovers, at the same time a sense of relief engulfed her; like the sudden feeling of freedom she'd experienced after divorcing Matthew. This too was a kind of release, an escape from the lingering uncertainty of the two years since, puzzling over whether or not she and Forman would have a future. In a way, she thought, they would have, even though it could never be in the way she'd hoped for.

As they left the park and started down Fifth Avenue toward Washington Square and the Village, she clutched Forman's arm tighter and said, "You know what?"

He could already sense a difference in her, an ease that seemed to have abruptly swept away what had been confusion and anxiety. This was her essence, he remembered; the ability to quickly accept changes, the ability to adjust to what was at the moment.

"What?" he asked.

"I'm beginning to think this is something special," she said. "A singular something between us that all those others have no clue about." She gestured around at passersby. "They'll just go on as they always have, in the ordinary way. Our way is different, something new, I think, don't you . . . best friend?"

"I think it is . . . best friend."

"Time to be crossin' that last t," interrupted a strong Irish brogue. "Half the ladies are on the way t' the seventh floor already."

I closed my pad and stood. "Perfect timing Mrs. Kelly," I replied. "I've just this minute finished."

"And was it some good writin' you got done?"

"I think so. Kind of a little story about a time in my past life."

"Past life, is it? You write about the past, do you?"

"Well, not all the time, but today it seemed important."

"Why do that, for mercy sake? The past is past, isn't it? I can't see meself gettin' on about yesterday, even if I had a mind to write. Which I don't."

I considered for a few moments then replied, "I suppose I look back so I'll be better prepared to look ahead."

The nurse's face screwed into a quizzical smile. "Well, each to their own, I always say, but it's inside with us now. Never know when another elevator might take it in mind to stop runnin', do we?" She deadpanned briefly, then let loose a mighty guffaw.

I joined in, laughing, as she took my arm and we headed up the steps.

22.

"I'll buy it, Dan," Henry announced as his Monopoly token landed on the B & O Railroad. "Two hundred dollars, right?"

"Yeah," I grumped.

"That makes three," Henry went on as he handed over the money. "I only need the Reading now then you'll be kaput!"

"I'll be what?"

"Kaput. It means you'll lose."

"You gotta land on it first," I shot back with a defiant shake of the dice, wondering if he was speaking German.

Almost daily during the free period after school and before dinner, my roommate and I sat on the floor of our room, doing battle over the Monopoly board.

Davy stood in the doorway, watching.

Though our fortunes seesawed back and forth over the week, today's game saw my bankroll plummet to a measly hundred fifty dollars. But even though (to my chagrin) Henry never landed on my big moneymakers, Boardwalk or Park Place, I wasn't giving up. "Anyways," I went on, "I've got both utilities."

"Doesn't equal four railroads," grinned Henry.

"You've only got three so far."

"Doesn't matter. You're still going to go broke."

Just along the corridor from our open door, I could see George, the ever-present cigar stub in his mouth, on hands and knees, diligently waxing the oak floor and apparently chuckling at our competitive banter. At the sound of footsteps, he looked up. As it happened, Morris, Gordon Arbuckle's loud-mouthed hanger-on, was ambling along the hall, stopping in at each succeeding room without knocking. George had a suspicious look on his face; something underhanded was obviously going on. No surprise. Arbuckle and his bunch were usually cooking up some crazy plan.

"Wat'cha doin' here, Little Bit?" Morris asked Davy as he appeared at our door.

"Just watching," my brother replied.

"Hey, Heinrich," Morris went on as he stepped into the room, "What're you and Shirley up to, huh? Lookin' over some secret plans from 'der fadderland,' yeah?"

"Your turn," said Henry without glancing at Morris.

Ignoring the intrusion, I rolled the dice and moved my token—only to land on Reading Railroad.

"Two hundred dollars, please!" beamed Henry.

I picked up my remaining stash. "I've only got one-fifty left."

"Oh, right . . . okay, one hundred fifty."

With a sigh, I handed over the bills.

"Der zourkraut wins again! Der fuhrer vill be zo pleased," taunted Morris.

I felt like socking the guy. In the corridor, George was shaking his head.

"Okay, look, you creeps," continued Morris. "I come by to give you some good news. You heard about the zombies in the cave, right?"

"What's a zombie?" quizzed Henry.

"The living dead, Heinrich!" replied Morris, bugging out his eyes and moving toward us stiffly with his arms outstretched. "Corpses brought back to life by some kinda voodoo magic."

"There's no such thing." I sneered.

"Oh yeah? Gordon saw 'em the other night. Three of 'em. Spooky they were, flesh drippin' off 'em. . . . Ain't that right, Little Bit?"

"Well, I—" Davy said before Morris cut him off.

"They live back there in the cave. They started for him. All three. He got out okay, but you don't never wanna mess with zombies."

"Stupid," mumbled Henry as he began to sort the Monopoly money into neat piles.

"I'm not kiddin'," persisted Morris, unaware that George was listening in the corridor. "And there's a way to find out—if you're not sissies, that is. We're givin' five bucks to anyone who goes in the cave and stays for fifteen minutes. 'Course, you gotta pay a dollar to go in."

"You don't own the cave," I said.

"Us older guys got dibs on it. Always have. Under fifteens can't come in unless we allow for special privileges. Like for Little Bit here," he added, putting an arm around my brother's shoulders.

I could feel my stomach churn. "How come you hang out with these guys?" I asked Davy.

"What's it to you?" growled Morris.

"He's my brother, you dumb jerk."

Davy looked at the floor.

"Well, fuck off, chicken shit! You're a mommy's boy, that's what you are. We know all about you. Gordon and us heard your auntie talkin' when you first come, about how your mama's in the nut house and all. She—"

Davy looked up, stunned.

I leaped to my feet. "She ain't in any nut house; she's taking a rest. She's just tired, that's all!"

"She's in the loony bin," Morris shot back. "'Takin' a rest,' huh? Gordon says that's just a cover. She's locked up on the funny farm."

I was close to tears. "No, she's not, she's not!" I shouted. "Gordon's a big dumb jerk, just like you!"

After hesitating for a moment, my brother turned and bolted into the corridor, past George, who had taken the cigar from his mouth and risen from the floor.

"Oh yeah? Well, see how you like this!" shot back Morris, shoving me backward across the Monopoly board, scattering the houses and hotels and play money. I almost fell over Henry.

"Hey, knock it off!" demanded Henry.

"How's about a knuckle sandwich, Heinie?" countered Morris, raising a threatening fist.

Instantly, George shot into the room, grabbed Morris's arms, and pinned them behind his back. "That's enough of that!" he commanded.

"Let me go!" shouted Morris. "Get your damn black hands off o' me!"

George turned the protesting boy around and frog-marched him into the hall. "You just be on your way," he said, pointing down the corridor. "An' leave these fellers be, you hear?"

"Fuck you, Sambo," muttered Morris, storming off.

George, trembling, watched until the bully disappeared down the stairwell. Quickly regaining composure, he looked back into the room. Henry was on hands and knees gathering the scattered Monopoly money, while I stood nearby, frozen in a combination of rage and fear.

"You gonna be okay, son?" asked George.

I didn't reply.

"New here, ain't ya? One of the Bessie boys, that right? Was that your little brother been watchin' the game?

I nodded bleakly.

Having noticed Henry and me around the school, George had already worked out that we tended to spend time alone or only with one another. He'd known plenty of others like us during his thirty years at Musgrove. "'f I was you," he suggested, "I wouldn't take no stock in what them like that Morris boy says. They're the kind likes to toot their own horn. You know what I mean?"

I nodded again.

"Well, look," continued George, checking his watch. "It's 'most dinner time, so I figure you both best clean up now. And Danny—that your name?"

"Yes sir."

"Okay. So, you ever want to talk about stuff, just know I'm around most all the time. You got that?"

Another nod.

"Okay. I'll leave you be now so's you can get this mess sorted," said George as he started out of the room. "An' don't be late for dinner. Turkey stew tonight, I hear tell," he added with a smile. And, sticking the cigar stub back in his mouth, he closed the door.

"I don't think I can put this all back the way we had it," said Henry as he sat on the floor surveying the Monopoly board.

"Who cares?" I mumbled. "I lost anyhow." And, choking back tears, I fell onto my bed and threw both arms over my eyes—the unknown puzzle of when David and I would get out of this place and go home overwhelming me.

After being silent for several moments, Henry finally sighed and said, "Okay, I'll just put everything away for a new game tomorrow."

Images swirled through my brain: lying in bed with the mumps, Mom kissing me goodbye. The recent memory of Morris shoving me brought to mind Rico doing the same in Danbury; David all muddy and crying after having gone missing for hours, images of Kenji and me hurling ourselves into a snow bank to blast away at imaginary Nazis.

Then this morphed into kind of a dream, with Henry wearing a swastika armband, his arm raised in a Hitler salute. And zombies, a parade of zombies coming toward me like in the film—but I knew they weren't real, that it was just a movie. The living dead, Morris had said, corpses brought back to life by voodoo magic. Maybe they were real after all? Then what Morris had said about Mom being locked in some dark fortress with a bunch of weirdos . . . What if it were true that she'd gone crazy? Would we ever see her again?

No, no, she's not crazy! shouted a voice in my head. *She's just tired. She came to see us, and we went out to lunch. She said she just needed a little more rest. . . . Two months, she said, and she'd come visit again . . . Maybe take us home . . .*

As my anxiety gradually faded, I thought about what George had said: "If you ever feel like you want to talk about stuff, just know I'm around most all the time. . . ." I needed that. I really did—someone to help me figure out stuff.

How I wished Mom were there. She was so good at that kind of thing.

23.

Following dinner and several rounds of gin rummy with nurse Kelly and a couple of patients, I'd been feeling cheerful. But it didn't last. As I prepared for bed, the recurring image of Davy and Dan lost in a big house crept in. "My boys," I sighed; how close I'd come to losing them. Or rather, how close they'd come to losing me, the mainstay in their young lives—half of the time with a mostly absent father.

As I dwelled on this, Alvah came to mind; his intermittent visits after our divorce, his endless political involvement, and a year in Spain fighting the fascist general Franco. Then home, marrying a new wife, spending most of his time churning out stories in order to earn a living, thus leaving less time for the boys.

Later, Harold came along. A kind, loving stepfather the boys adored, but who was taken from us far too soon. Once again, I was left to raise Dan and Davy alone.

Aware I'd need to examine all this in due course, I slipped under the blankets and turned off the bedside lamp. Overwhelmed by the responsibility that lay ahead once I was out of Payne Whitney, I began to think about my father. Dear Dad: he'd always been there for me, just as I now felt I needed to be there for the boys. *What are they up to right now?* I wondered. If only Dad had lived long enough to know them. . . . *He'd be so proud. . . .*

Noble Burnett in his early sixties

Then, as so often when I felt a need to bounce my problems off him, I began to feel his presence, as though he were in the room.

"Hi, Dad," I began, wiping away a tear. "Been a while, hasn't it? Seems like years since we last spoke, but it must have been only a couple weeks. Still, that's too long. I'm afraid I've been in a terrible funk since then and didn't feel like I had much to say that would sound rational. I'd probably have carried on like some moping crybaby, which is what I guess I was. But despite worrying about the boys, I've been feeling a lot better lately, so maybe now you can hear me out. Are you listening? Silly question—of course you are. . . ."

I paused. *Where should I begin?* There was so much I'd love to have hashed out with him; so much I wished we'd been able to chew over when he was alive.

"Well, there are probably a lot of things you didn't know about, and that I've only begun to understand myself of late. I suppose that's what comes of living in small town Michigan, in a home that, in spite of all its confusions and squabbles, its restrictions, still somehow felt like a safe cocoon during my growing years.

"Oh, we talked of course, you and I. You were a patient listener, Dad; sympathetic, always willing to hear us young folk out or try to patch up misunderstandings or smooth over whatever troubled us.

I guess the big problem is that we . . . well, me at least—I shouldn't speak for Harry, Leo or Verne. . . . I suppose I didn't know, deep down, what I really thought about much of anything way back then. I just coasted along and assumed life was ducky, and that how we lived and what we talked about and how we behaved and what we did or wanted was simply the way things were. What's that old saw? 'If I'd known then what I know now.' My, my, Dad, the conversations we might have had.

"There I go again, off on a tangent. I'll start over. I suppose—"

A light rap on my door interrupted the dialogue, and in stepped Martha, the young nurse I hadn't seen for several days. She looked pale and drawn. While I don't recall our exact words, the gist of our conversation ran something like this:

"I'm sorry to disturb you, Mrs. Burnett," said Martha, straining to scan the room, which was illuminated only by dim moonlight through the window. "It's nearly one a.m., you know, and, well, I heard your voice, and—"

"There's no one here," I explained as I turned on my bedside lamp and got up.

"Well, okay . . ." replied Martha, looking at me a bit oddly.

"I was talking to my father."

"Your father?"

"Yes. He passed on in 1928."

Martha seemed unsure how to respond.

"How can I? You're wondering, right? But I do. Not often, you understand, but when I'm feeling muddled or just can't find an answer, it's what I do."

Martha responded with a quizzical half frown.

I asked her to sit down, and though she demurred, when I patted the end of the bed, she betrayed an embarrassed smile, then crossed to the bed and sat.

"But . . . well, do you actually see him?" she asked.

"Let's say I picture him in my head. I see him as he was, as I knew him when he lived and as I knew and talked with him briefly on the day before he died."

"What was he like?"

"Oh, very patient. Gentle. I suppose we were each busy with our own lives most of the time. Except I always knew he listened and tried the best he could to answer any question I had."

Martha nodded slowly, thoughtfully.

I need to say something about what she's going through, I thought. So I continued: "He was a good man," I said. "Kind, loving . . . Something like your beau, I'll bet." Sensing a sudden tension, I asked, "Still no word?"

Tears began to form as she shook her head.

After pondering a moment, I asked, "What if you talked to him? Kind of like I talk with my dad, that is. Although you might get word any day that your beau is fine, just pretending someone you care about is there might be a great comfort."

"Maybe," she said, dabbing her eyes.

We sat quietly for several minutes before I tried to offer a few more encouraging words—until Martha rose from the bed. "I'd better be off; the staff will be wondering where I am." Forcing a thin smile, she added, "And if you're going to continue talking to your father, best keep it down a bit, okay?"

I smiled back and nodded.

At the door, Martha turned and added, "Thank you, Mrs. Burnett. I'm going to try what you suggested."

I thought for several moments after she left, then reached to the nightstand for my writing pad and pencil, and soon began to write:

> Well, Dad, it seems like chatting aloud might not be such a good idea tonight, and since I've rarely been able to keep my voice to a whisper, I'll just scribble instead. First, I should mention that it's 1943 now, early April. And I'm in a psychiatric ward in a New York City hospital. . . . Now, don't get all in a dither! How I landed here is quite a story, but I'll save that for another time. Since yesterday, my brain's been rattling around back in 1926; until just before (and even after) I got that scary message from brother Leo in '28—the one telling me I had to get to Detroit quick because you were dying. . . .

I briefly stopped writing to reflect. *There's so much Dad doesn't know,* I thought. *But maybe now's not the right time to get into any of that. . . .*

> Okay, Dad, I'm back. Yes, I know. You've listened to me endlessly over there in whatever mysterious world exists beyond, but there are still confusions it's taken me a long time to unravel. And I suppose some began even before I married Matt; maybe when I was a kid. . . . What kind of girl was I, Dad? Shy? Sometimes. Mature for my

age? About certain things, yes, but painfully adolescent about most. Was I interested in school? So-so. To be honest, I was looking more for love than for anything else. Was I inhibited? Yes and no. I'd been out with many boys, been kissed by many but somehow never connected even the most exciting kisses with sex or marriage; that's one of so many things you and I never talked about, Dad. Guess I hadn't truly come awake. So in spite of all those experiments, marriage was still sacred, the thing to be hoped for. I would have been insulted if someone assumed I'd have intercourse before tying the knot. Once I slapped a young man across the cheek for even intimating that he wanted to. Though I later realized that in my deepest nature, that's what I longed for. Does that shock you? I hope not. Sex and marriage were deep mysteries that my own inhibited outlook wouldn't allow me to consider. Love was somehow a "pure" thing, one woman for one man, and my notions about it were right out of *Snow White* or *Sleeping Beauty*. Makes me think of that old song; remember?

Tell me, little Gypsy,
In the days that are to be . . .
There's a boy for every girl in the world,
There must be someone for me . . .

I know you can see that I'm smiling, Dad.

Does this make me sound like an incurable romantic? Well, I probably am. Or at least have been. See what kind of daughter you raised?

On the other hand, how much of all that was a product of the times we lived in, society's puritanical view of man-woman relationships? And in particular, Mother's probably fearful attitude toward sex?

Glossing over my marriage to Matthew Parker and recalling that Dad had known about our divorce, I went on to write about Forman's invitation to New York; the invitation that ignited the hoped-for realization of my fairytale fantasy like a Fourth of July rocket—and that had come crashing down when he told me, "I am spoiled for any woman."

That was certainly my low point, Dad, but I knew I had to keep going, make some sort of life for myself . . . And it wasn't easy.

Continuing, I described Forman leaving for Europe, once stopping at the Italian restaurant we'd gone to, where Giovanni asked why he wasn't with me (I never went back), the loss of my job at Columbia's registrar office (budget cuts), then slipping into the aimless life of a somewhat bohemian artist (or at least an aspiring one), staying up all night, overflowing an ashtray with cigarette buts as I covered endless sheets of cheap paper with pencil and paint—without ever being satisfied with a damn thing.

When I looked in my purse one day and found just seventy-five cents, Dad, and with not even a can of soup on the shelf, I started going down the block to a delicatessen where I'd become friends with Mrs. Bronstein, the plump, talkative woman who ran it. She always seemed glad to see me, but had a sad expression too, because I still felt terribly depressed. And I suppose I looked it, wearing the old corduroy coat and dark blue felt hat I'd picked up in a secondhand store. Mrs. Bronstein gave me credit and never asked for payment, so I'd sit there and eat a pastrami sandwich and have a cup of coffee and smoke a cigarette; my meal for the day. When Verne or Leo sent a little money once in a while, I'd pay her.

I described roaming the lower East Side, mingling anonymously with crowds among the teeming shops and tenements, stopping to watch ragged, boisterous children playing stickball, or racing up and down alleys and streets and jumping off stoops as teams tried to catch one another in the apparently endless game of Ringolevio. How I'd drop a nickel in a subway turnstile and head for the Battery, where I'd sit in the park, gazing across the water toward the statue of Liberty raising her lamp "beside the golden door." Or how I'd track ships as they ended their long voyage, coming from . . .

> From where, Dad? South America? Portugal? The British Isles? Or France, where Forman surely was at that time; and doing what? He wrote me letters from there off and on, even before he arrived. . . .

Breaking off from writing, I turned to my folder to retrieve that letter. Having long since made my peace with who Forman was, it could still bring a twinge—though nothing like when I'd returned to the pond in Central Park, sat on the same bench we'd parted from all those years before and read it for the umpteenth time:

At sea, June 4, 1926

Dear Mary,

This letter, most of it, was written and rewritten many times. We land tomorrow, and I will mail it there before I catch the "rapide" for Paris. All the days at sea I have thought of you; your face, your sad mouth and deep eyes have haunted me, and I wonder if you ever can forgive me for what I've done to you, for this cruel breach of a friendship that has lasted so many years and been productive of so many things I like to think of as lasting beauty. If you could, it would mean forgiving me more than any man on this earth has ever been forgiven. Can you do it?

Have you reached an understanding of the matters I tried so gropingly, so poorly to convey to you in Central Park?

You told me you'd read the book I gave you. I do hope it made me understandable, helped you to see that I too have been helpless in this matter, but not through any desire to deceive you—only because I have been confused in my own mind for years, a confusion that will probably plague me till my death. I saw in you a means of rehabilitation (that sounds crude), but I grasped at you because I knew I loved you and I thought that with

> your aid I could accomplish the apparently impossible. You must not think I am ashamed of what I am; you must not think this is a disease of which one can be cured. It is not that, it is a state of being, as potentially productive of everlasting beauty as any state of being. . . .

Enough. I'd poured over it too many times. The years had long since passed when I'd tried, with little success, to tuck the month with Forman into my portfolio of memories. Even now, the letter did nothing but conjure up the exasperating mystery of what, at the age of twenty-eight, the fates ultimately had in store for me in that department.

But my mind, still back in 1926, continued to wander.

Finally, I got up and walked from Central Park all the way downtown to Brooklyn Bridge and across it, reaching the opposite side at twilight, and all the time wishing I'd stop thinking about him. My feet ached, so I went into a café and nursed cups of coffee until after dark, when the lights came on in Manhattan, just as Forman and I had seen them on our many jaunts.

It had been a hard month. More than a month, actually, more like a year and a half of aimless mental meandering. With a couple respites, fortunately, because otherwise I wasn't sure I'd make it through. Nights, I escaped into my diaries or tried to quiet my brain by more wandering around Manhattan. Mostly, I haunted the East Side, losing myself along Delancey Street, Rivington, Orchard, or Broom; or Hester Street with its pushcart vendors and army of Jewish immigrants trying to eke out a living. I loved everything about the area, with its angry, laughing, arguing, and jostling crowds, old clothes, scruffy but happy children, and the smell of raw fish cooking.

In a strange way, I felt at home.

In 1928, Harry finally arrived in New York—with Roddy in tow, the young man he'd met at Yale and who'd become a partner with him and Forman in his puppet shows. Remembering that year, I picked up my pencil again:

> From his letters, Dad, I had a sense that Forman and Roddy were now a couple. I realize you'd probably be shocked, but the world you knew is certainly changing.
>
> Anyhow, Harry talked Verne into putting up quite a chunk of money to launch his New England tour. For me, May and June of that year were something of a rescue. Harry rented a workshop on Bank Street, crammed in between a couple of stables (horses whinnied through the night), and I spent two harried months in the basement room next door, surrounded by mountains of colored rags, yarn, crepe hair, braid, and ribbons, snatching sleep between 2 a.m. and 8, and working feverishly to stitch costumes for the marionettes in a kind of Moorish version of "Bluebeard," the old French fairytale. Harry was haggard and bad-tempered much of the time, churning out puppets faster than a couple of volunteers and myself could possibly clothe them.
>
> Sounds frantic, doesn't it, Dad? And it was. I wish you'd been there to see it. But it was a rescue nonetheless, because at least I could pay the rent; it kept my mind off all that had gone on during most of the two

years before—and for a change I began to feel a bit useful. Even with the overwork, I loved not having any responsibility except for making the costumes, but also felt torn between wanting to do them right and a ghastly feeling of failing. I think it made me understand better what it must have been like for you when you had to close down the dry-goods store in St. Johns, and—

Hey, Dad, I just realized how that chimes with what I've been doing here at Payne Whitney these past few days—making puppets, not having any real responsibility except teaching the ladies here and feeling a bit useful. But you know, that fear of failure still haunts me.

Reflecting again, I suddenly felt free not to hold anything back from Dad.

There had been men along the way before working with Harry and after the disastrous tour of '28. Men who wanted me, that is: a policeman on the beat who kept dropping by "Just ta' see how you're gettin' on; we like to keep an eye on new folks on the block. You're not from New York, are you?"

Michigan, I told him.

"Well, you need anything just give a shout, Miss Michigan. I'll come by, maybe you can make me a cup o' coffee, huh? Gets lonely patrollin' at night."

I never invited him in, and after a few more attempts he got the idea.

I wrote about the friendly old man who lived on the second floor. He reminded me of my father. "I seen you come and go, all hours of the day or night," he said. "You got a feller?"

I said I didn't.

"Girl oughta have a feller," he went on. To my embarrassed laugh, he asked if I needed money, and before I answered he handed me five dollars. "As a loan. Give it back when you can."

I reluctantly accepted and made a mental note to pay it back.

He wanted me to come up to his room, said he'd give me more, that he gave all the girls money. "I can tell you're a nice girl, not like them perfume-smellin' girls you see, with their faces all painted up."

I wondered if I'd ever be desperate enough. But though there'd been plenty of hungry days, I never was. And the old man never asked for his five dollars back.

> I had one brief stab at something I hoped would be more serious, Dad; with a carefree kind of younger fellow Harry hired to paint backdrops based on the designs for the Bluebeard show. Bill had set up in the workshop, and we got talking. He was a jack-of-all-theatrical-trades, an actor too. Just the sort of guy I always seemed to get attracted to (for better or for worse). But it didn't last. I suspect that at twenty-three he was still "sowing his wild oats." We finally lost contact, but I've heard he went off to California and has been doing bit parts in several of those cheap movie serials. Ah well, it seems that except for

Matt I've always drifted toward younger guys. Guess that's another aspect of my character to take a look at, isn't it?

One more thing: when Harry and the boys and I returned from the 1928 tour of New England, something come along. . . . *Someone* else, I should say.

While gathering my thoughts to write about meeting Alvah and our life in Vermont, I glanced up at the window. With the curtains only half closed, I was stunned to discover the sun shining through. I'd been writing and talking to my dad all night.

Just then, there was a knock on the door, and in bustled the starched nurse, cheery and talkative. "Did we have a good sleep?" she bubbled.

"We" again. I resisted the urge to reply with sarcasm as she went on about what a gorgeous day it was, rushed to pull back the curtains, and, as she checked her watch, announced, "The other ladies are already at breakfast, and I'm afraid we're a bit late, aren't we? It's nearly eight."

"I'll be right along as soon as I get dressed."

Alone again as the door closed, I picked up my pad and a pencil. Then I smiled and put it down. "Gotta go, Dad," I said, softly. "I'll continue when I've got a bit more time. Writing is fine, but it's always so comforting to actually talk with you. And besides, I need to get a letter off to the boys right after breakfast."

Continuing the whispered conversation as I got dressed, I added, "I've told you they're at a boarding school, right? And though I've been to visit them once so far, I'm feeling kind of guilty just now; perhaps indulging myself a bit too much over 1926, 1928, and Forman and all that, and not being in touch with Dan and David as much as I should be. Well, that's going to change!"

Tired from lack of sleep but at the same time exhilarated after committing so much previously unshared emotion to Dad, I looked at myself in the mirror, applied lipstick, then, after blotting some with a tissue, lightly rubbed the residue into my pale cheeks.

"They're marvelous boys," I went on. "Survivors. But between you and me and the lamppost, I worry about how they're doing. What I most need is to become strong enough to get the hell out of this place, and the sooner the better. They need me. And I need them."

24.

As I lay in bed reading, my mind kept wandering to Mom. What was she doing right now? Did she have a radio in her room at the rest home? Was she listening to Charlie McCarthy and Mortimer Snerd, like we did right after supper tonight at the school? I hoped so, 'cause she'd be laughing.

As the door opened, I looked up. Davy appeared, wearing pajamas—he also had a worried look on his face, and he held a pencil and a sheet of writing paper.

"How do ya spell 'terrible'?" he asked.

"You're supposed to be in bed," I replied.

"Just tell me!" he carped.

"It's past lights-out on your floor," added Henry without looking up from the book he was reading.

"I snuck down," Davy replied. "Nobody saw me, so tell me how to spell it."

"Bring it to me," I demanded.

"Just tell me if it's spelled "t-e-r-r-a-b-b-l-e."

I threw off my blanket, jumped out of bed, and grabbed the paper.

"Hey!" cried Davy.

"Keep it down; we'll all get in trouble," whispered Henry.

"How come you're writing about this?" I insisted. Then I read it aloud,

Dear Mom, the big guys here like Gordun and Morris ar saying you ar in a crasy house or someplace like that. This is really terrabble but I don't know what to tell them, so please—

I sighed then added, "And you spelled a bunch o' words wrong! You can't write this, and even so, Mrs. Musgrove would never let it get mailed!"

"Well, that's what Gordon and the other guys said about her the other day."

"They're always making up stories," cut in Henry. "Just ignore them."

"Why don't you just write Mom a nice letter?" I said. "Tell her about the baseball practice, say you hope she's feeling well, and nice stuff like we always say. She'll like that. Oh—and maybe put in our secret code, like a smiling sun when we're doing good or a raincloud if we're worried about something."

"Very clever," whispered Henry.

Davy thought for a moment, then slowly opened the door and peeked out. Turning back, he added, "He knows I go out sometimes. George, I mean. And I tell him stuff too. He never says nothing, just usually kinda smiles."

After Davy left, I got back in bed and lay still for a while, thinking about what he'd said about his talking to George. And convincing myself that what the boys told him was nothing but a pack of lies. "Mom told us she needed a rest. She wouldn't lie to us," I mumbled as I turned my face into the pillow.

"Be quiet and go to sleep!" Henry whispered.

25.

Though still tired from lack of sleep, my meeting with Dr. Thomas left me exhilarated. So a few softly spoken words with my long-departed father seemed in order:

"Just had an interesting session, Dad. When I told my psychiatrist about talking with you, he said he thought it a most interesting idea, and that he'd maybe give it a try. He let on that problems with parents often lay behind the traumas of many patients. That had me feeling damn good . . . And I've got you to thank, dear Dad."

Parents, I thought. *Fathers.* Dad's image briefly lingered, then dissolved to one of my second husband, Alvah Bessie, father of my precious boys. *Time to sort out those eight years together . . . almost nine,* I told myself. This seemed important if I was going to build the kind of life for Danny and Davy that Alvah and I somehow never did manage to sustain—though we'd certainly tried, maybe even came close.

Or did we really?

I picked up one of my journals from the time Alvah and I were together and opened it to an early entry. Having transcribed thoughts about our first meeting to paper while the memory was fresh, I found myself comparing him to Bill, the short-term lover I'd mentioned to Dad in a letter, and who had, with no warning, dashed whatever hopes I might have had and hightailed it for California.

On the surface, at least, Alvah seems more promising, Dad. He's a writer, has translated a risqué book from the French, been an actor on the New York stage—in bit parts, he admits—and though I didn't know him at the time, along with Forman, I'd seen him two years earlier as a member of the chorus in *The Garrick Gaieties*. . . . And when Alvah told me he'd been in it, I let loose with, "We'll have Manhattan, the Bronx, and Staten Island too. . . ." I then said, "I love that lyric; it's never left my head. Were you really in that show? I must have seen you . . . Along with my cousin, I mean. He wasn't in the play," I laughed. "He took me to it."

"And in several others too," Alvah replied. "*Marco Millions* . . . *Processional*. I was a Klansman."

I felt my heart pumping. *Take it slow, Mary. . . .*

"A Klansman?"

"And a miner. We doubled up on parts. But my big passion is writing."

Letting it slip that he was thinking about selling his collection of a thousand books and heading for Paris to spend a year writing a novel, he was nonetheless telegraphing non-verbal signals that he was more than casually taken with me. I suppose he felt that an "experienced older woman," one involved in theater and the arts, was a person he could relate to.

Here, we both instantly decided without saying so, was a melding of minds.

Hmm . . . *Certainly doesn't hurt that along with a creative sensibility, he's got an infectious smile, the gregarious manner of a young raconteur, and—if I can forgive a slightly receding hairline—a marvelous head of curly blond locks.*

"My mother always called it my natural Marcel wave," he laughed.

Have to confess that my heart continued its flutter. It must have been fate appearing right here on Bank Street, and three days after we met there's landed in my bed a man who seems as though he might fill the role Forman never could. . . .

Fleetingly, however, I wondered if perhaps I was grasping at straws. Alvah was, after all, six years younger than me. Though I had a hunch he was, at twenty-four, still somewhat . . . how should I put it? . . . unformed . . . my concerns dissipated as I became swept into the same kind of artistic, literary life Forman had introduced me to. Within weeks, Alvah and I had taken in *An Enemy of the People*, *The Cherry Orchard*, and a performance of the all Negro review, *Blackbirds of 1928*, with its enormous hit, "I Can't Give You Anything But Love."

While no promises were made, we never seemed to tire of one another's company in bed. Yet we broke up once (on Alvah's initiative), quickly got back together, ruminated about the relationship (sometimes until dawn), spent long evenings prowling Manhattan and

> Brooklyn to take in the occasional film or play, and visited Greenwich Village bookshops where authors such as Sinclair Lewis read from their latest novel and autographed copies. There were all-night sessions where convivial and sometimes heated discussions took place over drinks at the occasional speakeasy or at the apartments of Alvah's more well-off friends.
>
> I found myself completely swept up into his circle, a world populated by young actors such as Lee Strasberg, John Garfield, and Elia Kazan; aspiring writers like James T. Farrell (*Studs Lonigan*), and other talents such as Alexander Calder. We visited his barn studio in Connecticut, where he was starting work on hanging sculptures that the French artist Marcel Duchamp would dub "mobiles."

Then, in December of 1928, after we'd been together for only three months, Alvah opened his apartment to a browsing parade of friends, sold more than half of his thousand books, and raked in enough cash to sail for France.

As deckhands cast off the SS *McKeesport*'s mooring lines on a rainy Brooklyn morning two weeks later, I found myself among a small clutch of Alvah's friends—along with his mother, dabbing her eyes—waving from the dock. Camouflaging my emotions with a buoyant smile had me confused. This was, after all, the second time I'd seen a hoped-for man disappear on his grand European adventure.

Well, here I am, I thought as the ship moved away from the dock and out into the harbor: *thirty, and still alone.* That night, I opened my diary and tried to express what my hopes had added up to until then:

I like to think that I have run
Swiftly naked
Through the forests of the new earth,
That I have danced,
Brown and gay,
Before some early potentate.
Then tonight,
If I have been these things,
My loneliness was less gigantic.

Buy a ticket and get on over here, Alvah wrote after roaming Paris for just a week. *Two can live as cheaply as one in La Ville Lumiére. What a marvelous, magical, magnetic city.*

I don't have the money, I wrote back. To survive, I had to keep working.

Besides, I'd rushed to Detroit in November to be with Dad. He was dying. Verne paid for the trip—and Dad's final admonition to "always live within your means, Sis," was a refrain I couldn't shake. In addition, I'd never been terribly fond of travel. Still, the frustration ate at me. I'd fallen in love with a man who was off to become "the American expatriate writer" he dreamed of being. His letters told of wandering the Latin Quarter, browsing Shakespeare and Company to buy a copy of James Joyce's *Ulysses*—still banned in the United States—and guzzling vast quantities of Spatenbrau in company with other literati at the Café Balzar—then being packed off to his hotel in a cab after passing out.

Sounds as though he's doing fine without me, I thought. "Have a good time, young man," I recalled muttering as I read about his experiences and awaited his return. If *he returns, that is. Might the year he said he'd be gone stretch into two?*

What was I doing, then? I asked myself that afternoon at Payne Whitney as I rose from the bed and crossed to the window. A mourning dove had landed on the sill but flew away as I got close. It reminded me of those perching on the roof ledge outside Harry's Bank Street studio in the spring of 1928, when I'd put papier-mâché puppet heads and hands out on the roof to dry in the sun.

So much water over the dam since then, I thought. But instead of the daily events so often confided to my diaries, I found that entries during the next year and a half, some dated and others not, were mostly brief notes or scattered impressions, sometimes mixed with emotion and gradually reflecting a mounting frustration.

> *December 1928*
>
> I'm feeling at loose ends these days. What to do? Nights, I lose myself in drawing, a little poetry, getting my hands sticky with clay.
>
> *December 31*
>
> Midnight. Happy New Year, Mary! I think I'll throw myself a party. Not too elaborate, you understand—the rent is due next week. Seven dollars left in the jar on the shelf, saved from helping dress Harry's little wooden creations. But if I hang onto it for the landlord, how do

I eat? Haven't been terribly hungry these days anyhow. . . . Oh, what the hell, seven's a lucky number, isn't it? How's about stepping across to the speakeasy for a bottle of beer?

Too cold out, you say? All right, I'll bundle in bed—and hope the super doesn't get so drunk he forgets to turn on the radiator by the time the building wakes up.

Early February 1929

Thank God the overdue rent is off my chest. (A loan from Verne. Good brother. He says don't worry about paying him back. I do.)

February 15

Rescue! The Henry Street Settlement needs a person to organize theatrical productions. Quite a feather in my cap, because I'll get to put on a couple plays. A short letter from Alvah. He's on the way home. Lost the Paris job, he says.

February 27, 1929

Working with the performers at Henry Street. Two plays—*Ain't No Use for Larnin'* and *People Who Die*, although this second sketch is just a rather peculiar two-person dialogue. I'm not sure I understand it. As for the first, how in the world am I going to cast a play set in a crude log cabin in the mountains of North Carolina with the odd group of New Yorkers who've showed up to audition—a couple of elderly ladies who say they acted on Broadway in the early days, a funny little fat Italian man who seems to fancy himself a singer (there are no songs in these plays; and anyhow, his voice is awful—though I'll never tell him that), and two rather eccentric young fellows who I'm sure don't fit in with their classmates. A challenge? To say the least!

February 1929

Poor Alvah. His year in Paris has shrunk to three months. He's been canned from the rewrite job he lied his way into, cashiered when he objected to the publisher editing his stories. And except for eighty dollars tucked into the lining of his suitcase for passage home, he's exhausted his funds. He writes that one short story, typed out on the voyage from New York, has been the extent of his creative effort. No novel; though he'd taken along one previously written, intending to fine-tune it. But on rereading its four hundred pages on the return trip, he apparently decided it was rubbish and relegated it to the storm-tossed Atlantic. Wish I'd read it.

What now? Here in America, few would have predicted, factories are closing, and homeless men roam the land looking for any work they can find. I guess Alvah's been more fortunate than most.

March 2

Alvah is home. We're living together on Sidney Place in Brooklyn, and he's making bookcases out of apple crates for the several hundred books he didn't sell and had left with me. I'll be glad to get them off the floor.

March 4

Lo and behold, he's already landed a job! Assistant manager at Dauber & Pine's on Fourth Avenue. Twenty dollars a week. A bookstore; just what he's cut out for. Things are looking up. Whoopee!

March 10, 1929

I get a strange feeling that Alvah's getting queasy about our being together. He still seems restless, agitated, like when he returned last month. I had thought that would go away when the bookstore job came through. Seems not.

Another page . . .

March 15

The ides of March! Alvah hates the job, says he's just filing invoices, stocking the shelves, and keeping the store tidy. He stomps around muttering, "I should be writing books instead of working in a place that sells the God damn things!"

March 18

Ten dollars from Harry posted from Florida. Kind brother. But it seemed to annoy Alvah; he made some kind of nasty crack.

April 10

First outing of the plays are tomorrow evening. Hope we get a decent audience.

Saturday, April 12, 11:30 p.m.

I'm writing this after the second performance. Friday was a fizzle, only six people showed up. We were all so disappointed. Tonight was a little better, around fifteen or so. Relatives, I think. They seemed to like *Ain't No Use For Larnin'*, though *People Who Die* had them as puzzled as it did me.

April 30

We had a raging argument about Swedenborg, the mystic. Now Alvah wants us to split up again. He says we're on different planets. And just when I was about to drop a hint about marriage. He's gone off to sleep at his mother's tonight.

And here I am, still awake at three in the morning.

No more plays for a while; there's not enough interest.

May 4

Alvah came in around 11 p.m. with an off-the-cuff apology. I wonder if his mother had words with him. I like her, even if she is something of a gossip. (Alvah takes after her.) Hmmm . . . Maybe he just misses sleeping with me every night?

A soft knock on my door brought me back to Payne Whitney. My door slowly opened. The gently smiling face that appeared belonged to Martha, the young nurse.

"Come on in," I urged, glad for a break. "Sorry I can't offer you a cup of tea."

"Oh, that's okay," Martha replied. "I just noticed the light shining under your door and thought I'd check to see if everything was all right. Did you know it's way after midnight?"

"I'm fine. Guess I lost track of the time. Been going through some old notes from way back when. My diary. I've kept one since I was about twelve. Do you keep one?"

"Uh-uh. Do you think I should?

I thought for a moment. "Well, I suppose that's an individual thing. For me, it helps to look back on the past and think about how I was then and if I've changed—or if I ought to change."

"Kind of like talking to your father?"

I nodded.

"I've been doing what you said. Talking to him. My fiancé, Peter, I mean . . . not your father."

I laughed. "I'd be pretty surprised if you did. I'll bet my father would too!"

Martha smiled then said, "And you know, it really does help."

"I'm so glad."

She was quiet for several moments. I'd half expected a flood of tears, but instead she bit her lip, smiled, and said, "Well, I'd better go on about my rounds. I just wanted you to know you've been a big help."

"Any time. My door is always open . . . even when it's closed."

She smiled again then left. A few moments thought before returning to my diary:

May 10

Alvah's quit the bookstore job. A friend introduced him to the owner of a new publishing house. He'll be editing their line of mystery books. Seems a bit happier now.

May 20

He says the books he's asked to edit are "crap." And they won't let him rewrite anything. No wonder he's been so crabby this past week. (I think it's the owner's brother who churns out the novels.)

Early June

Well, I had a hunch. One month and the publishing company has already folded, and here we are again, living on Alvah's final week's salary, and a much-needed twenty dollars Harry sent—from Los Angeles of all places, where they've just landed after their apparently quite successful cross-country tour. When I mentioned it, Alvah let go with another of his sarcastic remarks about "your limp-wristed fairy brother supporting us," and stormed out again after I told him, quite gently, I thought, never to say something like that again.

Until now, I'd been having that terribly nagging urge to start a family. It certainly doesn't look like that's in the cards.

June 15

Five days and Alvah hadn't come back. And then he did, but with no apologies this time, just walked in as bright and cheerful as you please, as though nothing had happened, and expected me to be all lovey-dovey right away. And (damn you, Mary!) I was.

Between me and me, I'm getting damn sick of this.

Then he tells me he's found a new position, working nights in the "morgue" of the *Tribune*, clipping and filing news stories. Paper pushing. It sounds kind of like the bookstore job all over again.

Late July

Alvah's not home until almost three in the morning, since the subways only run on the hour after midnight. Not too much happening except that he still blows hot and cold whenever the subject of marriage comes up. (I've hinted a few times now, finally came out and spilled the beans directly about my feeling a strong urge to have a child. I'll be thirty-one next month, after all.)

August 3 (my birthday)

Just when we seemed to be getting on again, we had another raging argument, mostly over his unwillingness to make a commitment. "Shit or get off the pot," I finally told him. Not surprisingly, that didn't go down so well. This time, we've both decided we need time apart. I'm taking a room in a lodging house in the Village. Alvah's staying at Sidney Place.

August 15

Up all night again, painting, messing with clay. Probably getting a lot less sleep than I ought to. Fortunately, something's come up. Sally, a young woman who helped out in putting the puppet show together last year, is going to New Hampshire. Her family has a

> farm outside Lebanon, and she's asked if I'd like to come along. Marvelous! I need a break. So even though I don't owe rent again for another two weeks, I've decided to give up the room and go with her. We catch a train tomorrow morning. What will happen when we get back? I have no idea, but something always seems to come up.
>
> I'll send a short note to Alvah.

New Hampshire was a spring breeze in a hot August. It helped me forget about Alvah's on-again off-again ruminations, our arguments, and his retreat into a sarcastic shell at the mention of marriage, proclaiming it an "archaic institution that simply legalizes what anyone is free to do even without benefit of clergy."

The countryside around the isolated farm felt almost like a return to my Michigan roots; my long walks with Forman across summertime fields dotted with daisies, purple knapweed, and goldenrod edging low woodlands behind a weathered red schoolhouse. Now, walking with Sally, I could see the hazy outline of the White Mountains. I loved feeding the chickens, waking to a rooster's far off crow, hanging on a fence to watch a sow suckle its newborn piglets, Sally and I laughing as we waded in a nearby pond. No more sleeplessness way beyond midnight. By nine, I'd drift off to the chirping of crickets and the mating calls of what must have been a huge colony of bullfrogs: "Ribbit, ribbit, ribbit . . ."

How pleasant it would be to live in the country forever, said one of the few lines committed to my diary during the two-week visit.

But soon after returning to New York, I wrote:

September 10, 1929

"You did go to New Hampshire, didn't you?" Alvah demanded.

I was slow to answer.

Though it had only been ten days earlier, New Hampshire seemed like ages ago; another time, another country, almost. Lonely, sure, but after New York, a lovely contrast.

"Yes," I finally replied.

"I called you," he shot back with a petulant scowl, "the moment I returned. You weren't there. Your phone had been disconnected!"

"Don't feel like talking about it," I mumbled. "Just spent some time with a friend, that's all."

"I called you," he repeated, frowning. "Why did you disconnect your phone?"

"I've moved."

"Your note didn't say anything about that."

"I decided at the last minute."

"Too damn spontaneous, I call it."

"Well, I'm back now. Are you?"

A full minute passed before his, "I suppose so."

Remembering that year, "that awful year," as I've thought of it ever since, and especially tonight before bed, I recalled giving up the room I'd taken under the elevated trains, even though there was still a week to go on the rent (the second time I'd done that in two months), and moving back in with Alvah.

Soon after, a classified in the *Herald-Tribune* for a bookstore assistant in Oyster Bay came up, so I took the Long Island Railroad out there and was interviewed by the store's tall, lanky owner, Phil, whose hangdog expression betrayed not the vaguest hint as to whether or not he'd found me a likely employee. Then, no sooner had I walked through the door at Sidney Place than the phone rang.

"Hello, it's Phil," said the funereal voice. "Can you start next Monday?"

A huge sigh as I recorded my memory of the man . . .

July 8, 1942

Poor dear Phil; the applejack he concocted, swilling it every night after the shop closed, the brown stains from cigarettes he'd left burning on the bookshelves; the deep lines in his face, the lanky six-foot-three of him, the knowledge of a messed up life at forty-three. The one heartbreaking attempt at Jones Beach to gather a woman (me) in his arms, and knowing as he did so it was too late.

I believe I'll ever recall his loneliness; loneliness

unmatched by anyone I've ever known. (No, that's not strictly true, for I've known others who could match his.) Perhaps he gave me the job because he recognized in me a female match. Did I have the same droopy expression he had, the one I saw in the mirror again three months ago when I walked through the doors here at Payne Whitney? My God, I suppose I did.

Mary outside the bookshop at Oyster Bay, Long Island, 1928-29

More than ten years between then and now, I told myself.

There was Alvah's displeasure over my decision to take the job—even with the thirty-dollar a week salary being sorely needed. The job lasted ten months, months during which Alvah continued to waffle over making a firm commitment, even though he fulfilled his grudging promise to visit as often as he could in the upstairs room

I'd taken in the home of an elderly couple who all the locals seemed to know as Grandma and Grandpa Rogers.

After work and on Sundays that Alvah didn't come, I'd walk for hours beside the bay, or, before November's chill winds arrived, scuff along the fine white sandy beach barefoot, picking up clam or scallop shells, the occasional sand dollar or scrap of driftwood. The screaming gulls along the shore seemed to mock my indecisiveness, spurred, of course, by Alvah's. *Should I call it quits? Take a year or so off, move in with Verne and Laura, and take time to reassess where I'm going?* They were family, after all. But then, their stuffy formality always quickly got to me. Much as I loved them, they weren't people I could really communicate with at any deeply felt level.

Maybe I should save some money and take a chance on California? Harry was there; dear, caring brother. And I had a good friend in Forman. But when the money ran out—then what? And Forman . . . Wouldn't being close again rekindle the anguish I'd mostly let go of? I'd unburdened myself to Sally about my lingering but fruitless attraction to him while she and I were in New Hampshire. Wise beyond her years, Sally had mulled it over and sent a note a couple weeks after we'd returned:

> . . . and I suppose it was no surprise that you and Forman were attracted. Sounds as though you were both blessed with intelligence and creative inclinations, after all. That the potential affair was never consummated kind of seems like those mushy movie romances we've both seen. (Does that sound too harsh?) I always hope my friends will find happiness, but all things con-

> sidered, it seems like this potential affair had the most satisfactory conclusion. Two smart kids, temporarily tempted to climb into bed together, but aborted for whatever reason, is the stuff for later reflection over the kind of heartache you expressed; destined, I suppose, for the same scrapbook with a dried, pressed prom rose; not to be ridiculed, but eventually judged in proper perspective about all it was, and all it wasn't—bittersweet but not high tragedy. Does that make sense?
>
> I hope you come to the kind of decision regarding Alvah that feels right.

Smart gal, I thought. I wish I'd had that perspective at the time.

And what about my continuing, almost desperate desire for a child, for children? If not with Alvah, with whom?

As winter dragged into spring, with occasional trips back to the city where he and I would take in a film or a play, where I'd occasionally meet Sally and talk out my feelings and could at least soak up a bit of the stimulating (if frenetic) New York atmosphere, I came to a final decision; a decision triggered by a loving yet frustrating Saturday night and most of Sunday with Alvah; a playful time in his bed, but also with his usual avoidance of any talk that remotely bespoke a mutual future.

The brief phone call I made the next evening after returning to Oyster Bay is still fresh in memory:

"I know that voice," said Alvah.

"I'm calling from the bookstore."

"You're still there? It's after eight. I thought you'd be home. . . .

But look, I'm kind of busy right now, tons of stuff to file here, and—"

"Phil's gone for the day, I told him I'd lock up . . . And I'm sorry to phone you at work, but I've come to a decision."

"Oh? About what?"

"About us. I . . . Well, frankly, I'm sick and tired of this affair. It's going nowhere. Look . . . come out here and marry me, or I'm calling the whole thing off."

There was a long silence on the line.

Finally I asked, "Are you still there?"

"Yeah."

"I mean it."

We married three days later, on Thursday July 3, 1930.

26.

Landgrove, Vermont

Wednesday night, October 28, 1931

Snowbirds. While picking up the apples, I saw the snowbirds darting over the fence and back again. Then the wind came, with the rain and hail beating against the windows, blowing the last three leaves from the maple tree in the yard, and sending the snowbirds to shelter.

Then the sun appeared, and walking out once more into the freshness it came over me again, this feeling of "a woman's capacity must be great, mustn't it?" And all the while beating against my brain the million whirling images of things that must be done, the things there's no escaping from, the little things that are even pleasant doing. Then wondering, *How, how?* And it suddenly seemed that I was strong enough for all those things, strong enough for marriage, for pregnancy, for the infinite details of domesticity, and even beyond that, strong enough to write a story now and then.

Late April 1943

Sunshine at last, I thought while sitting on a bench scanning the diary. How different from that spring some ten . . . no, eleven years ago. After being fired from the *Tribune,* Alvah picked up a position as proofreader and fact checker with *The New Yorker;* but since I'd also left my bookstore job, with Alvah's only other income coming from an occasional translation of books from the French, a gloomy future loomed for us both when he was told he'd only been filling in for the magazine's regular man, who had been on vacation.

With no savings, and getting by on little more than a bowl of fifteen-cent minestrone a day, salvation suddenly presented itself: scanning classifieds, I spotted an ad for a summer position in Vermont: "Bright young couple wanted," read the notice. "Including room and board. The wife to cook, the husband to do handyman chores." Plus, as Alvah discovered on our arrival, empty the garbage, pick up summer guests in the owner's station wagon, and play chess with them when they became bored or were nursing hangovers. A few extra dollars came in by helping the owner (who had bought the entire town of Landgrove a few years earlier for $4500) restore the community's seventeen ramshackle mid-1800s houses that he turned around and sold to acquaintances from his home state of New Jersey.

Our busy summer gave way to the radiant rusts and yellows of autumn. We liked Vermont, and with not enough money to move anywhere else, we rented an old house for seven dollars a month and scrounged up minimal furnishings at barn sales. Alvah began to earn a meager living by selling short stories, while also writing to

New York editors who might offer book review assignments.

But the winter that followed, with days often below zero, found us pining for the mild and pleasant mountain greenery we'd landed in that summer.

The next journal entries offered hints of the demons of isolation and hopelessness that would torment me a decade later, snippets that also offered insight into what our marriage had been like:

> *October 23, 1931*
>
> I turned to see my husband reading near the window, and it seemed as if I could say to him, "God, I'm comfortable. I suppose I ought to get up and put on a dress, but I'm damned if I will, for you or anyone else." It seemed if I could say that and stick to it, I'd feel better—and I grew angry with resentment toward the need of even so small a vanity as dressing for him. Then I finally got up and said, "Ho hum, guess I'd better clean up and put on a dress," and he said, "I should think it was about time. You've been around in those pants for two days now. Who do you think you are, Jeanne d'Arc?" Then I knew, as I always know just in the nick of time that the hour has come to scuttle about making more pretenses—to be the thing I'm not. . . . *Oh well, I guess he's put up with enough from me already, won't kill me to stir a finger for him now and then.* But God it's good to be yourself, to not give a fuck what anyone says or thinks; to be able, like Alvah, to go on day after day wearing the same old ragged britches and never bother to dress up.

November 2, 1931

No one comes to the house except Charlie Clendening. . . . Sometimes he'll appear from nowhere, turning his big old jalopy into the drive and steering it up the grade and around to the porch. Then he knocks until I call, "Come in," and he wings his big smiling blond youth into the kitchen, says, "Hello! Boy! It's cold," and then goes into the living room where Alvah is.

We can't know why he comes, two or three times a week. He comes.

Then Mrs. Slade shows up with Vernice, her defective teenage son, and I try to talk of things she knows about, and wonder (while I notice Alvah's bored expression) how I can get rid of them most easily without offending, since they own the house.

These come and go. That's all. And we don't go anywhere. Perhaps our contacts are too few? The Chadwicks, the Hansens, for a second now and then, for milk or to bring the garbage pail back up when it rolls down the hill after the wind has blown it off the porch.

Tonight Alvah said, "I suppose it isn't good for us to be so much alone."

"I suppose not," I replied.

We'd both like, I think, to live nearer to a few stimulating men and women, but curiously enough, recalling our years in New York with many acquaintances, there rarely seemed to be a time for "touch," for much real

> depth of communication. I suppose that only happens if the mood catches two people at the right moment. And so it would seem senseless to plant ourselves among a million people again, just to sit on our asses and wait for . . . For what? A "natural" mood? Better this, to accomplish our small duties undisturbed, to read, free from the thought of telephone jangle or doorbell buzz; to write, if need be, without the possibility of escape to the movies or a speakeasy when difficulties arise that we're afraid to tackle or don't know how to deal with. Here, at least, we must look ourselves squarely in the face and learn to accept it or overcome.

Something like the situation I find myself in now, I reflected*; struggling to find a clear direction leading to a better tomorrow for me and the boys—but at the same time not quite knowing what path to take when I leave the clinic.*

"The winter of our discontent," Will Shakespeare called it. That's how I remembered the long gray days ending 1931 and on into early '32. Scratching out a living found us both low in the gut. The delight I'd felt as April snows finally gave way to budding spring, and the bark of a distant fox calling its mate hardly fulfilled the romantic picture of the bohemian writer's wife I'd begun to imagine myself soon after I'd met Alvah that day at Harry's studio.

Still, even before the spring thaw, I'd had a sense those demons of the early 1930s were crawling back into their hole—and for a blessed reason:

February 7, 1932

All day the rain, and tonight the great black clouds moving across the sky, and the wind rocking the small house almost as though it were a ship.

And I am three months pregnant!

So, cramps, gas, swollen and sore nipples, nausea, dizziness, and an annoying bladder. Then from Dr. Clara Leach, pink pills, white pills, lime tablets, and cathartic.

But these are minor miseries; troubles I could tolerate because what was to come had been so long yearned for.

Saturday, March 19, 1932

More than four months now? Infant, we are poor, we are patched, but we are clean and hopeful, and because we remember the sunshine of last April, we don't mope too long through these weeks of rain and snow and dampness.

Wednesday afternoon, April 27, 1932

Alvah laughed at my great belly, and at my awkwardness in handling it. Then he came in to stir the whitewash for the chicken coop. All day we were happy and hopeful as children. He is good, and more cheerful than me; too feminine, me, these days, laughing now, and ready to weep in ten minutes for wishing a few more of the decencies of living. I think his good sense will keep me going, and with his hands rubbing my back when the ache is too much, I have much to be grateful for.

It was last Tuesday evening that I slipped and fell flat and complete upon the near born. Good it did no harm, because it was morning before the doctor could come. "Still alive, still kicking, good position now, about six weeks. Write to Springfield and make reservations for the first week in August."

So infant, I pray you be as gentle as nature will allow you when the day arrives. Your being seems inevitable. Whatever may come for you, I have wished for you for a very long time, and in spite of today's unexpected snow flurries, in spite of your squirming, in spite of the mostly hopeless outlook for a comfortable future your existence, even through these few long months, has brought more real delight to your father and me than has come to either of us in our lives.

I pray those words will be harbingers of hope for my about-to-be-born son. The signs are certainly there: the bursting buds of spring, maple leaves appearing; grouse are seen scurrying along the lower road, a hedgehog discovered in the outhouse, its frightened beady eyes staring up in the moonlight as I'm about to squat.

And once again, I hear a fox barking as Alvah and I walk out onto the porch.

July comes. There have been these few days expecting labor, and now, tonight, some relief from the strain of waiting. Old Lucy Chadwick, the kindly neighbor who will stand by to assist, is puzzled because my belly is so big.

"What does the doctor say?" she asks.

"She says it will come when it's ready," I answer.

"Well, be patient, dear, you must be patient. I'll be waiting tonight, as always, for the telephone or doorbell."

Oh, I can't think of being patient, really. What do you suppose? Can you picture me with this prize-winning belly, throwing myself from room to room and yelling, "I can't stand it"? No! Instead, every day I wash and press the blue smock, which is all I can get into—and when Alvah scolds me for working, I laugh, and we try to think of other things.

Saturday morning, August 13, 1932

The chickens are feathered and growing strong. The nasturtiums have blossomed three weeks, and even the black-eyed Susans are hard to find. The pansies are in their second blooming, but all these things do not distress me. I see the period and the consequence of each. It's life, and so with me and Alvah and the squirming womb child, the time seems right. I must try to allow neither my happiness nor my disappointment (whichever it be) to overweigh. Only remember, my will to live is greater than my will to die. . . .

In the clinic's garden, I sat back in the chair, thinking. *The will to live,* I wondered; *do I still have that? Do I still have the will to live? Is it strong enough?*

I glanced back at the diary—

> Yesterday we laughed when we decided it would be twins, and I said, "That will be reason enough for this huge belly."
>
> Now I see the smoke from Nielsen's chimney, and hear the voices from the morning meadow, and Lucy's chickens, cackling, let out to scratch and peck all day. Soon Ruben will come with the milk, and Alvah will stir, sleepy-eyed and scowling, until he too has come out and felt himself a part of today. Then we will be glad for today's sunlight and the small tasks to perform, free for a few hours from the sleepless or restless nights.
>
> Then the cat, whining for his breakfast; Alvah, waiting for his egg.
>
> *Thursday afternoon, August 25, 1932*
>
> We are rescued! Alvah's novel has been accepted and will be published next year by Covici-Friede. With a $750 advance! What icing could possibly be sweeter to top our domestic cake? Do I resent that he stole the idea during the long winter nights when I dredged up stories about the odd, puritanical, strivingly ambitious and yet deeply loving family I grew up among in Michigan? I think not. (Fess up, Mary, maybe a little.)

Thursday morning, September 1, 1932

August 25 through to August 28, there was labor. No need to recall the details of "so common a thing as childbearing." So at 6:35 a.m. on August 28 was born David Bessie, eight pounds seven ounces, who had been much too long in coming.

David: big, strong, dark hair. "He has black hair, Mr. Bessie," I had heard the nurse call to Alvah in the night. But later, I watched their faces, and when the nurse said to Dr. Leach, "Did you see the forehead?" I knew he wouldn't live.

Why didn't I cry?

Pains start for second twin soon. Feet come first, then shoulders push through, and pain gives out. Miracle of three-minute interval, and Lucy and the other two women praying, and all the while dead David lying in the corner, and poor Alvah outside, waiting. Afterwards I saw again, more carefully, and we both saw and were sad. And I kept watching Daniel (Danny) wrapped in his blanket, and saw his kicking and was glad. Mostly I was glad for Alvah. Danny's dear little purple lips, his peaceful smile . . .

Daniel Bessie, born to Mary and Alvah, Sunday, August 28, 1932, 7:25 a.m. Six pounds, nine ounces, twenty inches long. Much like his father: long, fine, and blond. Daniel, as unlike his brother in looks as Alvah and me.

A Vermont Sunday, the sun rising between the twin hills I can see from the childbirth four-poster. It was, oh, such a morning. . . .

32

116 September 17th 1932 THE SATURDAY REVIEW OF LITERATURE

Wm Rose Benet

The PHŒNIX NEST

WE have received a large green card from *Alvah C. Bessie,* the well-known translator, critic, and short story writer, which shows a bearded man —Bessie himself—scratching a bewildered head against a background of Vermont mountains, while next him sits his placid wife with *Daniel Bessie,* 6½ lbs., August 28th, upon her lap. But the interesting thing about the wood-cut is that under the place-name, Londonderry, Vt., "July" was originally printed, July 1932. Yet to Daniel, though slightly belated, we raise our glass, because we know few people who are punctual after all. . . .

The house in which I (Dan, the author) was born on August 28, 1932

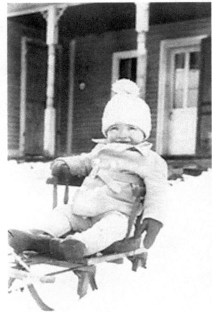

Christmas day, December 25, 1932

My father carved a woodblock Christmas card every year we lived in Vermont.

27.

While looking back on the immense joy I'd felt at Danny's birth, and the accompanying sadness at the loss of his twin, a voice interrupted my thoughts: "Had enough exercise for this morning, have you, Miss Notebook Lady?"

With a smile, I looked up from my seat on Payne Whitney's garden bench into the cheery face of Nurse Kelly.

Notebook Lady . . . Hmm . . . I guess that's who I am.

"Well, I—"

But she held up a protesting hand. "Don't say another word, dear. 'Tis plain you're busy with your book. A diary, is it?"

"Yes."

"Well, you just keep on." Checking the watch pinned to her blouse, she added, "For another fifteen minutes, that is, but then I'm afraid it's back upstairs I'll be shooin' you all." We both laughed.

And as she padded off, I called out, "You're a treasure, Mrs. Kelly."

Then a memory flash: Kelly. Brigid Kelly. Coincidence; the same last name as the young woman Alvah told me he'd been seeing on trips to New York to meet his publishers. He'd only let the cat out of the bag in 1934. Three years after the affair had begun . . . while I was pregnant again.

"I think I might be in love with her," he'd confessed when I finally pressed him about his frequent mood swings.

I'd stared at him for almost a minute, rose from the chair, and paced the room before sitting again. "If that's what you want," I suggested, "why don't you just hightail yourself back to the big city and see what comes of it?"

"Oh, for Christ's sake," he'd shouted. "We're about to have another kid!"

At the time, I'd meant it. If he wasn't going to be there for Danny and me and for this much-wanted second child, the hell with him! "Go find yourself, damn it!" I'd shouted back. "Go break down that 'dark wall' you keep telling me you see in front of you."

"I'm not imagining," he grumbled. "It's in everything I do. In writing, my first feeling after completing a piece of work is that it's what I wanted to say. Then comes the infernal darkness, banking up solid, impenetrable before the eyes of my poor mind."

I could rarely tolerate self-pity, even in myself.

But I'd soon dropped the subject and decided not to bring it up again; just let matters take their course. After all, I'd known from the start he had a lot of growing to do. If I'd just let sleeping dogs lie maybe he'd get over what I concluded was an infatuation. Maybe he'd wake up one morning and say, "What an ass I've been." Would he be likely to do that? Ever?

At that moment, I didn't know. I'd have to think it through.

Then Alvah went off down the road through the slush on some errand or other, leaving me with his confession to sink in. I could only sit, staring across the valley at the dark hills hidden by a thick smoky gray mist, and wonder what it is that's so wrong. In more optimistic moods, I thought I knew, and then it was all so simple, and I had only to be patient for a growth I was certain of. But today, with the troubled thoughts in my head and the knowledge of his "late" misery, I felt the darkness solidifying—while my feeble efforts to penetrate it only echoed in the emptiness of my head and left despair. Where once there was courage, turning in on myself now only brought on what I found there: nothing. Only the colorless images of a past, lifeless and meaningless, like a diseased appendix, or like the hawk, cold within an hour of its death.

Oh, Danny, what a stinking heritage. Do your best with it, and never allow yourself to regret.

"It's been going on since 1931," I recalled, Alvah telling me about the thing with Brigid. A whole year before Danny and his twin were born.

Where were we then? What was happening? I skimmed back through my journal, noting the record of our first year, the hard times, the scrabbling to pay the rent, even just to put food on the table:

> *Wednesday night, November 4, 1931*
>
> Waking before daylight, we heard the wind and the rain, and turning in bed felt the kitten move to make itself comfortable again. Then his purring, and we could scarcely hear the wind for the minutes he purred close to our heads. Then Alvah reached out and pushed him off the bed, and we heard the wind again, and the rain beating against the window.
>
> "I'll bet it's raining through the screen," I said.

"Hmmm," he said, and soon we were asleep again.

No letters come, no checks, nothing. So we begin the same old worries for ourselves, and drag out the butt box and take a stale puff or two. But today I couldn't bear that we should sit around and worry, so I said, "As long as it's not too cold, how about getting those spruce bows chopped down today?"

"All right," he said, and slung the ax through his belt.

I saw him going up the road and hurried to dry the dishes so I too could get out in the air.

For a few hours he chopped through the soft spruce wood and threw the branches to me, and then we both walked back and forth down to the road, carrying the boughs over our shoulders in great bundles. Mostly they didn't smell because of the wind—but sometimes it would be still for a moment, and there'd be a pine odor.

We came home through the pasture, and a bit later I went for a walk by the brook, climbing up the bank where Will Chadwick was. "Want a bottle of beer?" he asked.

"Sure!"

I didn't know Alvah was out looking for me, and worrying, while I was sitting in the dirty kitchen drinking McGinnis beer. It was cold and clear—and good.

There seemed to be no specific hints of hostility, just moods and our mutual inertia.

Sunday morning, December 27, 1931

What's happing to us both? Why?

This morning, rising, came again the monotonous routine of fire building, coffee making, and toasting bread. And in my mind, I rebel for the flash of a second against our dependence upon each other. But soon enough, I know it's what I really want, so "Lie still there within," I tell myself.

Now there is only the gray landscape before me, patched with a bit of snow, and the persistent images of a dead past march by, as bare and black through my head as the tall leafless trees on the near hillside.

Beyond trying to analyze or understand, almost beyond caring, there's only to stand here watching him as I might look at the twisted birch tree on the bank, and say to myself, "It's different from the other birches, the variations interesting," and thinking only this, to put aside all judgment and manufactured standards of right and wrong for man, and just let it be what is.

Landgrove, Vermont

Thursday morning, November 16, 1932

Asleep, the infant; Danny is three months old, and the room is warm and the wind beating against the few brown leaves still fast to the maple, and against the door that's loose in its frame. And over me passes the sickness that comes with Thursdays and Fridays.

"Sorry, Mr. Townsend, nothing today. Sorry, we can't pay you. Sorry."

Sometimes it's all I can do to keep from shouting, "Who ever asked you to trust us?" Suppose I have little right to complain, these good mountain folk are pretty much in the same sinking boat that we are.

On the opposite page, I'd sketched a meat deliveryman standing beside his truck. Next to it myself, hair in pigtails, as I walk away with Jobey, our German shepherd, on a leash.

"Sorry, Mrs. Bessie," says the deliveryman. "Only week to week."

"Okay by me. Come on, Jobey, come on."

Another entry brought back painful memories:

Sunday night, November 27

This afternoon, walking over the mowing, I came across the path that leads off toward the woods, and I stood there for a moment, knowing if I walked up it I would see again the bones of the dead horse lying beside the path—some scattered by animals that had long since feasted on the rotting flesh. And I didn't walk up the path toward the dark in the woods. I turned my face to the purple mountains and to the wind, and walked back across the mowing, over the frozen ground; not because of the gloom and the scattered bones, but because I couldn't forget so soon what Alvah told me last night.

"Is your stomach strong enough to hear something I thought I wouldn't tell you?" he asked.

"Sure," I said.

"You remember that Sunday my brother was here, the day two weeks after Danny was born?"

"Yes, I remember."

"You never knew where we went, did you?"

"No."

"Well, we went down to the cemetery."

"Why, what for?"

"Well, that morning when I took the garbage up to the Chadwicks, Lucy told me that word came to her something had been digging."

"You mean . . . digging in the grave?"

"Yes. So we dug about a foot. We covered it over with stones so nothing could dig."

"Oh . . ." It was all I could say at the time.

The dear little baby; David, Danny's twin; and I recalled turning my head aside and letting the tears flow. . . . As sitting again for a few moments on Payne Whitney's garden bench and brushing tears aside, I opened to a blank journal page and wrote:

> How strange. The resonance between then and now . . . Well, perhaps not so strange; the only exception being that just a few months back, I was on the verge of doing away with myself. While I hadn't quite reached that stage in Vermont, if the despair I was feeling had continued . . . Who knows?
>
> More insight, that's what I need. Wish I'd had a clue

then, about Alvah's affair, my confusion over his sullen moods, the growing estrangement between us, and the ability to recognize my own depression. Damn!

Well, no use crying over spilled milk; that was then, this is now. Try to hold that stronger grip on reality that seems to be coming in, Mary. Figure out why depression had me in its vice for so long, why I eventually landed in this place, and what I'll still have to understand in order to reunite with my precious boys, and find some way to reach the goal I've always dreamed about—to truly feel of some use in the world.

1931 to '34; almost twenty turbulent, exciting, confusing, frightening years ago. For Alvah too, I suppose. Can't say I blame him all that much, what with me moping around that ramshackle mountain house; my droopy mouth, hair pulled into a bun like some beaten down prairie farmwife.

I briefly flashed back to the day a few weeks earlier when Dan had asked if I slept in my clothes, and at the reflection of myself in the hall mirror as the boys left for the movies. And Brigid Kelly? How can I hold a grudge? After all, I wasn't exactly Snow White. No, not at all, I . . . I paused, thinking, before turning back to write again:

It was before we moved to Vermont; somewhere around the time our seaman friend Pete Glenn first came to visit—and that must have been, when? January, February '31. Alvah was at work that night, still at the *Tribune*, so I'd gone to see Pete off on his ship and was returning to take the subway back to Brooklyn and home. That's the afternoon (noon?) I saw you through the window of the restaurant on Sixth Avenue. Oh, I was glad to see you, Bill; it had been a long time since you walked out on the love affair I'd had hopes might turn into something that would last. Old joy at the sight of you, of being together that day, the first and only time since marrying Alvah, and the last for six or seven more years. I was, shall we say, unfaithful. (Or perhaps I was faithful to myself.)

When had I seen you last? I think it was New Year's Eve, 1929, the midnight when you came into the miserable dump on Bank Street. That was shortly after Dad had died. Alvah was in Paris. I had nothing to offer anyone . . . except all of me. My last image, the blue necktie you left hanging on the closet doorknob.

What did I live out? Who did I hurt beside myself?

Then, lo and behold, the balance of Alvah's payment for his novel arrived. The two thousand dollars not only rescued us but paid for my trip to the hospital in Bennington where, in March of the next year, our second son was born; a sturdy, gurgling boy who, honoring Daniel's dead twin, we both immediately agreed should be named David.

April 1935

The hell with Brigid Kelly. Let's get out of here while the getting's good. We've got the money (while it lasts), two happy, healthy sons, crocuses are blooming outside the door, and what'd'ya know, Alvah's friend Ed Cushing writes to say there's a job coming up as Sunday features editor on the *Brooklyn Eagle*. And he's recommending Alvah. The assignment won't start for a few months yet, but at least it's paying work.

Brooklyn, here we come!

PART III:
MORNING MIST

"The charm dissolves apace,

And as the morning steals upon the night,

Melting the darkness, so their rising senses

Begin to chase the ignorant fumes that mantle

Their clearer reason."

—William Shakespeare[5]

5 From Shakespeare's *The Tempest*, Act V, Scene I

28.

Looking back on our time in Vermont from the vantage of Payne Whitney in 1943, I'd seen it as a fresh start. But so too had been Alvah's and my return to New York, a refuge from what we'd only half-jokingly referred to when describing our years in the Green Mountains to friends as "four years of gracefully starving to death."

Now came the chance for yet another beginning, offered that afternoon by words from my psychiatrist. But the offer was perhaps not one I was quite prepared for.

"Well," said Dr. Thomas as he looked up with a smile after scanning my records, "I think it's about time we kicked you out the door. Are you feeling up for that?"

Ours had been a friendly interaction, increasingly spiced with light banter, so his joking way of asking if I felt ready to go home brought a responsive laugh—yet one accompanied by my furrowed brow and eyes searching in thought.

"Do I detect a note of uncertainty?" Dr. Thomas asked.

I smiled. "You're always very perceptive," I replied.

"Well, maybe not so perceptive." He opened a file on his desk and scanned several documents. "Every report I've had during the last four months has been positive." Then he went on, reading highlights from the reports: "'Relates well to patients and staff' . . . 'exhibits a sense of compassion when talking with several women who had previously been morose and withdrawn' . . . 'teaching puppetry in the craft class'—Bravo! I don't recall anyone having done so before. And . . . let's see . . . 'several trips out of the clinic with no apparent problems.' That's certainly an important plus."

While I've never been one to covet praise, to say I wasn't pleased would be far from the truth.

"Though I understand that several evenings have found you squirreled away in your room," he added. "Writing, correct?"

"I've found it's a great way to bring back the past," I replied. "Been looking at my life under a kind of 'word microscope' to see what makes all those amoebas and paramecium behave the way they do. Or *did*, since I suspect most are dead by now."

"A fine analogy," he replied with a smile, then went on to advise twice-monthly meetings between us for the next several months while I worked out plans for the future. "And I want you to know," he went on as he handed me a card, "that you can phone me day or night should anything critical come up and you feel a need to talk."

I looked at the card. As well as his office phone, it included his home number.

◆◆◆◆◆

"For your graduation," announced Nurse Kelly as she arrived in the dining room with a colorful cake frosted in pink.

Word had quickly spread, and the women at my table all chimed in, wishing me good luck, and God speed, and the hope that I'd never have to come back again.

"But we'll miss you," added the older Jewish woman who had only recently begun to be responsive.

"You'll do just fine," said the starched nurse, giving me a gentle pat on one shoulder. Even Mrs. Jackson, who had stayed an extra hour to wish me well, put in an appearance. "Would you take a look at something?" she asked.

Curious, I nodded.

Reaching into a large paper bag, she produced a stringed clown marionette. "Do you think it's good enough?"

"You made this?" I asked, quite astonished.

"I did. I saw what you were teaching the others and became inspired."

This meant a lot. I took the puppet, and to the applause of patients and nurses, pranced it back and forth along the floor, making a complete circuit of our table.

"Marvelous," I said, handing the marionette back to Mrs. Jackson. "Should I let my brother Harry in California know? Maybe he needs another puppeteer." Mrs. Jackson laughed. With the puppet dangling in one hand, she put both arms around me in a warm embrace.

◆◆◆◆◆

Though clearly pleased when I phoned to buoyantly announce I was coming home, Laura asked if she could pick me up at the station the following afternoon. Then she fell all over herself, apologizing that the spring cleaning had just begun, her maid Selma wouldn't be there until the next morning, and that "Verne and I are just back from the city you know, and I've got mail to answer, and—"

"Tomorrow afternoon will be just fine," I cut in. "Please don't go to any special bother."

"It's no bother," she replied, "but—"

"I'll take the Greyhound into Danbury and catch a taxi to the farm. It'll give me a chance to do some thinking."

"Well, Selma will have your room all ready," said Laura after a bit more hemming and hawing. "Nice and cozy, the attic room next to hers. You'll have to share the bathroom, though. That's all right, isn't it?"

After the call ended, a wave of apprehension swept over me. Supportive and caring as Laura and Verne had always been, being alone with either or both for any length of time could become wearing. This had come home to me again when Laura added, in a tone of voice hiding a shameful secret, "Of course, we won't mention to anyone where you've been. It's as though it never happened. We haven't told a soul where you were, we just told our friends you were away, taking a vacation for a few months."

Laura and Verne Burnett, along with their dog Lassie; Danbury Connecticut, 1940s

Damn it to hell, Laura! I thought. *Denial, always denial.* It would be like being back with Mother again; whenever something she'd convinced herself was embarrassing happened in the family, she'd blurt out, "What will the neighbors think?"

Still, the presence of Selma, Verne and Laura's warm, down-to-earth housekeeper who I'd always liked, would make the time bearable.

On the way to my room I looked up at the clock above the nurse's station. It had been an exhilarating day; another day of changes, like the move back to Brooklyn from Vermont. As I sat on the chair to take off my shoes, there was a knock at the door.

"I hoped you'd come by," I said, rising again as Martha entered. "I've been thinking about you."

"I just had to say goodbye," replied Martha. "I heard you were leaving. I'll miss our little chats. You've been so much help, what you've said and all."

"Oh, I haven't done anything, really; I just —"

"Yes you have, you have!"

I was sure Martha was about to burst into tears again, so I made a move to embrace her.

"I'm okay," she said. "Really. Oh, I know, I suppose I should be moving on, his folks have given up, they're sure he's never coming back. Missing in action. My parents too. They think it's time I started to look for someone else. . . . And I suppose I might, in time. But not now. Not yet. I just need to keep him with me, keep talking to him for a while longer."

I remained silent, listening.

"Like you talk with your father . . . do you talk to your boys too? When you're not with them, I mean?"

"Of course. And write letters."

"Well, you'll be seeing them soon, won't you?"

"For a while, yes; just a visit. But I've got so much to do. Find a new place for us to live. A job. Decide what I want to do with the rest of my life."

Martha was pondering. "I suppose I could write to Larry too, couldn't I?

"Why not? I find that it really helps."

"I wish I'd thought of it before."

"Well, whether Larry ever returns or not, you'll at least be able to look back and better understand what's going on with you now. What you were doing. What you were thinking and feeling."

She stood looking at me for several moments, then asked, "Would you mind terribly if I gave you a hug?"

Who can resist? I thought.

Moments after Martha left, I found myself sitting on the bed, writing:

> For Martha . . .
>
> One thinks of love. It comes in many shapes and many forms. It comes spontaneously, and joy abounds. And for a little while, there is such happiness. Cherish that, for it is real. When doubt, outmoded concepts, your friends, your ancestors, your deep anxieties, your submerged and undulating monsters begin to whisper in your ear, "Mistrust it," go ever so quietly into the forest of your imagination, deep where you will find the truth, and the joy will return. Shapes and forms will linger, but by now you will know, and you will begin to understand why you were born. And each day will be new, fresh. And beyond each day, no need to worry any more.

After several hours sleep, I woke suddenly and reached for my pad and a pencil again:

For my sons when you are older . . .

I woke from a dream just now, boys. I was on a train, looking for the both of you. "Where," I attempted to ask several different people, "is this going?" But everyone was busy talking, sleeping, or whatever in this well-lit and very long, homey, easygoing train. Walking through it seemed endless. But I suddenly felt I must return to wherever it was I'd left you both, playing with other children. I kept going back and back, from one car to the next, my eyes searching every seat, spot, or cranny where you might be. "Davy?" I called out. "Danny?" I was beginning to be concerned, but shed my worry, feeling you'd probably both curled yourselves up somewhere and gone to sleep, or would be wondering where Mommy had gone. Suddenly, I came into a car where a young man—you, Dan, all grown up and looking like your father Alvah—sat at a desk, writing. You looked up, and I was a little shocked to realize you had grown.

And curled up on a nearby seat, though more of a sofa, was a small dark-haired boy. "Who's the little boy?" I asked.

You turned to look. "It's David," you replied. "My brother." And this news shocked me awake.

I rose from the bed and stood by the window, looking out to

where a solitary tugboat was making its way slowly upriver. In the dim distance, a few lights flickered.

Returning to the bed, I picked up the writing pad again.

> *May 14, 1943*
>
> I, Mary Burnett, born Gladys Mae Burnett, August 3, 1898 in St. Johns, Clinton County, Michigan, hereby pull myself up by the bootstraps, and from this moment forward have every intention of dividing my energy between two separate existences; as different as day and night, but as irrevocably dependent on each other as the seasons. Over one of these existences I have control. The other must have its way with the remaining energy. David and Dan are my one life, the life I see and feel, the life I love spontaneously. The other finds its flowering through them, and it's as though my life with them was a symbol of all contact I have ever had with people, and through this life I find courage to grope, though for the recent past it's been groping along in solid night.
>
> Perhaps as I feel my way, the dawn will break before me again and I will both see and hear, see what I have always seen, smell the same smells, hear the sounds and sleep the same deep sleep—and find myself at last, like Jobey, the gentle German shepherd we had in Vermont, biting his own tail on the rug beside the warm stove.
>
> That will be all right. Then I will know, certainly, more certainly than now, what sort of woman I am to become.

29.

The Musgrove School, Birchfield Center, Connecticut

April 25, 1943

Dear Mom,

I hope you are feeling well. I saw a lot of gray squirrels around the school. Some of them live in the gym. What are you doing now? I just saw a pair of blue jays carrying some twigs in their beaks to build a nest. One boy has been sick, but he is better now. Another boy fell over a fence when we were playing a game, and he broke a bone in his shoulder. He had to go to a hospital and have it fixed. We had a big thunderstorm last night with thunder and lightning and everything. Danny and me hope you can come and visit us soon. We got a letter from Papa. He said he is going to write movies.

Love, David

Though mention of squirrels in the gym brought a faint smile, my younger son's drawing at the top of his letter, handed to me moments before I left Payne Whitney, pervaded a dull gray sky, with jagged lightning forking down across his penciled words.

Now, as the Greyhound headed toward Danbury, I read the letter for the second time, then sat staring out at the newly greening sugar maple, beech, and yellow birch. *That's a somber sky atop his letter,* I told myself; and, along with David's hope for a visit, a signal that the sooner I could get to the boy's school, the better.

I took the letter from its envelope again. Clearly, Alvah had written them from California (though David didn't say), for that's where he'd relocated a month earlier after securing a yearlong contract as a screenwriter at Warner Brothers studios. Writing for film had been his lifelong ambition, and since returning from Spain at the end of 1938, he'd picked up where he'd left off, writing book, film, and theater reviews for the *Brooklyn Eagle,* or the leftwing *New Masses* and the *Daily Worker.*

I hope you're truly living your dream, my friend, I thought. *Hope you'll make some generous space within it for Dan and David. Goodness knows they need a father figure in their life, even an occasional one. They've already endured your absence in Spain for a year, then the tragedy of Pennsylvania and the sorrow of losing Harold. . . .*

Enough! I scolded myself; *that's in the past.* Though this was something I knew I'd yet to make my peace with, only one thing was important right now: seeing my boys.

30.

"How come?" demanded Davy.

"I already told you, I don't know," I replied.

"But how come you don't know?"

I stopped on the stairwell and plunked down my suitcase. "Listen, will ya! All I know is what Mrs. Musgrove said. They're driving to here right now, and we're going home. That's how come we had to pack our stuff and clean up and get dressed up nice and everything."

"But you told me she said we've gotta come back. How come we have to come back?"

"Gosh, Davy, stop asking questions! She told me that Mom said it was for a vacation. Most of the kids have already gone for the summer, so I guess it's our turn," I growled as I grabbed my suitcase.

My brother hesitated, then blurted out, "We gotta find out how come she's in the nut house!"

"No we don't."

"That's what the big guys said, so I'm gonna ask her."

"Come on, let's go!!" I shot back. "They could be here any minute. And don't ask Mom about that!"

His jaw firmly set, Davy lugged his valise down the stairway after me. At the time, I didn't realize how obsessed he was over what Arbuckle and his pals had said about Mom. Or about riding me around on a timber, and how he could possibly keep that from happening.

Nor was he the only one with foreboding thoughts. Ever since Mrs. Musgrove had relayed Mom's message the previous afternoon, I'd been fretting about how long this vacation would be, and whether Mom had got over whatever was bothering her. And if we did have to return to Musgrove, how much longer we might have to stay. For a while, however, one thing was certain: I could forget about Arbuckle and his gang daring us to go into the zombie cave.

Dumb Arbuckle, I thought. *Dumb zombie cave.*

Still, I was worried that Davy would blurt out his question about the crazy house, and I didn't want to see Mom upset.

Then again, what if the older boy's claim was true?

31.

As Laura's station wagon arrived at Birchfield Center, my thoughts were with the boys, so my replies to her endless chatter were unfortunately somewhat curt.

A variety of concerns unsettled me: what kind of mother would the boys expect? How would they seem after my several weeks of absence? Could I allay any fears they must have about the future? Would it be a return to the days when they'd given up playing with other kids and announced, "Maybe we can earn some money, Mom," in a touching effort to help me through hard times?

Vivid images floated through my mind: the Brooklyn summer of 1937, with Dan, just turned five, at a little table on the sidewalk offering a few discarded clothes of David's babyhood, a broken toy, chipped dishes; and after a full day of running in and out with pennies and an occasional dime he'd accumulated seventy-five cents, so off we'd gone to the store for milk and ice cream.

Then Pennsylvania and the flowers, with Dan picking stalks of lilacs on an April day and offering them along a roadside; lilacs no one bought because no one drove by except a neighboring farmer on his way to town. Then New York again, on Barrow Street in Greenwich Village, after we left Pennsylvania in 1940; Dan at eight, David almost six, trying to sell discarded Superman comics. And finally, both handing me fists full of nickels earned at their lemonade stand on hot summer days.

Though it had almost been a game for them, I told myself that from now on I'd need to provide enough security to insure that if they ever wanted to do such things again, it *would* be a game, not a necessity.

As I half expected, Danny and Dave, abandoning their suitcases, rushed to meet the woody as Laura pulled up next to the steps at Musgrove School's entry. I had barely rolled down the passenger side window before Davy blurted out, "Are we going home, Mama? I wanna go home."

"You both look wonderful, grand, and I've missed you so much," I replied as I climbed out, smiling cheerfully.

Immediately, they were both in my arms.

"Are we going home now?" David persisted.

"We'll talk about that," I said. "We will. But first Aunt Laura and I need to say hello to Mr. and Mrs. Musgrove, then—"

"—and then we thought we'd stop by that nice restaurant we went to last time before we all drive back to Danbury," added Laura.

"We're gonna live in Danbury?" asked Davy, beaming. "In the same house?"

Dan caught my frown and clenched his teeth.

"Don't worry, boys; we'll talk about it. You see, someone else is living in the house now."

"Who? Who's living in our house?" exclaimed Davy.

"I'm afraid I don't know. And I'm really not sure we'll even be living in Danbury, but—"

"The big guys said you were in a crazy house. Is it true?" demanded Davy.

"I told you not to ask her that!" growled Danny.

"Nonsense!" chirped Laura. "Your mother's just been taking a long rest, but soon she'll—"

This won't do, I thought. "Why don't you go on in and tell the Musgrove's we're here, Sis?" I cut in, attempting to stifle her irritation.

Laura glared at me then, in a huff, disappeared through the entry.

Crazy house, I thought. *So that's it. But now's not the time to get into this.* I crouched down in front of both boys and pulled them close. "What would you say if I told you that the three of us are going to have a month's vacation?"

They looked at one another then at me. "Where?" they both asked.

"I'll give you a clue. Aunt Laura's bought our groceries and paid for our little wooden cabin."

"A wooden cabin?" asked Davy.

While trying to look solemn, I nodded.

"Waubeeka! I bet it's Lake Waubeeka!" exclaimed Dan with obvious delight.

My answer was a big grin, at which they threw their arms around my neck and laid their heads on my shoulders.

◆◆◆◆◆

As the station wagon glided past Danbury's Candlewood Lake, the boys jabbered happily away about previous summers at

Waubeeka. Despite Davy's crazy house question, neither, of course, had any idea of what had been going on with me a few months earlier. But I felt my heart quicken for a moment before turning to happy memories:

Waubeeka! The lake had always been magic for the boys. Secluded and seldom visited except by local fishermen, and boarded with thick stands of pine, oak, and occasional birch, Waubeeka had a modest dam over which water spilled after heavy spring rains. Off shore lay a small, swamp-like island so tangled with vegetation growing from the lake bottom that it was impossible to land on. Recalling the two incredible weeks I'd spent there with the boys the previous summer, memories of the place swam through my memory.

◆◆◆◆◆

My brother, David, and me at Uncle Verne and Aunt Laura's farm, where we stopped on the way to Lake Waubeeka

Moments after we'd arrived, unloaded our groceries, and waved Laura goodbye, the boys changed into bathing suits and raced for a dinghy tied up to the boat dock. Soon after, they were navigating the shallow waters near shore as I looked on, a bit anxious, though trying to remind myself they'd both learned to swim the previous summer and were as comfortable in the water as the lake's ubiquitous painted turtles.

Am I ready to give them a happy time here? I wondered. *Be the mother they need?* Trying to shake off the self-doubt, I nevertheless watched nervously as they rocked the small green boat from side to side until it began to fill with water.

"Be careful," I shouted. "You might sink it!"

"Yeah, we will, we want to!" Dan called back.

left: Dan and Davey at Lake Waubeeka
above: Mary, Dan, and Davey at the lake

As the dinghy submerged, they laughed uproariously, then leaped from the boat and dragged it to shore, where, now laughing myself, I helped them tip out the water. Then they were into the dinghy again, repeating the operation; and repeating it again. And again.

By now my concern had dissipated. *Can't panic,* I told myself. *I have to trust them . . . and myself.* But would David's question about my sanity come up again? *Or should I just let it slide? And hope we can all forget about the crazy house . . . for now.*

◆◆◆◆◆

The month sped by for us all. So eager was I to make sure their reprieve from Musgrove would sustain them after their return, I encouraged almost anything they wanted to do, and often joined in fishing for crappie, perch, or bass—usually from a rowboat. I helped bait hooks with night crawlers, scaled the fish they caught, and baked them over an open fire. Sitting among the reeds in a nearby swamp, I watched as the boys, along with Dennis, the sixteen-year-old grandson of the lake's elderly caretaker, patiently waited for a bullfrog to poke its head above water, then whacked it with Dennis's "frog bopper," a cut-off canoe paddle. (Neither of my boys cared much for the fried frogs' legs I served for supper, though admitting they "tasted sorta like chicken.")

With Dennis and his grandfather sitting in, I often let Dan and David stay up until eleven, playing poker for matchsticks by the light of a kerosene lamp. Tagging along as the boys blazed a trail around Waubeeka's perimeter, we all oohed and aahed as Dennis's grandfather had the boys' hair standing on end with his graphic tales of ". . . bobcats and copperheads. And even bears in the old days! You never know. There might still be one or two of 'em hangin' around in the woods." During the entire month, they saw nothing more terrifying than an enraged chipmunk chasing another. Though one afternoon, Dan, alone in the old dinghy near shore, almost fell overboard when a huge snapping turtle glided past on the lakebed below.

On our final day, after arguing about it all morning (and after insisting I row alongside), I agreed to let the boys swim the length of the lake. "A good half-mile," Dennis (stretching the truth) said it was. Beginning their quest by leaping from a high platform at Waubeeka's western end, and with me monitoring from the boat and ready to pull either boy out at the first sign of trouble, my exhausted sons, manfully refusing to admit defeat, splashed the entire distance. Well, almost . . .

"You didn't swim all the way," chided Davy. "I saw you stand up and wade in before you got to the dock!"

"It was too shallow," replied Dan, breathless. "I couldn't keep swimming. Besides, I was only about ten feet from shore. And I got there before you did!"

Bed that night came at dusk for the boys, earlier than usual. It had been a long day, a strenuous day. By the time I finished reading them a chapter of *Treasure Island,* David was fast asleep and Dan was struggling to keep his eyes open. Laying the book aside, I leaned over and gently kissed my sons, whispered my nightly, "Sleep tight; don't let the bedbugs bite," and tiptoed from the room.

Lying awake, my thoughts dwelt on how fine those weeks had been, how much my boys had enjoyed their reprieve from Musgrove, and how my own sheer joy had replaced the anguish I'd felt when I was torn from them.

Still, I couldn't avoid the need to start planning for the future. I'd soon have to find work, locate a place for us to live, and make plans toward what I'd do with the rest of my life. In the meantime, as a temporarily absent mother, I'd need to do my best to make sure the boys had the emotional support they'd need while still at Musgrove; for how long? Perhaps until Christmas?

32.

After sleeping for what seemed like ten minutes but was likely an hour, I was awakened to frightened voices.

"Mama," pleaded David, "we want to get in bed with you."

"There's a big storm," cried Dan, "with lightning and stuff."

I shook myself awake to thunder echoing nearby, my room illuminated by lightning flashes.

"Sure, get in," I said.

As they did, I got up to light the kerosene lantern, then crossed to a window to look out at the lake. Lit by nature's electrical wonder, waves such as I'd never seen on Waubeeka lapped at the shore. Nearby, birches and willows bent to the force of a violent wind. Frightened, Davy urged me back to bed. In moments I was beside them, snuggling under the quilt, with an arm around each.

How to reassure them? I knew how terrifying storms could be, especially for children. Hadn't I lay awake endless nights in St. Johns, worried that Verne or Leo would call me a "fraidy-cat"? Hadn't I bundled with little brother Harry when he too crawled into my bed seeking refuge?

And once more, David's question about my state of mind began plaguing me. Perhaps the storm was some kind of omen, an excuse for me to deal with the issue.

"Sure is some storm, isn't it, Davy?" I asked gently. "Kind of like the drawing you made on that letter you sent me, huh?'

"Like when I asked about the nut house?" asked David.

"David!" said Dan, rolling his eyes.

I hugged both boys close. "It's okay, Danny," I replied. Then, to Davy, "Uh-huh, kind of like that." Then, after a pause, "Where did you get the idea that your mom was in some kind of crazy house?"

Their reticence quickly dissipated. "It was Gordon Arbuckle and his friends," Dan blurted out, "Davy's dumb pals."

"They're not my pals!" exclaimed David. "I just—"

"Then how come you hang around with 'em?" snapped Dan.

"Maybe that's something we can talk about later," I suggested. "But first, I should set things straight for you both; and for Gordon and his friends too."

The boys waited expectantly.

"It's true that I've been away," I began. "But not to somewhere anyone would call a crazy house. Or at least not anyone who understands that sometimes people like your mom, who've been going through a difficult time, need a long rest. Maybe someplace where they can take it easy for a while and just talk to friendly people who listen to the things that have been bothering them."

"Like what?" asked Dan.

"Oh, like feeling bad after Harold died, or like the time when you could tell I had a headache, Davy, and you brought me an aspirin. Remember?"

"Yeah. Or like when Danny and me had to sell stuff on the street so we could buy milk or something?"

"That's it. But only people who don't understand that other

people sometimes need help would call a place like that a crazy house. At least, that's what I think."

"Then why do they call it that?" asked Dan.

"Well, maybe because since they don't know any better, they're afraid of the whole idea, so they make jokes about people who have problems."

"That's pretty stupid," said David.

"Yep, it sure is. But I guess being afraid is easier for some people than taking time to find out the truth."

Then an incident more than ten years earlier came to mind. "Why don't I tell you a story?" I began. "A story about being afraid. Because, you know, there have been times when your mom's been afraid too."

Dan looked up at me. Davy snuggled deeper under the covers.

"It was when your papa and I lived in Vermont. We had storms there all the time, and let me tell you, some of them were terribly fierce like this one, with lots of thunder and lightning. Some of them would go on for hours."

"Is this one gonna go on for hours?" asked Davy

"I don't know," I said. "Maybe. But probably not. And we're safe inside here, aren't we?"

"Yeah 'course," replied Dan, doing his best to sound brave.

"Anyhow," I continued, "it was a day in summer, and your papa was away on a trip to New York, and I was minding three children from our little village for two days while their family was also away. We had gone out for a walk, and—"

"What were their names?" asked David.

"Oh, well . . . let's see. . . . It was a long time ago, even before Dan was born. . . . There was Janie, and . . . Skipper, and Shorty . . . all from one family, and—"

"Was he short?" David interrupted.

"Actually, he was tall. And his name was David, like you. But everyone called him Shorty."

"It's sort of a joke," cut in Dan.

"Anyway, we were out for a walk and had come to a little brook. I was glad to feel the cool water through my canvas slippers, and I wished that the children, who were chattering and running around, were somewhere else. Even their excitement over the pool of pink rock we found, then a frog, and a piece of petrified wood Janie picked up, didn't last long. They seemed to be pretending to be happy, and I guess I was pretending too, so I think they were pretending because they thought that pleased me. . . ."

"How come you were pretending?" asked Dan.

"Well, I suppose it was because we were all tired. Anyhow, when we got back to my house, Janie said, 'Didn't we have a good time, though, Mary?' Yes, I said, such a good time. And I said this even though I knew that none of us had enjoyed the soggy tomato sandwiches I had made . . ."

"Yuck!" said Dan.

" . . . or the difficult time we had scrambling up the rocks in the hot sun, and the steep climb up the hill to the house. Then, while we all lay in the shade outside, resting, I thought how much happier we were just lying there, each of us free to do what we felt like doing. Janie borrowed my thin scarf to pretend she was a fairy. And Shorty dreamed about the trout he was trying to catch in the spring while

Skipper popped imaginary stones into the air with his slingshot.

"But later, when a thunderstorm suddenly blew up, we all became afraid. Then a funny thing happened—for quite a while not one of us was brave enough to say, 'Let's go in the house.' Until Janie announced, 'I'm going in,' and pretty soon we were all inside, standing in the doorway and watching the lightning fork down the sky and laughing to hear it crash—because I think none of us wanted the others to know we weren't brave. In a minute or so, the rain and the hail came scampering in, and Shorty said, 'Better close the door, Mary.' 'What for?' I asked. But at the same time, I was thinking I really should close it because sometimes people do get struck by lightning. And even though I was afraid I was telling myself, *Don't be afraid, Mary."*

By now, David was almost asleep.

"Were you really afraid?" Dan asked as he began to yawn.

"I was. But when Skipper moved back from the door and said, 'My ma says people do get struck,' I said, 'Oh, bosh.' But just in case, I got up casually and closed the door and bolted it. 'No use getting the floors wet,' I added. In a minute or so, Shorty said, 'Come look out the window at the lightning; it's far off now.' He was the bravest of us all, and I felt ashamed for wanting to go bury my nose in a book and just wait for the storm to pass. 'Look, Mary,' he went on, 'the sky's all blue over there. Come look out the window.' It cheered me to see the blue, and when the storm had spent itself, like they always do, I opened the door and we walked out onto the wet grass, and I wondered why my fear of lightning was so great, and why my dread of wind was so strong. But all the time I was thinking, *I have to get used to this, I must get used to this. There's going to be more storms ahead, perhaps many more. I will get used to this!"*

I glanced at Dan, who was trying to stay awake. What I didn't know then was that his thoughts had begun to drift back to what awaited him at Musgrove . . . the older boys, the zombie cave . . . and in the back of his mind, his concern about me and the uncertainty about whether or not we'd all be together again soon . . . or ever.

I spoke more softly now, quietly. "Then we saw a snake moving beside the house. I knew it was harmless, yet I feared it; but I followed it closely, for I was ashamed to let the children know my fear. Skipper picked it up, and we watched its red tongue flick in and out. We had all thought Skip was the greatest coward, and I almost cried for the shame I felt, because even then, when he handed it to me, I knew I was pretending to be unafraid. All kinds of reasons came into my mind for my fear of the storm and of the snake. But I put them aside because I really didn't like what I had become."

Unsure if he'd understood what I was trying to say, I glanced at Dan again. But I continued anyhow in a whisper, as he'd finally nodded off.

"When night came and all the village was asleep, my good feelings started to come back again; my self-respect. Outside, I could hear their dog barking mournfully. Shorty came close to me then, trying not to show his feelings, and Janie said, 'The nights are so creepy here when Jethro howls.' And it was then I could let go of my fears, for I needed to find a reason for them. I needed to understand why I was afraid. I saw the children all to bed, then sat quietly, listening to the wind. After the lamp flickered out for lack of oil, I sat a long time in the dark and the stillness—and dreaded nothing."

◆◆◆◆◆

Both boys were sound asleep. The storm had passed, with only the soft rumble of distant thunder and the comforting sound of the boys' breathing. I gently reached across Dan to lower the wick in the kerosene lamp then lay back, quietly thinking; thinking about fear, about how it had consumed me that day in Vermont, how I'd been able to conquer it then, how I'd dealt with the legion of fears clawing at me before and since. And although there were some demons of the past I still needed to kick back into their holes, this month I'd spent with my boys had better prepared me to get the job done. I'd already put some important confusions to bed: my mother's bitterness, the failed marriage to Matthew, the shattering disappointment I'd gone through with Forman, the collapse of my expectations about Alvah. And I felt I was getting closer to an understanding of why I'd come so near to ending it all.

Still, there was much to sort out before I could finally make my peace and move on; before this long look into the mirror of my life's journey was complete. Before I'd become a mother capable of helping David and Dan to grow into healthy, forward-looking young men.

33.

Summer 1943

Except for biweekly sessions with Dr. Thomas to discuss my progress, Payne Whitney was behind me. With tearful goodbyes, David and Danny had returned to Musgrove School.

Moving into the comfortable attic room at Laura and Verne's and puttering about to make the space my own felt much like it did on leaving Vermont for Brooklyn years earlier. That was 1936, and it meant neighborhood children for Dan and Davy to play with, renewing old acquaintances, perhaps theater now and then if Alvah's fifty-dollar-a-week salary at the *Brooklyn Eagle* would allow it—and perhaps some kind of productive work for me if I could persuade his mother to look after the boys part time.

Abandoning unpaid bills, selling our furniture, and with Vermont friends to whom we owed money telling us, "Forget it, we're doing okay, just get yourselves set up," we had rented a basement apartment just blocks from Brooklyn's waterfront.

My initial hopes, however, had soon petered out.

True, there was an occasional play, film, or a house party with friends. There were children on the block, but since Dan was not yet four and David still in diapers, I found myself alone with them all day while Alvah pounded out copy at the *Eagle* and spent most evenings at the Newspaper Guild or at left-wing political meetings. And his mother, a kindly soul, lived on Eighty-Third Street in Manhattan. While she adored the boys, Brooklyn was a long subway ride. Forever anxious since she'd once had a purse snatched en route, she preferred not to travel that way.

Then there was our marriage. Like Alvah, I'd long recognized how threadbare it had become. Was he still seeing Brigid Kelly? Was she still in love with Alvah? Well, I didn't know and didn't much care. In Vermont, when his friend Pete Glenn had visited and stayed for several days after Alvah went off on one of his New York trips, on his return I let drop that I'd developed a strong attraction for this merchant seaman. Though nothing physical had happened I recognized the admission as my own frustrated way of getting back at Alvah's infidelity; reversing the old saw: what's sauce for the goose is sauce for the gander. It had solved nothing; a goose I certainly was.

Hearing Alvah frequently lampoon the institution of marriage before we'd even tied the knot, I was well aware that neither of us had entered the union with any great enthusiasm. (My own words at the time popped up: "I don't know how it will work out, but let's try it and see.")

Hardly a promising start, I told myself.

Having curled up in an easy chair next to a small window in the attic bedroom, I reached into a cardboard box Verne and Laura had been keeping for me and began sifting through an envelope stuffed with photos. Mostly snaps from Vermont. Several of Alvah and me, bringing back images of the "starving scarecrows" I'd felt we were in '31. Dear sons; Dan at two in his little overalls and looking quite somber under a wild mop of blonde curls. One of myself feeding David from a bottle while Dan looked on.

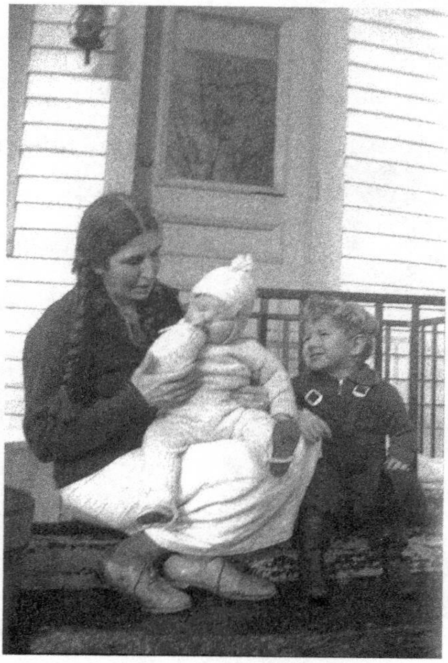

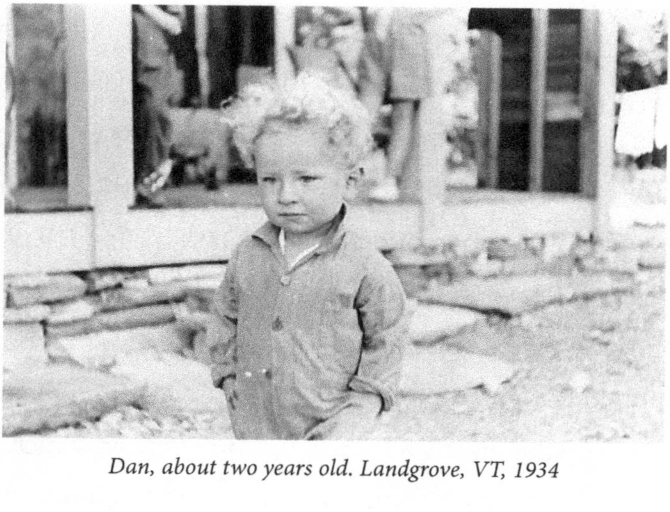

Dan, about two years old. Landgrove, VT, 1934

Another envelope held shots from 1936: Dan atop a pony in a photo taken by the street photographer who owned it. Another with Dan dressed as an Indian, aiming a bow and arrow he'd received for his birthday. Then David, looking content while nursing an ice pop as he sat on the front step of the small grocery store across the street in Brooklyn, a Coca Cola sign in the window next to him.

On reflection, I decided that perhaps 1936 wasn't so bad after all. Though initially feeling isolated after the move, and even with our marriage teetering on the brink, in some ways it had been an uplifting year, at least for me. Though I kept no diary from the period, no notes, I could bring it back in memory:

I recalled listening to a dynamic seaman from Jamaica discuss the strike that had recently broken out and tied up shipping along the East Coast; about his description of working conditions aboard ship, how seamen often received inedible food, had to deal with lice and other vermin in their bunks, and regularly worked long, grueling hours for barely enough pay to sustain them ashore until they shipped out again—if they were fortunate enough to land a job. Hiring usually meant a "shape up," an event in which jobless men crowded together for hours on a pier, each hoping to catch the eye of the company's agent. Odds were, those who got picked had slipped the agent a few dollars.

The Depression made things worse. Dockworkers and seamen on the West Coast had already won wage increases and better conditions. But most sailors belonged to the conservative International Seamen's Union. Along with the U.S. government, ship-owners saw any attempt to change things as subversion by dangerous anarchists and communists.

I'd come away from the meeting determined to get involved.

Hardly a dangerous radical, I'd nevertheless always been drawn to people I felt were getting a raw deal, to anyone down on their luck. Though reluctant to seek praise for doing what I felt any halfway decent person ought to, I'd always been ready to lend a hand: sewing sweaters for the boys fighting in France during World War I, supporting children as a teacher or friend, listening sympathetically as Forman unburdened himself. Or, with Alvah, making helpful suggestions whenever he'd agonize over his writing during those endlessly snowbound Vermont winters.

In my mind, the seamen got the dirty end of the stick, and their strike seemed like a worthy cause, something in which becoming involved might provide the sense of purpose I'd found lacking for too long.

As I lay back in the attic room chair and closed my eyes, the images of 1936 flickered past like a Movietone newsreel: While Alvah wrote publicity for the strikers, I plunged into organizing a Citizens Committee to support the seamen, which met in our small Pineapple Street apartment; visited restaurants and other suppliers, often with David and Danny in tow, to secure donations of anything those out of work or on picket duty might need; set up a soup kitchen at the local seamen's headquarters, where three hundred men were fed three meals a day, and spoke on the men's behalf to groups in private homes and at clubs and organizations to help raise money for strikers' families.

And my God, the drama! There were nights when strikers showed up at our home, bloody from an encounter with police or with International Seamen's Union thugs. Just before midnight one night, while Alvah was still at a Newspaper Guild meeting, a pounding on our door woke me. A sailor who had become a good friend rushed in, and with a look in his eye that frightened me, paced the living room repeating over and over, "Gotta get a gun. Get me a gun." Between cups of coffee, I spent more than an hour talking him down.

The strike ended with little resolution, then flared up again. From October into the following year, fifty thousand seamen struck. By early 1937, rebels from the ISU had formed a new organization, the National Maritime Union.

For almost a year, attention to our troubled marriage had been shoved into a shadowy corner that neither of us talked about. It had been a busy time. And exhausting. But for me, strangely exhilarating.

1937 began pushing its way into my thoughts, with the memory of Alvah indulging in a lifelong ambition: learning to fly. Made possible by a raise to seventy-five dollars a week at the *Eagle*, he'd begun lessons at Brooklyn's Floyd Bennett Field, soloed quickly, obtained his pilot's license, taken Dan for a ride in an open cockpit Stearman biplane, and, one evening, brought home for dinner Lee Gehlbach, a romantic figure with the dangerous vocation of a test pilot. Gentle, handsome, and a charmer, Gehlbach was also given to drink. Just the kind of lost soul, Alvah may have thought, that I might be attracted to because of my compassionate need to "fix" lost people, . . . "Like your consumptive first husband or your fairy cousin," he'd said in one of his more cynical moods.

Gehlbach had seen better days and couldn't pay his rent, so he stayed with us for three weeks. And, damn it, Alvah was right: Lee and I became close, and when he finally left, I told Alvah I was deeply in love for the first time in my life.

Looking back now, my understanding of what love is had a long way to go.

Alvah had no response. Until the next evening, that is, when he stormed in after work and after David and Dan were in bed, went directly to the bedroom, and began to pack, muttering, "I gotta leave. Gotta get out of here."

Not exactly stunned, since I'd felt it coming for months, I suggested he sit down and we talk it over. "I'll make some coffee," I said. "After all we've been through, we ought to—"

"There's nothing to talk about," he shot back. "You're in love with someone else."

"Maybe not. Maybe yes. I don't know. It just came out. After all, you've been seeing Brigid, and . . ."

But he'd made up his mind. Within minutes, he'd stuffed shirts, socks, and toiletries into a valise and was on his way to the door, with a hasty, "I'll come by to get the rest of my things later."

"What do I tell the boys?

He froze for a moment, then turned, "Tell them I'll see them on the weekend."

And he was gone.

◆◆◆◆◆

In the attic bedroom, I'd begun to drift off—to be woken moments later by a knock at the door. I called, "Come in."

The door opened to Laura's and Verne's housekeeper, Selma, greeting me with a broad smile and an apologetic, "Oh, sorry, Ms. Burnett, I didn't mean to disturb you. I can come back later if—"

"It's Mary, remember?"

Selma laughed. "I forgot. Sorry. All right then . . . Mary. But don't let on."

"To my sister-in-law? No, of course not. She's a bit formal, isn't she?"

Selma chuckled. "I s'pose she is. Most folks we work for are like that."

"Anyhow, you're not disturbing me at all. I was looking forward to seeing you."

"I just come by to see if you've got any washing. Be doing a load first thing tomorrow."

Accepting my invitation to sit, she agreed, "But just for a couple minutes, I got a roast on. Lamb. Mister Burnett's favorite, asked for it special he did, 'cause tomorrow he's off on a business trip I don't know where. Someplace."

I nodded then said, "About the washing; I just have some underwear and a couple pair of stockings. Maybe a blouse, but I can just as easily rinse them out in the bathroom sink, and—"

"Oh, Ms. Burnett—your sis-in-law, I mean—wouldn't like that. Wouldn't like that at all. She'd know. I've got a big load, won't be a bother."

Selma looked off, hesitating then added, "Wouldn't take to me sittin' here talking with you, neither. You know how she is about the line between white folks and the help."

"I won't tell her if you don't," I replied with a wink.

We looked at one another for several moments, then burst out laughing.

34.

Tuesday, March 8, 1938

Dear Poppy,

Someday we are going to make a strawberry pie with baked apples in it. And, dear Poppy, Mommy told me that you are in Spain. We're just going to tell Frankie and Emilio and Jaime that you're in Spain.

Uncle Harry has been here three times.

I brought four papers with colors home from school today. I want you to know, dear Poppy, that I'm going tonight to send a picture and it will be a tent and you will have it in about one month.

Pooh! Pooh! Pooh! Write that all over the letter, and he'll laugh.

Do they have this Indian tent in Spain?

Love, Dan

My then five-year-old had dictated the letter. Below the signature, he'd drawn a triangular shape vaguely resembling a tent, nestled among trees.

Why did I keep this? I asked myself—*and the other letters we wrote to Alvah? Good question.* Perhaps because Alvah had returned them to me while he was still in Spain. How had he put it? . . . Oh yes: "If I don't come back, you might want to take a look at these someday to see what was going on in your head." *Well, no matter now; here they are, and with it all I'm glad Alvah and I stayed on good terms. Will these letters prove insightful for the boys one day, or end up in their own furnaces?*

Though Alvah had been in Spain since February, I'd known six months earlier that he'd go; begun to sense it the night we'd gone to see Charlie Chaplin in *Modern Times.* As much as we'd looked forward to the film, the newsreel preceding it recording the market day devastation of the town of Guernica by Germany's Condor Legion had been almost too much for either of us to deal with: dead children, grieving mothers and old people, buildings torn apart, and hundreds of civilians killed.

Driven to tears by the courage of the Spanish people in the face of overwhelming firepower, Alvah had left the theater determined to get involved. Early in 1938, he joined the Abraham Lincoln Battalion of American volunteers, part of a contingent of forty-five hundred *brigadistas* from more than fifty countries rushing to help defend the Republic.

Before leaving, he filed for divorce.

What now? My mind was in a tizzy. *What about the boys? What if he doesn't come back?* Early battles had decimated the American battalion. How would we get by? While Alvah helped pay my bills before shipping for Spain, the meager sum he left us would soon run out. Still, I respected his decision, the reasons for which he spelled out in a note: " . . . to work for the first time in a large body of men; to submerge myself in the mass, seeking neither distinction nor preferment; to achieve self-discipline and learn patience, resignation, and unselfishness." *Well,* I agreed, *a noble ambition;* one in line with his often-expressed hatred of his stock-market-driven, buttoned-down father.

Still, to me, his motivation seemed to come more out of the kind of person his new political perspective told him he ought to be rather than from the kind of person he actually was. His determination to fight fascism certainly felt honorable, but his need to "complete the destruction of his early training in order to build a life geared to other men" (and so on) did seem at the time—and even now, from the perspective of my attic room in rural Connecticut—just a bit . . . *How should I describe it . . .?*

Pooh! Pooh! Pooh! Like Dan had written in that first letter to him. Exactly how a five-year-old who didn't know how to vent his frustration over his father's sudden disappearance had put it. Well, I could make notes too; wasn't I the Notebook Lady, as Nurse Kelly had called me?

I opened to a blank journal page:

> I suppose I sensed it then, that he wanted so much to be a man. Just as Matthew did, trying to support us by tramping all over Chicago with his vacuum cleaners. As my father did into his sixties, hefting rugs in the department store . . . something akin to me, with my struggle to become the woman I need to be. I wonder what kind of a world this is in which so many people have to spend the first forty years of their lives "finding" them-

selves; and why it is that so many never do?

What then? Tough decisions. Even though we were divorcing, I did what I could to support Alvah along his journey.

We all go through our own struggles, I'd told myself. And if we're lucky, we eventually choose a path we're convinced may lead to inner strength and greater fulfillment. Laying aside any doubts, I had to let this man I cared for, whatever his faults and whatever my sadness, know I was there for him—and to do so without recrimination, vengeance, or perceived wrongs. These were never a part of who I am.

March 22, 1938

Dear Alvah,

This afternoon we were surprised to find the Loyalist hats in the mail; also the copies of your battalion newspaper. Dan and David paraded with their hats all afternoon. On Saturday there was a noble anti-fascist parade and gathering here on the corner. Four ambulances were displayed, purchased with money raised practically overnight. Last week's bad news from Spain has left its mark on plenty of us. Too many have probably already forgotten, but it was a stimulus nevertheless. We have to do more. Except for a trip to the airport Saturday with the kids, just haven't seen anyone for weeks. Your old flying instructor, Tom, was busy now that the weather's warm. He sends his best to you. I expect to see Brigid K. this Saturday. She wrote that she planned to be in New York and would be over. Am looking forward to meeting her.

I read your letter to your mother. Good letter. Write us all as frequently as you can. Your letters are swell. You do sound so happy and so alive.

The kids are well and happy and busy. They'll have a snapshot with their new hats on one of these days, and I'll send that along.

Will be anxious to know if any of our letters have come through.

Salud, Mary

Just as important, I knew, would be the boys' letters to him.

March 22, 1938

Dear Poppy,

The Loyalist hats and slippers came today. We wore them out and everything, and I didn't let anybody touch it. I'm wearing the slippers. Davy's feet are too small for his. You're a good Poppy to send them. Please send Davy some more slippers.

Yesterday Mommy sorted all our clothes, and we took a big bundle over to the place where they will be sent to the Spanish children. Mommy's writing this with a pencil. My finger is sore so I can't draw a boat very well, but I made one on the other page.

Davy sends a hunk of hugs, Poppy. Someday Davy and I are going to Spain. When you come home, buy a bag of ice pops down on the corner for us all to eat.

Big hugs and a kiss. You're a bum. You bum, you bum, you bum!

Dan

As he dictated, I asked Danny if he really wanted to call his father a bum. "Yeah," he'd answered, "because it's funny." So it stayed in—just like "Pooh!"

◆◆◆◆◆

During a late summer lunch spread out on a rustic wooden table next to the brook flowing past Laura and Verne's Connecticut home, I was hardly surprised when my brother began to press me on what I planned to do next. "Perhaps you might think of learning some kind of vocation," he suggested. "What about nursing? Or teaching. After all, you survived the little monsters that year in . . . where was it?"

"Manchester," I replied.

"Yes, Manchester, just outside Ann Arbor."

"My teaching credential would only be good in Michigan, and it was so long ago I'm not sure they'd honor it. Besides, I'm not qualified for anything but elementary. For more than that, I'd need an M.A."

"How about nursery school?" Laura asked Verne. "She had the little playgroup in Danbury, and—"

"Well, that was pretty much a bust, wasn't it?" he huffed.

"She did try, dear. It wasn't Mary's fault she only enrolled a few children."

"Five," said Verne. "And it never made any money."

I started to gather luncheon dishes. Best to keep my peace.

"Selma will clear those," said Laura as she reached for a little silver bell used to summon the housekeeper.

"I'm going in anyhow," I announced. "The lunch was lovely, but if you don't mind, I think I could use a nap."

Starting for the house, I noticed Laura glare at my brother.

"What?" he said, apparently catching her look.

Laura folded her arms and sighed.

After a snort, Verne reached into a pocket for his pipe and tobacco.

That's hardly what I needed. True, along with Leo and Harry, Laura and Verne had come to my rescue time and again; for supplies at my backyard playgroup, fees at the clinic, and even for the boy's tuition at Musgrove School. Yet there had always been a stuffy quality about my middle brother, a kind of small-minded Babbittish manner that I found grating. Well, I'd make the best of it. I had to concentrate on more important things: communicating with David and Dan on a more regular basis and continuing to resolve the long journey through the years that landed me in Payne Whitney.

Alone once more in the attic room, I drifted back to 1938; back to Alvah and Spain. Rather than detail his weeks of training, harrowing battles, or the names of comrades killed (news accounts made the horror immediate for me, anyway), his letters were mainly designed to allay our fears. Most described the Spanish villages, the rocky, olive-tree-studded countryside, the peasants he met, and the everyday life of a soldier—often sleeping on bare ground, washing infrequently (the boys got a kick out of his description of bathing in a cold mountain pool), and perpetually running short of food or cigarettes.

Though maintaining a steady correspondence had often been difficult.

> *Sunday, May 15*
>
> Alvah dear,
>
> I haven't written you for such a long time. Only yesterday, word came of change of address for the American volunteers.
>
> Needless to tell you of the concern we have here, and how anxiously we await word of your whereabouts. Nothing has reached us from you since April 6, which was the time when Herb Matthews's piece appeared in the *Times*, mentioning you among six who escaped miraculously.
>
> Brigid was here a few weeks ago. We had a good time together with the kids. I like and admire her tremendously. A letter from her just yesterday says she hasn't heard from you either. . . .

That Alvah had found another love was simply a reality I needed to accept; *Why let it drag me down?* Clear too was that Brigid had to deal with the anxiety of knowing that any moment might bring news of the death of the man in her life; I quickly came to see her as a sister.

> The kids are splendid, talk about you and wonder when you'll be home to see them, and aren't forgetting

you for a minute. They spent a week with Grandma at Ada and Chuck's in Connecticut while I drove out to Michigan with Harry to see Mother, badly afflicted with angina. We came back through Pennsylvania at night, watching the eclipse, and so much went through my head during those long hours. Out of it all, however, we must be strong—and we will be—and with it all keep a sense of humor about ourselves.

All of you there should be heartened by the relentless efforts being made here on Spain's behalf. Even brother Leo, awaking to something or other, sent me a check stating, "to help along a good cause." Which made me happy.

When I was home, Mother asked me, "Just who are the Loyalists?" which gave me an opportunity to really reach her for the first time in my life. As long as I am able to enlighten anyone, to make them begin to see, I shall thoroughly enjoy being alive.

Until we hear from you then—

Mary

Just days later, the boys and I received four of his letters. Immensely relieved to know he was alive and well, I got off two replies in as many days. Assuring him again that the boys were fine (though just getting over whooping cough) and raring to see him, I went on to say he should forget about Lee Gehlbach (the test pilot I'd been enamored of). I'd read in the papers that he'd married and

*Alvah Bessie in Spain; Darnos, Catalonia,
April 1938*

was getting famous. "After all," I wrote, "it's of no importance, really, so let's just not mention him again, okay, pal?"

By way of telling him our divorce had been finalized, I ended with a P.S.:

> And please know that you are now legally a free man and I a free woman (ho!)—for all the good it does anyone. That was about three weeks ago. What a lot of bullshit. Haven't told a soul. . . . Don't see much of any-one.

But alone and awake on a Brooklyn morning, I recorded a flurry of free verse daydreams and recollections of Alvah . . . or perhaps of another? Ships passing in the night:

When I lean on the window ledge before the dawn,

And the breeze coming up from the docks
Rustles the crumpled papers below me in the street,
Then, piercing, sharp, and quick, is for a single moment
The dream . . . the dream of two that never can be one . . .
Sharing and working and loving for the little while remaining.
And even while the dream is there, suspended,
Still, escaping once again with that moment's moving,
Come voices, children early waking, to tie me surely
To the earth, to all the manmade creeds of all the
Centuries. . . . And this, I know finally, between this dreaming.
And the next is best for women; best for women, and best for men.

Poetic meditations seemed to be my only release; I'd sunk into a mild lethargy ever since the divorce. Now that I was able to look back objectively, I could recognize it as an early sign of the coming depression. Except for raising the boys, with the end of the seamen's strike, the end of the marriage, and Alvah going off to Spain, I'd certainly felt once more that my life had little meaning.

The strike had been a high point, providing a strong sense of purpose, involving me in an important way in action that might help make life better for thousands. But though my own spirits were flagging again, with Alvah in combat and with the real possibility of David and Dan never seeing him again, I somehow managed to continue sending him reassuring letters:

May 29, 1938

Dear Alvah,

The kids have been digging up the empty lot. "Mom," says Dan, "sometimes people find gold and all sorts of old things when they dig."

I wish you could have a peek at your sons; they're pretty hot stuff, and I think you'll be right proud of them someday, as they will be of you.

I've started a file of clippings on the Americans in Spain; some literary instinct, I guess. Sort of thought you might want to be having them someday. And though we all miss you terribly, please know how proud I am that you've joined the "good fight." Even the boys must be. I look out a window and see the neighborhood kids lined up in two armies, the "Loyalists" versus the "Things," with Dan, the only blonde on the street in this mostly Spanish neighborhood, darting back and forth, taking care of himself like a regular fellow. He's one of the gang now. It's a good school for them down there on this tough but lovely block, and when I see him coming forty miles an hour down the street on his bike, missing cars with a seventh sense, my heart ain't where it ought to be, but I let him go, because he needs it. David can run him a pretty close second; especially today

> when he climbs up the ladder off the fire escape right on to the roof. Oh well, it's all in a lifetime. In spite of everything, they're a great pair of guys. And try not to do any worrying about your sons. I do the very best I can in teaching them to take care of themselves, but tie them to my apron strings I will not.

In a letter written days later, I added to the thought:

> Don't be getting the idea that they are growing up to love war. It's a game to them. I suppose if their father were a G-man or a racketeer, the same would apply. Kids are like that, and it's right that way, I guess. Far be it from me to try to make anything out of kids. But more and more am I determined to do everything that I can to see them help themselves, and fit themselves for whatever sort of world they'll be growing up in. That, I guess, for the moment, is the best job I can do.

My secret fears for the boy's future, however, only my journal knew about:

> My sons! Sons of all fathers now in Spain!
> Sons of all fathers fighting in China!
> Sons of fathers everywhere, fighting for their jobs,
> Their lives, yes, and for their souls!
> Will you know better what it's all about when you too,
> Armed with rifles, with machine guns,

Rush at command across some unplowed field at midday?
Or will you too, like these fathers of today,
Who, half bewildered, half afraid, trying to answer
The question for you with their lives . . . will you too,
Half bewildered, half afraid, rush at the enemy,
The flesh and blood enemy, who, also half bewildered,
Half afraid, come to meet you at midday in the unplowed field?
And will that be the heritage, that the substance of
Your sons' inheritance . . . forever a question . . .
Never to be answered?

While the pre-dawn hours raised a fear about their lives ahead, the boys could also sometimes drive me crazy:

Wednesday night, June 8, 1938

To Dan—

Cradle Song

Mama's little man sings only one tune
All day long.
All night it pounds in Mama's ears.
"You know what I'm going to be
When I grow up?
I'm going to be a man who fixes faucets,
A man who sells ice pops,

A candy store man.
I'm going to be a streetcar man,
A man who fixes stoves,
A restaurant man.
Or maybe I'll be a man who makes boats go,
Or a truck driver,
Or a man who's a barber.
A barber's a good thing to be, isn't it, Mom?
You know what I'm really going to be
When I grow up?
I'm going to be a policeman
Who rides a horse.
I'm going to be an aviator, and my airplane
Will be the biggest in the whole world,
And I'll drop bombs on the old rebels.
Mom, you know what I'm really truly
Going to be when I grow up?
I'm going to be a soldier like Pop and
Go to Spain and shoot the old rebels.
Mom, you know—"
STOP!

At the sound of barking, I looked up from my writing to glance out the attic window. Below, Verne and Laura's immaculately groomed collie Lassie (what other name should it have?) bounded after her master and mistress, who, decked out in freshly laundered *Better Homes and Gardens* attire, trowels and cultivating forks in gloved hands, were on their way to attack an infantry of weeds now parading through the flowerbeds bordering their broad lawn. In the driveway next to it stood Laura's Ford woody station wagon.

I smiled. The idyllic American scene. If I'd had a Kodak, I'd have snapped a picture. It looked like an ad from *Colliers,* or *The Saturday Evening Post.*

Continuing to chew over 1938, I recognized that my "everything is fine" declarations to Alvah continued to flow; by early fall, other feelings had also been creeping in. We hadn't been out to the airport again to visit his flying instructor Tom, because . . .

> . . . there aren't many pennies for Coca-Cola and peanuts. Shoes and socks are more to the "pernt."
>
> You ask—
>
> 1. How do we live? Well sir, that's always been a puzzle, but I never was much on anatomy, and while I've read the Bible, I've yet to discover just where the breath of life comes from.
>
> 2. How much do we get from relief? $42 per month.
>
> 3. How do we manage on it? We don't. Verne and Laura send $7.50 a week, bringing the monthly total up to $72. $22 goes for rent, approximately $8 to $10 per week ($40 monthly) for food, cigarettes, soap, stamps, toilet paper, mosquito cream, ad infinitum. The remaining ($10) buys our clothing, haircuts for the boys, and pays the light and gas (with the gas getting periodically turned off).
>
> 4. Are we in debt? No. I've scrupulously avoided such, which I consider wise in present circumstances.

5. Are we well? Yes.

Last week, the kids spent a few days with Grandma, so I went out to your cousin Simon's and had dinner with him, and we drove to some friends' of his in Mount Kisco, up north of NYC about fifty miles. Ever hear of it? It was a nice change. Almost too close to home, but it's not easy to get away and no place to go particularly. One of these days I'll get moving. Never was much of a butterfly, as you know, and conditions are not ripe for my even attempting any kind of work at present.

I guess I am pretty much a hermit. Guess I always was. For one who loves people as much as I do, it's a pretty sad mess. One of these days, though, I'll get stirring. Guess the Vermont years didn't do for me what they did for you in keeping the body in shape. Don't know. Can't figure it out. Don't want to try figuring out anything anymore except how to make a living and be of some use....

You speak of the rainy season. All the good Catholics in town swear we're in for forty days of it. We've had eight straight now; what a difference from what you're going through. We sleep in beds, most of us, and have coffee (provided the gas hasn't been cut off) with cream and sugar, and can dry our clothes in the cellar. Funny how you get used to anything after a while.

Call this "dopey mom" night (no dirty cracks now) . . . and perhaps the spirit will be gayer and stronger next time.

> Salud and best of luck, kid, Mary
>
> P.S. Dan comes home from Grandma's saying, "Poppy is coming home safe and sound because Grandma prays to God every night to bring him home safe and sound." I heard the two of them in their beds tonight talking about God and the devil, Dan saying, "The devil's in you. There isn't any other devil." "Oh yeah," says David, "I'll tell the devil to come and he'll show you."

In another, written just days later, I noted a passage that I now realize Alvah may well have taken as a hint of my darker feelings:

> All the home news seems so trivial and unimportant, but there are so few times when the big things can actually be said on paper. More and more I realize the need for action of some sort. It will come soon, I think. How, I don't know, but one thing I do know, as I have for a long time, is that unless the rest of my life is directed toward some service to humanity, it's not worth living.

As I finished looking over the words, the buzzer in my room sounded. I pressed the intercom's respond button. "It's me, dear," chirped Laura. "Dinner in half an hour. Be sure to dress nicely, won't you? Verne's off again . . . to California tomorrow, some publicity campaign for Bing Crosby of all people; can you imagine?"

"I'll be there," was my response.

I clicked off, sighed, shook my head, then chuckled. *Dress nicely? In what, for God's sake? I'm still ten pounds underweight, and what little I've got hangs like a rag and makes me look like a Dust Bowl refugee.*

But dress for dinner was *de rigueur* at the Burnetts' of Danbury, even if the only guest would be myself. Thank goodness this wouldn't be one of those occasions where they'd invited Verne's business associates and their wives, or other stuffy neighbors from along the road. Then I'd have to smile politely at inane small talk, stifle myself when someone carped about how badly FDR was managing the war—or listen to my brother describe Selma's children, whom she'd brought along when her mother was sick and couldn't mind them, as "those adorable pickaninnies."

How to get off on my own? I wondered. *To a place much like the peace and quiet here in rural Connecticut, but without the necessity to listen to conversations that went nowhere, dress for dinner, or have to put up with that infernal tinkling mealtime bell.*

Well, enough of it; I needed space, thinking time. Breathing time. Since I had an appointment at Payne Whitney the following afternoon anyhow, and since Laura would be driving Verne to the station for his train to New York, I'd ride into the city with him.

Dr. Thomas had already helped me through the major crisis of my life. Perhaps he'd offer some advice on how I might escape this much smaller one; gracefully, if possible.

35.

"Woodstock," Dr. Thomas suggested. "My wife and I go there almost every summer. It's a delightful place. Secluded, quiet."

"You'll recall me telling you about my time in Vermont," I replied. "I'm not sure I want to go back there right now, and—"

"Not the one in Vermont. Woodstock, New York. It's kind of a refuge for artists; has been since the late eighteen hundreds, I believe. We stay at a big three-story boarding house there, the Homestead, run by a sweet old woman named—"

"Sarah Birdwhistle! Is she still there?"

"Indeed she is . . . but how did you—"

"We went through Woodstock in the mid-twenties, when I toured for a season with my brother and his puppet troupe. It was only for one night, but who could forget a name like Birdwhistle? She was charming. And I recall really liking the town, though I only had a glimpse. We got in late and left early the next morning."

"You said you've been writing. Drawing too, I believe?"

"I have."

"Well then, Woodstock would be ideal. And since you've met Mrs. Birdwhistle, it's not as though you'd be a complete stranger."

"I'm afraid it's been quite a while."

"It's just another little step," said Dr. Thomas, smiling. "One step at a time, remember."

◆◆◆◆◆

Why go back to Danbury? I thought as the bus headed through Connecticut toward this weekend visit with Dan and David. *I've got everything I need, enough for a couple weeks: comfortable slacks, walking shoes, blouses, socks, underwear, and my journals from 1938 through '41. I'll phone Laura and let her know what I'm doing. . . . Shit! She'll probably think I'm not being sensible, but what the hell. . . .*

I smiled, recalling Dr. Thomas's advice. *One step at a time. So what about a bit of bravery too?*

And for now, money would be no problem. As Verne dropped me off for my Payne Whitney appointment before catching his flight for California, he had handed me two crisp hundred-dollar bills. "For your birthday," he'd said, "since I won't be here to help celebrate. I'm sure you know how proud we are to see you get over this delusion, or whatever it was, so quickly."

I forced a gracious smile.

Excited about seeing the boys again, I'd not slept well the night before. But no sooner had I dozed off than the bus bounced over a large pothole and jolted me awake. So, having decided to continue making my peace with 1938 and the years with Alvah, I shook off the drowsy feeling, opened the valise stowed under the seat, and pulled out the packet with our exchange of letters.

The first was from his year in Spain:

> Feeling low today, with the sudden crystallized and final realization of how dear the kids are to me, and how deeply I'm feeling their absence. I think of them asking, "When is Pop coming back?" and "Is Pop ever coming back?" and I realize too with shame that it is largely self-pity that brings tears to my eyes at the thought of possibly never seeing them again. This possibility rises again and again to consciousness and yet is too appalling for long or steady contemplation. Wherein lies the horror of this consideration? The thought of my own end? Or the pity I should feel for fatherless kids if I were able to imagine my own death?

Unusual for him to unburden himself like this. But how well I could empathize. Because what he'd expressed echoed what I'd gone through myself after the first days at Payne Whitney, when, with suicidal feelings subsided and bouts of remorse over, I realized how close I'd come to leaving David and Dan motherless.

I'd penned an immediate reply:

> You must know, kiddo, that we've all been with you in spirit, and I'd venture so far as to say in the flesh, such has the agony of mind been these past few weeks. As you say, it's hard to relate the whole business to your self-pity. Still, it is something that has to be related sooner or later, if we're to function at all, I guess. . . . Your young'uns are in the street teaching themselves. They're good enough. Might be worse, might be bet-

ter. Don't belittle the part you have played in their existence. God knows they haven't much from me, and if I'm trying to teach them a little, it's no more than any mother hen (probably less) would instinctively do for each new brood of chicks. . . .

Somehow, Alvah unburdening himself had given me permission to do the same:

Brooklyn
Monday, September 13, 1938
Dear Alvah,

You complain about no letters from us. What, I ask you, can be done about that? Since I'm the only one who can do anything, and since I never was one to write letters that raved about the beautiful fall days we're having. What the hell. Pearls, you beg for yet. Pearls from me? Shit Ma, I can't dance.

I sighed at the memory. Until recently, I'd managed to flood him with nothing but upbeat news, when every day had been a struggle to keep the boys and I afloat; when instinct told me that, though never expressed directly, Davy and Dan harbored a resentment that their father wasn't there for them:

And Danny's just waiting for you to get back so you can kill me and throw me in the river. David's going to help him too. Says Dan tonight, "I'm awful mad at you. You're the best Mommy in all the worlds, and in the world on top of all the worlds there are, but I'm mad at you just the same because you won't get the roller skates. When Poppy comes home, I'm going to tell him to get a new Mommy."

Now what in the name of the good God Pan can you do about such things? Here I am writing to you by the light of a store candle because the lights have been turned out these three days (non-payment of bill, in small voice), and your sons want to wring my neck. I can always have a good laugh about it.

Dan's back in school. Mama has to keep his shoes shined, his nails clean, his clothes proper these days. He seems very happy to be back. Nice kid, that boy.

Tonight the street is buzzing. War is in the air. Read the piss-pot's speech (Hitler's) in this morning's paper, polished my weapons anew, and will sleep with them under my pillow.

Signing off tonight. As long as open battle has not come to State Street, I'll keep on letting my kids believe that life, while perhaps not always rosy, has to be lived, and can even be enjoyed at rare moments. God damn it!

It wasn't long until I heard that, with Franco's forces on the verge of seizing the entire country, the International Brigades were withdrawn, and Alvah, along with the remaining Americans, were due to sail from Cherbourg for New York in December 1938. Realizing he might be home by Christmas, I felt an enormous relief for us all. And though of small importance compared to what it would mean to David and Dan to have their father back, was the knowledge that the huge pile of news clippings, magazine articles, and other material about the war I'd managed to compile would be there for him in anticipation of the book about his experiences he'd told me he hoped to write. "If I come through this thing in one piece."

I selected another letter I had written during the biting Brooklyn winter of 1938 while Alvah was still in Spain. I'd told him about the boys and I walking on Atlantic Avenue in the early dark, their happy, eager faces peering into lighted windows, the security they felt. Wasn't their mother walking with them? Didn't she get them clothes and food and sometimes toys, and tuck them warm in their beds?

Like Alvah, we too had survived.

I started to read one more, but the bus was only fifteen minutes from Birchfield Center, and the letter dealt with a Pennsylvania memory from that year or so, and I hadn't time, or perhaps the emotional strength, to deal with it right then. *Maybe when I've got a few quiet hours in Woodstock,* I told myself, hoping it would turn out to be a place with the restful calm Dr. Thomas suggested I'd find there.

I laid the file aside, then lay back and closed my eyes. Images floated past: people and places I'd known, experiences from childhood in Michigan, to the uncertain years with Matt, and on to Forman, my struggles in New York with poetry and paint, the poverty of Vermont, and then the divorce while Alvah was in Spain.

"Let it go," I whispered. *Except for the boys, that's all yesterday. What's done is done. You've survived the decades, weathered so many storms and made your peace.*

Or have you?

I shook my head. There was still Pennsylvania to deal with, 1941, the year with my third husband, Harold. But gradually the past was beginning to make sense. Though I was still fitting the puzzle pieces together, many didn't quite seem to connect just right. *Perhaps,* I thought, *if I keep working at it, they'll fall into place. And don't forget: right now, it's the boys, always the boys. Dear David, dear Dan.* I'd booked a room and would take a cab ride to Musgrove School to visit them early the next morning.

"Birchfield Center," the driver called out.

I opened my eyes.

Yes, things will fall into place; I'll make them!

And give yourself a little credit, please, Mary; though you've been through rough times, been in and out of depression and nearly ended it all, you're still here. You've gone through so much, you and the boys, but you're emerging from the morning mist and beginning to discern a clearer road ahead.

As the bus rolled to a stop, I retrieved my valise, stood, and smiled. *What's been my greatest joy?* I asked myself, moving toward the exit; *the one thing giving me the most satisfaction through all these mixed up and too often confusing decades?* The answer was immediate: children. Being with children. Seeing them flourish, seeing them take chances, watching them grow strong and brave, watching them learn to cooperate. And not just Dan and David. *Maybe there's a wider role for me to play in that,* I thought. *I've done so in the past—at least a little; in Manchester, the playgroup in Danbury. Perhaps this is something to hang onto for the future. I'll have to think more on that.*

The sky had clouded over. Rain pelted the ground as I stepped from the bus. *Children. My children. They're my agenda for the weekend... only them, my boys, David and Dan,* I thought again as I quickly unfurled my umbrella.

36.

"No, Henry isn't a Nazi!" I growled. "Don't you remember Mom talking about that on her last visit? How come you think he is?"

"The guys told me it's true."

"You trust what Arbuckle and his creepy friends say more than Mom? Dumb jerks, all of 'em!"

As we sat on a bench in the entry hall awaiting Mom's arrival, George the maintenance man was busily sweeping a nearby stairwell.

"Henry's a German, that's all," I went on. "I asked him about it. Doesn't mean he's a Nazi, though. And what about this zombie stuff Arbuckle and his friends keep talking about? You know, trying to get everyone to go into the cave and all."

"Some of the guys already went in, and—"

"And what? How many of 'em got the five dollars Arbuckle said he'd pay if they stayed there for ten minutes?"

"I don't know."

"There's no such thing as zombies."

"There is too! I went in there and saw 'em!"

"And they got a dollar from you to go in, right? How stupid."

"I didn't pay any money, and—"

"Bet they didn't give you five dollars neither."

Bolting to his feet Davy shouted, "They didn't need to, they said I could do it for free, 'cause I was the first one to try it out. But you better not go in; they'll get you. The zombies. So you're the one that's stupid! They were all in rags and with white faces, dead guys, groanin' like monsters and stuff, they—"

"Whatever it was, I'll bet you peed your pants."

"I didn't neither! I wasn't scared!"

"Hold on a minute, boys," said a voice. We looked up. George stood above us, arms folded across his chest. "Now, what's all this talk about zombies?"

"I saw 'em, I did!" Davy insisted.

"There's no such thing," I protested. "Is there, George?"

George scratched his head, considering. "Can't say as I've ever seen one—"

"There are too!" snapped Davy, his jaw set, his eyes narrowing. "You go in there, and they'll tear you to pieces. I saw 'em!" With that, he turned and ran down the hall and onto the front porch, slamming the screen door.

George shook his head, lowered himself to the bench, then took a cigar from a vest pocket and said, "Looks like we got your kid brother kinda upset."

"He gets that way, but he'll be all right in a while. I can't figure how come he got so mad this time though."

George nodded, lit his cigar, then asked, "You think maybe he's afraid for you?"

I shrugged. "Dunno, but he doesn't need to be. Even though we heard them talking about bouncing me around on a railroad tie."

"They said that, did they?" George looked off thoughtfully.

We sat silently for a while until I asked, "Do you think there really are zombies?"

"Young Davy seems t' think he saw 'em."

I avoided a reply.

"You're not sure about if there is or there ain't, huh?"

George eyed me for a moment, then offered, "You don't suppose someone coulda snuck in the storeroom one night where there's costumes and old clothes and such that are kept for plays them older boys put on come winter time? Maybe found some big old speaker box, microphone, and electric wires and stuff too?"

He seemed about to say more when the *beep beep* of a horn sounded.

George looked up. "Must be your mama, son," he said, "That's ol' Ted Wilkerson's taxi, only horn I know 'round here what sounds like a sick goose."

I jumped up and raced for the door. By the time I'd bounded down the porch steps, Davy was already at Mom's side, demanding to know when we'd be going home.

"Just a minute, dear," Mom said. "Let me pay the cabbie. Then I want to hear about everything you've been doing, and—"

"We got zombies here, Mom!" cried David.

"Uh . . . well . . ." I cut in.

As the taxi drove off, Mom gathered us both to her, looked from Davy to me, and asked, "Now, what's this about zombies?"

"Danny doesn't believe I saw 'em. They was in the cave."

"Zombies don't exist!" I chimed in. "I know they don't."

"You better not go in there," warned David. "You'll find out!"

Back and forth we went, me accusing Davy of falling for lies by the "big guys," and he accusing me of not trusting him.

"They were there!" Davy insisted. "Two of 'em! Dead, and with their skin hanging off."

◆◆◆◆◆

Clearly, my boys were upset. All at once the knot of guilt I'd been feeling about leaving them in this place, a school I'd had a queasy feeling about from the moment Laura told me she'd enrolled them, began tightening. Unsure how to handle the heat of their argument, I suggested, "All right, all right, let's both calm down, okay?"

As David turned aside, arms at his side with fists clenched, I asked, "Now, you say you went into a cave and saw a couple of dead men who were alive, is that it?"

"Yeah, zombies."

Turning to Dan, I asked, "And you claim there are no zombies, right?"

He nodded.

"Well, how do you know if you didn't go into this cave?"

"I just know."

They're waiting for me to take sides, I decided. I had to say something. "Well, how's about we just spend the day being together?" I finally suggested. "For two days, actually. I've got the hotel room until Monday morning."

"Yeah, but—" Dan began.

"We'll talk about it later . . . and you know what? I passed a theater in the taxi just now, where there's a double feature playing. *The Jungle Book* and *Tarzan's New York Adventure.* What say we go have lunch then take in the show?"

"Okay," said David, relaxing a bit, "but the zombies are—"

"Let's let the dead rest for a while, sweetie. Okay?"

He stuffed his hands into his pockets.

"Can Henry go with us?" asked Dan. "He's back from vacation."

"He might be a Nazi," piped up Davy.

"He's not!" replied Dan.

"The guys said he is. They told me—"

"Hold on," I cut in, "Hold on. Let's not argue about it right now. But Davy, do you really think your brother would ask a friend to spend the day with us if he was a Nazi?"

Davy shrugged.

"Well?" I asked, "Do you?"

"S'pose not," he mumbled.

"Okay, then let's go see if it's okay with Mrs. Musgrove for Henry to come. And you know, I can't think of anything more fun than spending the afternoon with three such handsome young gentlemen."

Davy betrayed a grin. Dan groaned. When I tousled his hair, he griped, "Cut it out, Mom!"

As we went inside to fetch Henry, I noticed George standing quietly by the porch. Obviously, he'd been taking in our heated exchange, for he gave me a welcoming smile and a knowing nod.

37.

Mrs. Musgrove must have spotted us coming in, as she suddenly appeared in the hallway and exclaimed, "How lovely to see you, Mrs. Burnett. I do so appreciate it when folks arrive on time."

I smiled and offered a polite "Thank you."

"Lunch is about to be served," she continued. "You will join us, won't you?"

Feeling a refusal would seem impolite, I replied, "Why certainly. How kind of you." But noting David and Dan's crestfallen reaction I whispered, "Right after lunch, we'll head right off to the film. I promise."

While the boys reluctantly took their regularly assigned places in the mess hall, I joined Mrs. Musgrove at the staff table in an adjoining alcove. As she held forth in a flat monotone about how trying it was to manage forty-five rambunctious boys, how tedious she found it to see they all showed up for meals with combed hair and clean fingernails, and having to remind them to brush their teeth and say their prayers before bed, I offered sympathetic nods, and tossed in an occasional, "Oh, certainly, I do understand."

Little wonder it felt like I was back home in Michigan, being bombarded with the anxious tribulations of my self-pitying mother.

From where I sat, Dan was out of sight. But I could see Davy picking at his food and ignoring his boisterous tablemates. Catching my occasional smile seemed to cheer him, though it was clear he was impatient for lunch to be over. And soon it was.

Along with Dan's roommate Henry Smith, who Mrs. M (as I'd begun to think of her) had agreed to let accompany us, "As long as he's back by dinner," one-thirty found the boys and me scurrying along the street leading to Birchfield's small cinema. We arrived just as a newsreel with the latest war reports concluded, so I hung back in the lobby and asked the boys to save a seat, while a pimply-faced usher guided them to their places. Minutes later, jumbo bags of popcorn in hand, I joined them, and we all settled in for *Tarzan's New York Adventure*. As the opening credits finished, a plane carrying a crew looking to trap tigers for a circus landed in Tarzan's jungle.

While the boys became engrossed, my thoughts wandered from the film to their argument about zombies. Where had all that come from? Zombies didn't exist, said Dan. But Davy claimed to have seen them. He'd taken the older boys' dare and gone into a cave and seen . . . what? Something certainly. I wasn't sure what was going on, but knew I'd have to try to find out, because their agitation felt real. At least Dan's was. But David's outraged response seemed way out of proportion. Why so? Whatever it was, I resolved to get them out of the school as soon as I could.

To reach that point, however, I felt a need to further explore the origin of my own fears. Not of zombies, of course, but (as I'd later write about it) the part of me that's so volatile but so unformed; so certain yet so confused; so kind and so stupid; so bold and yet so fearful; so certain yet so unsure—sort of joy mixed with fear. *What crazy contradictions! Something like the boys sitting here, lost in these flickering images yet likely to see their anxieties come roaring back when whatever it is that brought them on intrudes again; a common human condition, I suppose.*

Then my thoughts turned back to the previous night. I'd lain awake after dinner, disturbed, as the downpour from a violent electrical storm beat a relentless tattoo on the hotel roof. *How is that different, my fear, my uncertainty about the unpredictable elements of a storm?* I thought back on several incidents: the story I'd told the boys at Waubeeka when, so frightened, they'd crawled into my bed; my grandmother's recollection of the raging gullywashers she'd known as a girl in the middle west, of lying awake after her tales and wondering if one like that would come and wash me away; of the one Harry, Forman, and I had driven though while touring New England. I recalled the lightning flashes during last night's storm, the loud thunderclap as the streetlight along with lights in the hotel's hallway went out. And how, determined not to revisit a wilderness of past fears, I'd reassured myself that the storm would soon abate.

Haven't I gone to sleep with elevated trains rattling practically across the roof of my tiny room in New York? Haven't I slept through neighboring tenants' raging arguments, survived the wailing of an infant, sick somewhere in a nearby apartment, and somehow ignored the challenging barks of neighborhood dogs, set off by one single jittery pup?

No need to fear, I now told myself as I sat in the theater with my boys and their friend. The lights will come on again. And even if they don't, morning will come; it always does.

A gasp from the boys interrupted my introspection. Glancing at them then at the screen, it seemed Tarzan and Jane had died in a fire, while a band of kidnappers, having taken their child, were racing for a getaway plane with a band of spear-hurling natives in hot pursuit. In moments, a raucous cheer went up: Cheetah the chimp had awakened Tarzan and Jane before the fire took hold. Much relieved, the boys went back to stuffing themselves with popcorn. When Davy held his bag up toward me, I gratefully took a small handful.

Thinking back on the talk of zombies, a similar fear came to mind. It was 1918, and I'd taken off a year from college to teach and rented a room in which, I'd been told, two of the family's children had died during the influenza pandemic of that year. The memory haunted me. I can picture it still:

> The dishes are done, the sad couple and their sad little boy who has been spared all take off for bed at dusk, and I go to my room to read or sew, to sleep then face another day. But there is only fear for what seems to go on for hours, and the paralysis, the need to have something or somebody to hang on to. But again, somehow, there is not daring to scream out.
>
> I knew that people just didn't do that. You had to fight those kinds of internal battles yourself. It made me feel crazy to not be able to run out of the room and down the hall and across it to the stairway and rip the door off its hinges and holler, "Help!" The odor of carnations still filled the house, and the children's mother still

wore black and tried to smile, and her big-jawed, broad, beef-backed husband was still silent too.

What did I know of grief? I asked myself. *And what was the fear? What was I afraid of? Waking up in a room where the two children had died? Of looking toward the end of my bed and seeing them standing there, white, pale, like transparent ghosts?*

No, there were no ghosts. And certainly no zombies; I'd never even heard the term back then. It can only have been the fear that I'd fail, that I was a piss-poor teacher and incapable of doing the job I'd been hired for. Maybe because I wasn't so far removed from childhood myself. I loved playing games with the boys and girls and delighted in Tag, Keep Away, or Lay-Lo; however, when it came to balancing that with the need for the discipline necessary to keep their noses in their schoolbooks, I was an utter incompetent.

Probing more deeply, I realized that with three years of college behind me, and fully aware of what I was supposed to be doing, I should have known what was expected. But having never taught before, I'd somehow let fear of the unknown creep into my then nineteen-year-old consciousness.

How different, then, can it be for Davy with his zombies? Or for Dan? It all boils down to the same thing, I decided: *fear of the unknown, fear of failure.*

The moment the film let out, all three boys began play-acting; mixing scenes from *The Jungle Book* with the Tarzan film and swapping remembered lines. David and Henry took turns as Mowgli or Tarzan. Dan was quickly into a Cheetah imitation, bending over with his arms hanging down, hands almost scraping the sidewalk chimpanzee-style, or waving them wildly in the air as he let go with a string of pant-hoots—much to my amusement and that of other exiting patrons.

As "Mowgli" charged up the street after "Cheetah," Danny became Shere Kahn, the tiger; and while Henry transformed into Kaa the python, I spotted Birchfield's single taxi parked nearby and arranged for Ted Wilkerson, the rotund driver, to take us out to a nearby state park my hotel's proprietor had mentioned.

Soon after we got there, the boys trudged up the park's steep hill to where a tower of rough-hewn stones immediately became a fortress, and they were suddenly medieval knights defending against the onslaught of an invading army. By then, exhaustion had set in. Well, almost. There was still time to rent a rowboat, in which they splashed around for an hour much as Danny and David did at Lake Waubeeka.

"Are you okay?" I yelled as the boat tipped over.

"Uh-huh," Davy called back. "It's warm; we'll dry off quick."

There you go again, I told myself as the old fears began to surface. *Stop that now! They know how to swim, the lake is calm, and there are dozens of people nearby. Anyhow, kids need to be trusted, how else do they learn?* With that, I felt able to command the ugly toad of anxiety that surfaced now and again to crawl back into its black hole.

"Are you still gonna be here for the baseball game tomorrow afternoon?" Davy asked hopefully as we set off back to the school.

Baseball? On a Sunday? This was news to me, considering that the Musgroves had more than once mentioned how crucial it was for them to "keep the Lord's day."

"Sure," I answered, "But I thought you had church on Sunday."

"We don't have to go if we don't want to," Dan replied. "Just to Bible class."

"I think Mr. Musgrove cares more about baseball than the Bible," added Henry. "But please don't tell him I said so."

"Of course not," I replied with a smile.

"They choose up sides, and the big guys decide who gets to be on each team," said Dan. "Arbuckle always chooses Davy, so we won't be on the same one."

"Arbuckle is a crumb," piped up Henry.

I turned to Davy and asked, "Is he really such a crumb?"

He answered with a shrug.

"Davy's kinda their mascot," chided Dan.

"Hey, cut it out!" shouted Davy.

This was something else I wouldn't find out from Davy until months later: he'd figured that if he told me what Arbuckle might have in store for Danny—the whole gang riding him around on an old wooden railroad tie—that would only worry me. So he'd decided to say as little as possible and not mention the zombie cave again.

Though at the time I still couldn't fathom the apparent animosity between my sons, I decided to let it drop. I knew they'd always rushed to help one another when necessary. Especially David, who, in spite of being two years younger, was developing an increasingly rugged bravado that the more sensitive Dan seemed to lack. Though either boy would defend the other when a threat seemed imminent, I knew that the first to come to his brother's aid would always be David.

"Well," I finally said, "I guess I'll be rooting for both your teams, huh?"

"If I get picked," said Dan.

◆◆◆◆◆

As I sat in the bleachers the next afternoon, it became obvious that Dan would be the last boy chosen. So, catching his eye, I gave a quick thrust of my fist and a broad smile as if to say, "Chin up; you'll do fine."

Sitting in the warm sunshine and waiting for the game to begin, I began to doze off. Sleep had been slow to come the previous night, with my mind a mélange of what still needed to be sorted and put into place in order to assure a secure future for the boys and me. The big nut to crack would be our two years in Pennsylvania, my marriage to Harold and the horrifying events that had become the final straw leading to my near suicide. Once beyond that, I could perhaps begin figuring out what the next steps would be, what kind of job I could find, where to live, and how to scrape by during the months it would surely take to put everything together.

While visiting parents cheered the teams as they took the field for warm-ups, I sat quietly, mulling over the tension between Dan and David. Memories of my brothers, Leo, Verne, and Harry, growing up came into focus. The elder two, striving and ambitious (to my mother's delight), were a contrast to Harry, seen by her as "a strange boy," forever expressed in her inability to understand his "ways." Though Dad too had been a bit puzzled at times, Leo and

Verne, despite their preoccupation with success, always loyally accepted him as merely being "different."

Harry was always my favorite, and years later, when he, like Forman, revealed his homosexuality, sharing this long-hidden secret with me brought us even closer. A plus was that I reveled in his artistic creativity.

Sibling loyalty runs strong in our family, I thought, reminding me too of the unquestioning (albeit mostly financial) support Verne and Leo had given me over the years. *Deep down, I know that Dan and Davy also have their backing. But while here alone together, they may need what support I can give them.*

I turned to look for George. He sat by himself, eyes on the warm-ups. And his reaction to my conversation with the boys earlier had set me thinking. As I stood and climbed the steps toward his row, George spotted me and was immediately on his feet, his cap off and offering a friendly, "Afternoon, Missus." After a bit of small talk and his recognition that Davy and Dan were on opposing teams, I decided to seize the bull by the horns.

"This might seem like a ridiculous question," I asked, "but . . . have you heard any talk around the school about . . . zombies?"

George coughed loudly several times.

"Are you all right?" I asked.

He nodded, then narrowed his eyes before replying, "Well Missus, uh—"

"Because I know about this cave with zombies . . . or whatever it is," I cut in.

At first he seemed reticent, wondering how to reply.

"Well," he finally began, "You know how boys are, what kinda mischief they gets themselves up to.

"Of course."

"Now, can't say for sure, but I did have some talk with your older boy . . ."

"Dan."

"Uh-huh. An' the young'un too. David, ain't it? He had some words 'bout a cave. Told his brother he better not go inside it."

"Did he?" I replied with some surprise.

"Sure did. Said he went in hisself there and saw . . . well . . . sumpthin'."

"Yes, he told me that too."

George seemed to be studying my reaction. He could tell I was worried, and I sensed there was more he wanted to say. Did he suspect that the Arbuckle boy was capable of some kind of mischief? Of a kind that might affect Davy or Dan?

"Tell you what I think, Missus," he continued, apparently reasoning out what he felt he could reveal. "Some of these boys here, 'specially the older ones, they was itchin' t' be let loose back when summer was comin' on an' all. And I s'pose they took out some of that energy by raggin' the younger ones. Kind of a game for them, I guess. Thing is, the little ones they don't have the same kinda ideas t' mind, so they get scared easy. Might frighten them t' death they saw somethin' comin' at 'em, all dressed in a costume or such, and maybe with a lotta scary sounds. 'Specially in a cave—'cause there is a sorta cavern back there, where the echoes would bounce around. A bit weird, you know."

"Then that's what you think it is?" I asked. "Just some of the older boys dressing up, like a Halloween prank?"

"Couldn't rightly say. I can't be sure. But it's likely the way I'd figure it if I was wantin' t' play tricks on somebody."

I studied the man. He seemed to be avoiding my inquiring gaze. Then he looked at me again. "I did say one thing to your older boy . . . Dan . . . that if he had some worries 'bout anything, he could come talk t' me if he wanted to. I don't like to see my boys afraid of nothin', you understand. 'Specially the littler fellas."

I was about to respond when the cry, "Play ball!" rang out on the field from Abner Musgrove, refereeing the game. Clearly relieved by the interruption, George raised the cigar he'd held until now in a clenched fist, took a deep drag, and said, "Looks like we got us a game, Missus."

"Looks like it. And thank you so much for talking with me about this."

"Oh I didn't say nuthin'," replied George with a smile. "Just some speculations."

I smiled back, then looked out at the field. David's team was at bat, and he waved to me from his place on the Blue Devil's bench. Dan sat on the Falcon's bench, in reserve, one of two who had been picked last. As he looked around, I could see he was smiling. Watching the game, I couldn't help dwelling on what they'd both said. Especially David, who had been so vehement about what he'd seen in the cave, about his brother facing grave danger if he took up the dare by the older boys to go in alone and stay there for ten minutes.

I'd have to think more on this, on Davy's version of events, and on what George had implied about the older boys' bark being worse than their bite. Mainly, I had to be certain my sons were safe between now and the weeks or months later when I could liberate them from the school, when we could be a family again.

But I also knew that both boys, especially Dan, needed to stick up for themselves. Davy, of course, with his feisty demeanor, was already ahead of the game. And they had one another.

38.

The baseball game, the talk around the Monopoly board, and last night's tearful goodbye to the boys were still on my mind as I came out onto the hotel porch, where taxi driver Ted Wilkerson rose from an Adirondack rocker to greet me.

"Had a good visit with your young'uns, did ya?" he asked

"Very fine," I replied, adding a few details before mentioning that I hoped Dan and David would get along all right until they'd be home for good; "By Christmas, as I've promised them."

"'Spect they will," said Ted, pulling thoughtfully on his pipe. "Kids is tough. They endure."

Endurance, I thought. *Maybe that's the key?* And as the cab pulled away, my thoughts once more drifted back to the previous evening spent sitting on the floor of Dan's room as he and Henry and Davy huddled over their Monopoly game, probably the last time in months I'd be with my boys.

As the taxi navigated its way toward Kingston, where I'd catch the train to Woodstock, my conversation with George about the crazy idea of zombies popped up again. Davy, I knew, was keenly observant. Even by six, he'd developed a sharp sense of the real and the unreal, with a logical way of forming ideas and making decisions that often amazed me. I recalled the time he'd been recruited for a minstrel show at school.

"What is it?" he'd asked.

I told him I thought it was a kind of show that made fun of Negro people, "But it's your decision." I'd then added, "You can be in it if you want to."

He quickly decided not to. I was proud he felt that making fun of people because of their color was pretty stupid.

And would older boys in costumes have fooled him into thinking they were anything but that? I didn't think so. Maybe his inflated protestations of having seen the walking dead were a coverup having to do with fear about what might happen to his brother. Keeping Dan away from the "zombie cave," I felt sure David had decided, would protect his brother from some other kind of threat made by the Arbuckle boy and his hangers on. Since I wasn't there to keep them safe, Dan was Davy's one link to any sense of security while they were alone together in a troubling environment.

As the Monopoly game ended and the boys began to count and put away their money, something Dan had said provided the opportunity I'd been hoping for; to talk a little about Harold. "Remember when we lived in Pennsylvania?" he'd asked. "How I used to play Monopoly with Harold? And how I used to beat him every time?"

"Who's Harold?" Henry had asked.

"Our father," David replied.

"No he wasn't," insisted Dan. "Harold was just our stepfather."

"He died," David added. "In the army. He was killed in the war."

None of the boys noticed my eyes beginning to tear.

"He wasn't a very good Monopoly player," Dan went on. "He

had to ask me all the time about the property cards. He couldn't tell about the names, 'cause he couldn't read."

"How come he couldn't read?" asked David. "I can read."

"Well," I answered, "he . . . he really didn't have much of an education, and—"

"Remember how he told us when he saw Hitler?" Davy butted in.

"That's impossible," Henry replied, frowning. "Hitler's in Germany."

"He did too see him!" argued Davy. "And he—"

"He *was* in Germany," added Dan. "Bombing Berlin and stuff, wasn't he, Mom?"

Henry shook his head.

This is tricky; should I rush to my sons' defense? Defend Harold's memory? Two years earlier, unwilling to let on that their kind and caring substitute father had also had a dark side, half-truths had been enough. But right then didn't seem the time to get more deeply into it.

"Well," I began, "he did tell a lot of stories. . . ."

"He had a gas station," said Davy. "He told me."

"And he sold cars too," Dan added. "It was Studebakers."

"I'm really not so sure all those things were exactly the way it was," I added, trying cautiously to judge the boy's reaction.

Davy seemed puzzled. Danny frowned. "Well, if it wasn't true about seeing Hitler and about the Studebakers and all, how come he said so?"

Here was the moment I'd been waiting for. Here was a question that might let me reveal some of Harold's hidden side, but in a way that might provide a bit more understanding. Especially for Davy, if it could cut through his tale of zombies and maybe serve as an analogy in his attempt to protect Dan. "I guess you remember the hard times we were having in Pennsylvania, don't you?" I began.

"I had to walk half a mile through the snow to get to school," said Dan.

Davy was silent.

"My parents told me we had a difficult time in Germany," Henry interjected.

"They most certainly would have, dear," I replied. "The year or two the boys and I had in Pennsylvania was just another kind of difficult. Not better or worse, just different." Answering their questions as best I could, I explained how I'd lost a part-time teaching job, how millions of people were out of work, and how Harold couldn't find anyone to hire him. "I don't think he was a bad person for boasting about the things he probably hadn't actually done."

Dan expression signaled his uncertainty.

"I think he told stories to make us feel better. And maybe he told them to make himself feel better too. Maybe he sort of needed to feel stronger, to tell himself that no matter how hard it was for us, he'd somehow get a job, find work that would support us so we didn't end up in the poor house."

"What's the poor house?" asked Davy.

Clearly, Davy had been paying attention. But did he get what I was trying to say? Would he understand the link between Harold's effort to protect the family and his own effort to protect his brother? After explaining what a poor house was, I added, "Sometimes, when someone is in danger like we were during that time in Pennsylvania, I suppose it's natural for the head of the house to make up stories. And if telling the truth is hard to do, they keep it all inside and think they're protecting everyone."

I'd noticed that Henry was listening intently and wondered if he was thinking how his father protected their little family and brought them out of Germany to safety.

"Do you think that's what Harold did?" asked Dan.

"Maybe so. Maybe he was frightened too."

"Frightened about what?"

"Oh, afraid he wouldn't actually be able to find work, that me and you boys wouldn't have enough to eat, and maybe have to move out of our nice home on the farm. So perhaps he made up those stories about some of the things he'd done, like owning a gas station and selling cars. I think it was probably a way of helping us to feel that something would turn up. That we'd all be okay."

"We'd better finish clearing up," interrupted Henry, sounding a bit anxious. "We're supposed to be in bed with the lights out by nine o'clock."

Did David get what I'd hoped to convey? It was hard to tell. But he seemed to have gone deep inside himself; a look that indicated he'd been listening carefully. While it was impossible to know for sure, something, I told myself, was certainly going on deep in that seven-year-old brain.

◆◆◆◆◆

As Ted let me off at the Kingston station, his words came back to me: "Kids is tough. They endure."

His words struck a hopeful chord. I knew there were resources my boys could count on. For Danny at least, since George had already told him he was always around to talk with if a problem came up. And after our goodbyes, I'd asked Davy if he understood about Harold, and how his tall tales were probably designed to help the family feel safe.

"I guess so," he'd replied. "But still, lying isn't no good, is it?"

"No, it isn't *any* good," I'd replied. "And I'm afraid that lies usually come back to bite you."

Davy had looked so serious as I left that I could only hope what I'd tried to get across had sunk in. If not, well, for the moment I'd done what I could . . . though mixed feelings of guilt and frustration at my inability to do more for them continued to stick like glue. Still, I had to rely on Ted's final words.

How else do children learn except by confronting their fears? And how else do I move ahead except by doing the same?

◆◆◆◆◆

Autumn's first subtle breath had begun tinting the beeches, oaks, and birches as my bus rolled west through Connecticut's Mohawk and Housatonic forests. Patches of witch hazel and mountain laurel spread among the trees. Hobblebush flourished beside streams, along with maple-leaved viburnum with its blue-black berries, a shrub I recalled from walks with my dad in the Michigan woods.

After last night's long talk, the taxi ride to Kingston, then an hour-long wait for the bus to Woodstock, I was a bit worn out, so I had been looking forward to climbing aboard and taking a nap. But curiosity got the better of me. Retrieving a folder from my valise, I first took a quick peek. An envelope among the papers stuck out. On it I'd noted, "Photos, PA." On opening it, I smiled; it held several snapshots I'd forgotten about. Two pictured the boys and me on the flagstone porch of the old Pennsylvania farmhouse I'd rented. Another caught us standing amid a pile of boxes stacked near the front door. A fourth showed Dan manipulating an iron pump handle that drew water from a well in front of the house. On the back of that photo, in brother Harry's hand, were the words, "I took my sis and children to the country to start life anoooo! May 1939." One of two slightly larger photos taken at a later date found me sitting on the porch with the boys, Dan with a cap pistol. In the other, Harry sat between the boys, his arms around both. All three wore striped t-shirts, though Harry's was but partially visible beneath his broad-lapelled suit jacket. In both photos, the boys were forcing grim, resigned smiles as if to say, "How come we have to sit for these stupid pictures?" Both also needed haircuts.

There were other photos, including a shot of Harold and me standing in front of the ready-to-fall-down barn that sat across from the house. Harold wore a necktie, his shirt collar unbuttoned at the top. I'd forgotten about the picture, but since he never wore a tie, it must have been taken on our wedding day. As for me, hair up in a bun behind a bandana, even with a thin smile I still looked like some Kansas farmwife; the same somber lack of concern for style or appearance I'd affected in Brooklyn before and right on up to Payne Whitney. I reminded myself to stick it into another envelope and not let myself look like that again.

Bucks County, Pennsylvania, 1940

So much to chew over about Pennsylvania: what chain of events had brought me there with the boys? Why the retreat to the country? There were letters to read, but so many that instead of sifting through them plus exploring a small bundle of diary pages that had escaped the flames in Danbury, I lay back against the seat and, as I started to doze, let my thoughts blend into a montage of images:

More of Alvah's letters while in Spain; a reply from friends Burt and Marion in Pennsylvania in answer to my having asked them to be on the lookout for a peaceful country place where the boys and I might relocate; Alvah's return home, our attempt to renew the relationship with a couple nights in bed (while enjoying the closeness, we both agreed it was a lost cause); a lovely Christmas at the swanky Manhattan apartment of Alvah's doctor brother, Everett, and the lovely photos taken there, one of Danny rolling a big toy truck he'd been given underneath a coffee table he'd decided was a tunnel. Spending weeks working with Alvah as he relived the trauma of Spain, and plumbed his memory to craft *Men in Battle*, his memoir of the war (unaccepted by any publisher until Ernest Hemingway stepped in and recommended it to Scribners). Wonder of wonders, I received a modest sum from Alvah's advance. I wrote a poem to celebrate:

Paid in full! This month's light bill,
Yes, and telephone.
I owe the grocer nothing,
And the milkman only for today.
And when I see how often
Mothers do neglect their young,

From too much of self-seeking,
I think my job is not too badly done.
It might be better, truly, that I know,
But it is good, and I can sleep well on it.

Serendipitously, that same week another letter arrived from Burt and Marion in Pennsylvania. A nearby farm couple owned a hundred-year-old stone house they'd been renting out to "summer people," but with the Depression discouraging short-term tenants, they'd decided to look for a steady occupant; fifteen dollars a month. Would I be interested? I phoned immediately and learned the owners were in no hurry. Still, anxious to get out of the city, I asked Burt to tell them we could be ready to move in two weeks.

◆◆◆◆◆

"Woodstock!" called the driver. "Next stop is Woodstock." As I gathered my belongings, my thoughts turned to David and Dan, and I promised myself I'd write them in the next day or two, maybe even phone.

And there was one more crucial promise to myself I'd have to keep: to recapture and weave together a deeper and more personal understanding of the year and a half on the Pennsylvania farm and all that had happened there. *How to begin? With writing, perhaps? A story about Harold?*

Don't dwell on it, I decided. *Time enough over the next couple weeks. For now, turn off the old brain and get ready to enjoy what happens next.*

39.

Woodstock morning

September 1942

Old faces long ago;
New faces come and go;
Ice is ice
And snow is snow.
Time and the river
Just flow and flow.
Wherefore art thou, Romeo?

Interesante! Just awake, and saw myself with the red leather notebook of 1928-29. The all-night struggles to rub my fingers through paint until the sun should come through. And the light (the magic answer?) that I sought would shine with sudden brightness to show me to myself and lead the way. What way? What a way.

Not a time to think about a new Romeo. Let them rest for now, those old faces: Charlie Britton, my first date; Forman, dear Forman; poor Matthew, whose dreams I crushed; Bill and then Alvah; Lee, the test pilot . . . and Harold; my tired brain will shortly be filled with you, my friend.

The partially raised shade at my second-floor window revealed the foliage of a huge oak, an occasional leaf blowing away, branches crisscrossing up, down, around and around against an etched grey sky. And as I looked and studied from my bed, two little birds flew into the drawing, hopped about, then flew away. This scene recalled the frosted windows of childhood, where a fairyland of fern-like lace fascinated me on a cold bitter morning—while inside, the kettle steamed on the range, and I anticipated the business of Mother making breakfast before I'd leave for school.

New faces come and go,
Old faces long ago . . .

New faces, that's the thing. When I checked in, Mrs. Birdwhistle had only a vague recollection of our puppet troupe having stopped here. *Well, can't blame her, it's been fourteen years. New faces . . . guess I need to get out and explore the town.*

Laughter and horseplay echoed down the hall as I closed the door and headed for the stairs. *There must be children about. Some who can make an impersonal corridor come to life with the joy of just being alive.*

I awoke late. Other guests had already finished breakfast, but since coffee and toast were my usual fare, I'd declined my hostess's smiling offer to "scramble up a big mess o' eggs . . . or poached or fried if you'd rather. We've got our own layers, you know, so we don't have to bother about the war ration'n'."

After small talk about the changing weather, I asked if there was a shop in town selling art supplies.

"Darn tootin'. Have to, what with all the painters and such who come by. It's on Tinker Street, right by the Green. Called the Little Art Shop. You can't miss it. Fixin' to do some paintin', are you?"

"Perhaps a little drawing," I told her.

"Well, there's plenty to draw around here, that's for sure," she replied.

Stepping onto the porch of the rooming house I'd be at for the next two weeks, I paused to take in the scene. *What a world of traveling one does in twenty-four hours,* I thought; *with the boys at Musgrove School, back to my childhood memories and on to Forman, Alvah and the rest of the Romeos, and now to this creative waystation.*

Images of yesterday mingled with those of the here and now: across the street, a bent old man raking leaves; small black storm clouds; patches of sun through the trees, white puffs then all at once a light wind. As the leaves scattered, the man sighed and started to rake them again. Behind me, a door opened, and a young girl in a maroon stocking cap emerged, a poodle leading the way. They bounded down the steps and quickly disappeared; a morning mosaic, a sketchable feast for the eyes.

Either Woodstock is always like this, or I'm emerging from a long tunnel into a brighter, more alive, more exciting time.

Strolling past Tinker Street's wood frame houses alongside the village green, I discovered the Nook, a small café with an inviting, rustic feel. I immediately sensed it would become my habitual choice for afternoon coffee and a cigarette.

The Little Art Shop was an equal delight. Well stocked with supplies, there were also a few chairs in one corner where patrons could sit and examine the shop's selection of books on painting and drawing. On a bulletin board, notices for local exhibits and events were tacked, along with a large card featuring an abstract design of Canada geese flying through a snowstorm. The card advertised a twice-weekly art workshop, and along with a phone number was the instruction to call Adelaide.

After paying for a sketchbook and colored pencils, I asked the elderly clerk, "That workshop listed on your bulletin board . . . is it for professionals or for anyone? I'm really just a beginner, you see, and—"

"Best you talk t' Adelaide," the clerk interrupted with a smile. Then, indicating a heavy-set woman wearing baggy slacks and wearing her hair short, he added, "She's just over there, lookin' at the canvases."

"Join us, why don't you?" replied Adelaide when I asked her. The workshops, she explained, were loosely structured, and along with other students, I could follow the assignments, or just do what I felt like. Sessions were three hours, each one ending with a discussion of the day's work, and "the fee is fair, I think. Just a dollar. Artists don't have much money."

What a stroke of luck! My mind buzzed with the prospect of a creative way to delve more deeply into the past by using the writing and drawing skills I'd always enjoyed. No longer feeling quite so daunted about exploring the year and a half the boys and I had spent in Pennsylvania, the marriage to Harold, and all that followed, I hurried back to my room, laid out the new supplies on my table, and began to plan.

Best if I start with images. Notes, sketches . . . whatever crazy stuff my mind dredges up. Don't try to make sense of them right off the bat, just let 'em flow. Free associate. Make a start. . . . Jot down the memories.

- What were their names? My landlords . . . right: Gunderson. Dortha and Johan Gunderson. The old man would joke with the boys when they'd run down to the barn to watch him hitching one of his horses to the plow. Or milking a cow, he'd squeeze a teat, then roar with laughter as a stream of warm milk squirted into their faces.
- That first summer, I boarded three children of New York friends. Helped a bit to meet the bills. Had a substitute-teaching job in Doylestown for several weeks.
- David and Dan riding on the hay baler with Harold, and on the harrow before winter wheat was planted.
- Harold and the boys hitchhiking into town to see Charlie Chaplin in *The Gold Rush*. They came back all excited. "He cooked his old shoe and ate it!" said Dan. "Warn't that sump'n!" exclaimed Harold.

I was on a roll.

- My sketch of a man on a bicycle recalled Harold calling out, "I used t' be a trick clown inna circus one time . . ." as he'd climbed onto his battered Sears Elgin and circled in front of the old barn—before tumbling to the ground as he tried to ride while standing on the seat:

Up from New York in August, Alvah and his new wife, Helen Clare, a copy editor for *McCall's* magazine. They brought along a brand-new Schwinn for Dan's eighth birthday. I'd invited Harold for dinner; he seemed resentful, probably because he couldn't afford such a gift. When Alvah talked about having completed his first solo to earn his private pilot's license, Harold let on that he'd owned a garage once and an auto agency. "And I been a flyer f'r a time myself, might get called up, now we're fightin' them Nazis." When Alvah questioned him about what kind of planes he flew, Harold didn't "rightly rec'lect." *Bucking himself up,* I thought; I could tell from Alvah's sarcastic expression that he regarded Harold as a fool.

- Another memory: Harold sitting on the overstuffed living room sofa. He plays a harmonica as David snuggles next to him, Dan on the opposite side, both listening.

The day the boys and I came home from lunch at Burt and Marion's, Harold was behind the wheel of the Gunderson's big hay truck, grinning. "Why don'cha go on in'a barn," he said to Dan and David. "I fixed up a little surprise." I followed them inside. Harold had stacked the bales in such a way that a maze of tunnels ran through the hay, creating a "secret fort" for the boys to play in.

I thought back on what he told them, his whopper about having seen Hitler. ("Seen Mussolini too," he said.) What stories he had to tell; what a yarn spinner.

Earlier that fall, Harold was let go by the Gundersons. I let him fix up a place to sleep in what had been a small tack room in the barn.

He lined it with tarpaper, decorated it with photos cut from magazines, and told me it was "right cozy." At my insistence, he began taking meals with the boys and me.

His unlettered backcountry speech and poverty of intellectual conversation didn't bother me; the direct and simple way he worked things out and quickly pegged people as honest or phonies actually seemed refreshing in contrast to Alvah. Still, there was one issue I needed to deal with: over breakfast one morning, Harold pointed to a *LIFE* magazine photo of Japanese emperor Hirohito on the cover.

"What's the story about?" I asked.

He flipped through pages. A long silence followed.

Looking up from buttering my toast, I asked, "Harold?"

A long pause, then he admitted, "I can't read, Ma."

"Ma?" Not surprising. Country husbands often referred to their wives that way. I answered his admission with a smile and said, "Well, I'll just have to teach you."

After breakfast, we sat at the kitchen table and drew up a list of places he might look for work. Before he set out for the day, I made a sandwich for his lunch and gave him a dime or so to buy a soft drink. Looking for work, he'd walk or hitch rides for fifty miles in every direction, visit farms, shops, or garages, any place that might take him on.

Evenings or weekends, he built furniture from scrap wood, spent hours puttering in the barn, and had even helped me nurse the boys through chicken pox. Sometimes he'd disappear for days, then suddenly show up again and hand over a few dollars. "I sweated m'self t' get this. Twenty-five cents a hour it was, fillin' potholes on the roads."

There was the day I picked up the party line phone before realizing it was Dortha Gunderson's ring, not ours. Just about to hang up, I heard a voice I didn't recognize:

"Hear tell your renter woman's took up with Harold Frisbie. Word is, he's moved in!"

"Don't know nothin' about it," Dortha replied.

"No tellin' what some women will get up to," said the other voice.

"I mind my own business," huffed Dortha.

Good old Dortha, I thought as I gently replaced the receiver.

One day, rent two months overdue, I'd walked down the road to pay her ten dollars from a small sum Alvah had sent. Stopping at the postbox on the way back, I found a letter from an attorney threatening legal action if several small bills weren't promptly paid. I lay the letter on the kitchen table and went upstairs briefly, returning to find Harold looking concerned as he tried to read it.

"Were you able to make it out?" I asked.

"Some," he replied. He headed for the door and announced, "I gotta go feed the chickens."

"That damn gun!" I exclaimed. *Wish I'd known what he had in mind right after reading the attorney's letter.*

I had uttered those same words one day at Payne Whitney while crafting.

Other patients around Mrs. Jackson's crafts table had looked up. "Sorry," I muttered. "Just thinking . . ." At Mrs. Jackson's suggestion, we'd all closed our eyes and drawn something from memory. Mine was a sketch resembling a pistol. Looking back on the drawing years later, I saw that I'd written below it: *"Souvenir." Pistol Alvah took off a dead fascist officer while in Spain, which Harold borrowed so he could shoot porcupines getting under the house.*

Pausing to gather my thoughts, I realized how valuable Adelaide's workshop had been in helping me delve into the past—the imaginative exercises she suggested, a fresh way of looking at things. Still, even with several sessions under my belt, I felt unable to sort out the problem rattling around in my head: the months with Harold.

As I came back to the present, my tears welled up. *How did it begin?* I wondered. *What attracted me to him? We were so different, so little in common. Was I really that desperate? That lonely? Have to reason it through.* Now wasn't the moment to sift through the past, but that evening in Woodstock my memory returned to our first weeks in Pennsylvania. Even before Dortha told me she'd hired a man to do odd jobs, I'd seen Harold working in the fields; as he'd stripped to the waist, I couldn't help noticing how lean and muscular he was.

"He could do that shinglin'," said Dortha. "I'll send him along soon as he finishes with the plowin'."

Two days later, Harold drove up in the Gundersons' old flatbed, toting several bundles of shingles. While he unloaded and prepared to get to work, I stopped hanging laundry to listen as he beguiled David and Dan with a story about a polliwog that had no tail. From then on, the boys took to following him around like puppies whenever he came by to repair a loose door hinge, or right the outhouse that had blown off its foundation, or nail down the corrugated tin roof the summer's eastern seaboard hurricane had nearly ripped off the main house.

One afternoon, I invited him in for coffee. We talked for an hour.

He knew I'd been a teacher and asked, "Why'd you come t' live way out here t' hell 'n gone, an' don't you miss your folks in the city?" Before I could answer, he suggested that it wasn't a good idea for a woman to live alone in the country, "'Specially she's got young'uns."

"Kind of you to say that, Harold," I replied, "but you know, I'd become so used to living alone in New York that I actually feel much safer way out here in the country."

"Well, sure ain't much t' be skeered about here in'a sticks," he replied with a chuckle. "'Specially with me hangin' around."

Accepting his country speech and clear lack of education, his tales of having been a flyer who had "cracked up a plane agin' a hill in'a fog," run an auto agency and other seemingly implausible occupations—I have to admit it wasn't only the boys who were drawn in, but me as well. Though I did probe a bit:

"Where did you go to school?" I asked.

He looked at the floor and admitted, "I on'y got t' the third grade, Missus."

When I told him I hadn't meant to embarrass him, he shook off my reply, stood up, and said, "Got chores t' get to, Missus."

After an abrupt goodbye, he stepped onto the porch, slid the screen door shut, then turned around and, with the sudden grin of a Cheshire cat, added, "You don' know about me, Missus, but if I was a mind to, I could spin you a yarn . . ."

Looking back, I wondered why I hadn't seen the signs. Mainly, I decided, there were aspects of Harold—and of my own history—that allowed me to ignore too much.

My loneliness? Certainly, but there was something else that

attracted me: Harold exuded a robust virility, a manliness I'd rarely experienced with other men. Oh, I'd felt it with Alvah on occasion, in Vermont, when he became frustrated with his writing and went out to chop wood, or set off to tromp four miles or more through the snow for needed supplies; or on returning from a New York trip, buoyant because payment for a book review or short story had rescued us for another few weeks. I felt it with Lee, the flyer Alvah brought home for dinner and with whom a hint of us being together promised a world of adventure I only dreamed about.

Forman gave me something entirely different: the passion that came from a deep sense of companionship based on a constant give and take, with the melding of similar minds and sensitivities.

With Harold, there had come a clear turning point in my willingness to consider a relationship. One morning, I had to catch an early bus to interview for a secretarial job.

Harold had shown up the previous day to arrange to repair our rain gutters.

"Could you be here tomorrow when the boys wake around seven-thirty?" I asked. He had readily agreed. By nine, I was back. The job had been a dead end. "They were looking for a younger woman," I told Harold, who was standing at the stove, his back to me.

"Sorry 'bout that," he said. Then, without turning, he added, "I scrambled you up some coffee 'n eggs."

"Scrambled coffee? Don't think I've ever had that before."

A momentary frown, then he guffawed. "Eggs, I mean. I done scrambled the eggs."

I made an effort to smile and thanked him, but wasn't really up for talking much. He looked at me. I noticed, and looked back. Neither of us said a word. It was as though we were taking stock of one another. I smiled faintly again and said, "Think I'll just sit in the living room for a bit."

"Kids is playin' upstairs. I'll bring the coffee in to ya."

Somehow, this simple act evoked for me an unspoken understanding between us, and it felt comfortable.

It all happened so quickly, this mutual affection. There were so many aspects to it: I was a woman alone, and with a mostly absent father, Dan and David relished the attention Harold paid them. The nurturing instincts I always felt toward those that "polite" society regarded as outcasts or underdogs was also a part of it. As too were my feelings for Harry and Forman as "outsiders," and for my Uncle Milt, who showed up at his mother's funeral in his threadbare but medal-bedecked Civil War uniform. And for my much loved and always compassionate dad, who had invited Milt home to "sit by the fire a spell" and warm himself—while Mother bustled about preparing dinner, her jaw set and her lips clenched in a resentful scowl.

Clearly, I told myself, *I'm my father's daughter.*

I suppose our coming together was finally cemented one evening after dinner, when Harold said to the boys, "Let's wash up the dishes for your ma." As I watched, he put on my apron, tied a towel around Dan's waist, and with David joining in, the three chattered through the dishwashing like a clutch of old women, laughing back and forth, the boys making kid jokes and Harold joining in with his own.

Later, I read them all a story, we tucked the boys in bed, and

Harold, who owned a cheap guitar, strummed and sang as the boys drifted off to sleep:

Oh, a grasshopper sittin'
On a railroad track
Sing'n Polly wolly doodle all the day
A-pickin' his teeth
With a carpet tack
Sing'n Polly wolly doodle all the day. . . .

We returned to the living room. The evening was chilly, and Harold made a fire. We chatted about the boys, with Harold saying how much he cared for them. "It almos' feels like I got me a family here." He went on to describe how cozy he felt.

I'd been warmed by his admission. Drawn in even more.

Then he looked into the fireplace and in his rough country twang. recited a poem, "The Cremation of Sam McGee," about a sourdough from Tennessee seeking gold in the Klondike. Always freezing cold and on his last legs, he'd made his best friend swear that after his death, he'd cremate his remains.

Obliging, the friend did so, and as he opened the oven door to add more wood:

" . . . there sat Sam, looking cool and calm, in the heart of the furnace roar. And he wore a smile you could see a mile, and he said, 'Please close that door. It's fine in here but I greatly fear you'll let in the cold and storm. . . . Since I left Plumtree down in Tennessee, it's the first time I've been warm.'"

I had laughed at what I considered doggerel, but also understood what Harold was trying to say. Thinking perhaps to introduce something more uplifting, I retrieved my copy of Milton's works and read his poem about Samson.

"Oh yeah. Had his eyes put out, didn't he? I feel like that sometimes: blind."

As Harold went on to admit he had a lot of secrets he'd never told anyone about, I offered, "You could tell me."

"I don't aim too," he replied. "Never tell no woman nothin' you want kept quiet!"

We laughed together, and then he said, "I do know one secret, though." He leaned close then and kissed my ear.

Is this it? I'd asked myself. *Do I dare? Do I take a chance?* Heart pounding, I paused before responding . . . then decided to seize the moment.

"That's a lovely secret," I said. "Do you know another?"

"Oh, I do," replied Harold. "I surely do!"

40.

"What's this I hear about you getting married?" demanded Alvah, having driven up from New York early one Sunday morning. "To that farmhand character, I gather?"

"Where the hell did you 'gather' that from?"

"Burt and Marion. They said they were worried, so I thought I'd better—"

"You thought you'd better *what?* Rush right down here and put a kibosh on it? When in God's name are you ever going to stop interfering with my plans? Probing into my life, snooping, wanting to know things. You've done this forever, Alvah, always been a busybody. I even remember coming home once to find you reading my diaries, and—"

"Well, you let me read them."

"Only because you decided to write a novel about my family. And anyhow, you were reading them before you even asked me if you could. Why don't you just let me live my life the way I want to?"

"Calm down, will you? Why get so belligerent?"

Oh, I was belligerent, all right!

There was more. With me close to tears, we sat arguing for half an hour. Alvah hotly denied my assertion that he didn't think Harold was my "type," and couldn't understand why I'd take up with someone without at least a university degree. I told Alvah he'd had his nose stuck in a book so long that he had no idea how to accept people for who they are. "People who aren't just like you, that is."

"Wrong!" he shot back. "It's simply that you've never talked about marrying him. Not even a hint."

"Why should I have? It's none of your business. Spill the beans, Alvah, and admit you're a damn snob. You and I came out of the same class of people: intellectuals, interested in a lot of the same things. Look where it got us."

He seemed to be trying to form a response. Finally, I sighed, rose from the chair, and crossed to the window. In the yard, Harold was playing tag with the boys. "Just because a man doesn't have an education . . ." I began, my voice breaking.

"I don't look down on anyone who hasn't been to college," he finally said, defensively. "Everyone should have an education."

"Damn right," I answered coldly. "But not everyone gets one."

Looking back now, I recognized that I'd probably been more hostile than necessary. But this was an old story, with Alvah frequently mining me for tidbits of information about my life, quizzing me about men I'd been with, where I was, and what I'd been doing at any given moment—even when we weren't together.

I recalled my New Hampshire trip with Sally, and how Alvah had grilled me on my return. And the afternoon in Vermont when I'd felt a need to be alone and spent two hours walking through the woods; then his annoyed diatribe when I came back, his worry and concern—but in an accusatory tone, as though his anxiety was my fault.

Would it have made a difference if he'd told me what his friend

Burt had written to him—that when he'd learned I was going to marry Harold he was sure there would be "tragic consequences"? Alvah only confessed this a year later in what I felt at the time was an "I told you so" manner. And I have to admit that I'd given little forethought to the idea of marrying Harold. My boys seemed quite happy when he'd moved in, my loneliness had been greatly alleviated, and even with Harold unemployed, at least it would be two against the world instead of just me alone.

The day after Alvah's visit, Harold and I married.

I still remember our August wedding as a special day. Special and simple. Harold had traded his old bike to the owner of a gas station for a loan of the man's Dodge sedan, complete with a full tank of gas. I'd come close to tears then, and once again later, when, after handing Harold the plain gold wedding band I'd kept since marrying Alvah, he'd replied, "Don't need it, Ma, I got one here." He'd reached into his pocket and produced a cheap dime store ring. But neither of us had the three dollars to pay the local Methodist minister. "Just pay it when you can," he said kindly. Harold promised he would. Coming down the steps of the minister's white frame house that afternoon, I saw Harold hand David and Dan each a dime and a nickel as he told them, "Call yer ma Missus Frisbie now, ya got that? *Missus Frisbie.*" For a honeymoon, he drove us all to the nearby Doylestown airport. "So the kids c'n watch the airplanes take off n' land. I figure they'd like that, and it don't cost nothin'."

In the airport's café, the boys each spent their fifteen cents on ice cream cones and Coca Cola.

41.

How did it all fall apart? What was going on in Harold's head; in the mind of this man who'd tried as hard as he knew how, when no jobs were to be had, to find work to help support the wife and two kids he'd come to adore? Maybe if I try to crawl into that mind, I can make sense of it in the words he'd use, in his rough, "country" grammar. It might work, I decided as I sat in my Woodstock room with notebook and pencils at the ready.

Imagining Harold's voice, I began to write:

> Well, there ain't much to tell 'cept pretty soon after we was married, I carried her over the doorstep like in the movies. Three months we was married. And we was happy too. But things was pretty hard. Word got 'round how she and me was married, and some folks knowed about me, and she lost the teachin' job she had, and purty soon winter was a settin' in without a nickel 'tween us. 'Cept the man she'd been hitched to 'fore me, he sent a little now'n again, but it went fast. I kept tryin' for work, diggin' ditches and on the roads like before, but with the cold they stopped that, so it was no good. Nobody had no need of me.

With a sudden impulse, I picked up my sketchpad. Shortly, an old-time sailing ship appeared; something from the 1600s. Not what anyone would call accurate, so I wrote under it: *The Mayflower. David helped Harold put together one of several small models of this ship, hoping to sell them. I bought a sheet of green cellophane for the windows. Weeks he spent making them. He asked ten dollars each. After all that labor, he only sold one.*

Needing time to mull over what I wanted to write, I got up and went down to the boarding house kitchen, made myself a cup of coffee, then returned to continue.

> Twice I just walked off in'a middle o' the night when they was all asleep an' got as far as Doylestown, thinkin' they'd be better off without me, but I come back both times, hopin' we'd make it. Guess that's when I got the idea'a telling' her 'bout the house I owned over t' New Jersey. "I kept it a secret," I told her, "'cause I didn't want you should marry me for my money." She sure laughed at that, and I laughed too, just to see her grinnin'. But there weren't no house. There weren't nothin' but that pistol Alvah loaned me. I told him I wanted it f'r shootin' porcupines and such, but that were a whopper. I never used it, mostly I kept it in a old shoe box in the bedroom closet, but by and by I stuck it in a pocket o' my old winter coat and carried it 'round, just in case one of them times would come I'd have a need for it.
>
> Anyhow, it all happened real fast. She kept naggin'

> me to see the house in New Jersey so's we could maybe sell it, so I quick told her one mornin' I was going t' see a real estate man and unload that house. Funny, I knowed I had to get out'a there right quick. She was upstairs makin' the beds and I hollered "I'll be seeing yuh," and run down the road like wild horses was after me. I could hear them kids callin' me. When I got down past the Gunderson place and I knowed she wasn't comin', I sat down and had a p'culiar turn'a mind. I wanted to go back and tell her everything, 'bout the times I was in stir, 'bout all them stories I made up, and 'bout how much I liked her and her kids. But I couldn't go back this time. She owed them bills, that letter I made out the readin' of, where the lawyer said 'bout comin' after her, and there was almost nothin' t' eat in the house, and well it all got t' me and I had to do summit'. Just had to. So I just keeps on walkin' and hitchin' rides and sleepin' wherever I found me a place.

It felt accurate. I had tried to retrace the events and fit the puzzle pieces together the best way I knew how; set the background as I thought Harold would have framed it had he been able to write. But there was so much I didn't know, so much I was never sure of. So many things he told me that might have been as they happened, but then again might have been a mishmash of half-truths, confusion in his mind, or downright lies.

I turned to the sketchbook again.

The next drawing I did was a crude representation of a new

1940 Oldsmobile driving along a country road. Two figures sat in front, Harold and me. In the back, Davy and Dan. I stared at the sketch, remembering. . . .

Harold had been away for two nights and most of the following day when the Olds suddenly appeared in the drive, him at the wheel. At the sound of a motor, I'd come out the kitchen door. "Belongs t' my brother," he called out the car window. "He's in'a navy air force, don't need it whilst he's off on duty, so he let me use it." When I asked about the house, he seemed nervous and confused, but then abruptly grinned and added, "Been t' see that real estate feller in New Jersey. Gonna go up f'r sale soon. Why don't we all drive over t' see it?"

"Now?" bellowed Dan and David, who'd come running from the barn. "Can we go there now?"

"T'morrow be soon enough. Got me a bum foot here," he replied, limping as he climbed out of the Olds. "Stepped on a big ol' nail over t' my brother's place."

Indoors, I asked to see the injury. Harold took off his sock, revealing a blood-soaked bandage covering two shattered toes. Momentarily stunned, I said I'd fix a pan of hot salt water to soak it in, and that he'd probably need to see a doctor.

"Done that already," he replied. "Over t' Doylestown. Put iodine and such on it."

The next afternoon, the boys and I piled into the Olds for the drive to New Jersey. The boys were thrilled, a long ride in a brand-new car. But when we arrived, Harold had trouble locating the house. We cruised up and down several streets until he finally

In later years, my mother often created pictures of past events—with her eyes closed as she drew—as in this one, recalling Harold soaking his feet after claiming he'd stepped on a nail.

announced, "That's the one right there, I think. Been a long time since I seen the place." The windows were shuttered. No car stood in the drive or on the street in front.

"Be right back," he announced. "Gonna see if anybody's t' home."

As we watched he hobbled off across the street, returning moments later to say, "Guess they's gone off somewheres."

"Are you sure this is the place?" I asked.

"Stop pest'rin' me about it! Don't ya think I don't know my own house?"

Better keep my mouth shut, I decided as he got back into the car, started the engine, and turned back the way we'd come.

The boys had fallen asleep and it was after dark when we reached the farm. A plain black sedan was parked next to the barn. Two men, one tall and one short, both wearing jackets and fedoras, stood on the porch. As the Olds drove up, they turned and—cautiously, it seemed to me—approached as Harold and I climbed out.

After Harold confirmed his name, the shorter man directed, "You'll have to come with us."

"What's this about?" I asked, suddenly unnerved.

The tall man flashed a detective's badge. "Just routine. We need to ask him some questions." He led Harold down the steps.

Steady, I told myself, *keep your nerve, Mary*, as, with Davy in my arms and trailed by Dan, I headed into the house.

"Who are those men?" Dan asked.

"They've just come to talk with Harold, dear. Time you were both in bed now, okay?"

"Okay, only—"

"Harold might be away for a little while, honey, but don't worry, everything's going to be all right."

We headed upstairs, and after tucking them in and a quick kiss for each, I hurried back down.

When I arrived, Harold was in handcuffs and limping toward

the detective's car.

"Hurt your foot, did ya?" the short detective was asking.

"Stepped on a nail."

"Uh-huh."

"I don't understand," I said. "Where are you taking him?"

"It's all right, Ma," Harold called, as the detectives put him into the back seat of their sedan. "Be back soon enough."

Slamming the screen door behind him, one of the detectives turned to me with a brief but chilling announcement. "A man's been killed over in the next county, and we're taking your husband in on suspicion of murder."

Suddenly, I felt as though my body was made of glass. Somehow I managed to hold myself together as both detectives began questioning me. Had Harold been away lately? For how long? Where did he get the Oldsmobile? Did he own a gun? Where was it now? I answered as honesty as I could, but never volunteered the dark suspicions beginning to surface in my mind. And I decided not to mention the gun, or that it was, as far as I knew, still in an old shoebox, upstairs in the bedroom closet.

As the detective's car drove off, I stood in the yard for what seemed like forever. *What should I do? Who to call? A lawyer? Should I phone Burt and Marion to drive me to the Doylestown police station? What about the boys?* I couldn't take them along, and Dan had school the next day; what if the other children heard about this?

Finally, I hurried into the house, ran upstairs, and checked on the boys; they were sound asleep. Downstairs again; I went into the kitchen, picked up the old wall phone's receiver, and asked the operator to connect me with Alvah's number in New York. "Please reverse the charges," I added, my head reeling as I waited. He answered in minutes. "Alvah," I said, my jaw set in a determined effort to remain composed, "could you come out and get us? I think we need to be in the city."

I could sense the frown in his voice. "What's going on?" he demanded. "Is there some emergency? Are the boys all right?"

"They're fine, Alvah, but look . . . I don't really want to talk about it over the phone. Can you come and get us? Please?"

A long pause at the other end; a slight sigh, then . . . "Okay. When? Tomorrow?"

"No. Right now."

◆◆◆◆◆

I shuddered. Even now, in my room at Woodstock, and even though it was two years in the past, the memory was still fresh. Once again came the urge to commit my feelings to paper. I picked up a dark green colored pencil, closed my eyes, and let my hand sketch what it would. Opening my eyes, I discovered a round face. No mouth, no ears; just two enormous, transfixed eyes staring straight ahead, like a ghoul. Somehow, even without the mouth, the sketch resonated; it called to mind *The Scream* by Edvard Munch. Beneath the drawing I noted, *October 1940, night of terror.*

42.

Adelaide's Woodstock workshop was a blessing. The return to capturing images on paper quickly found me understanding how to create shapes and textures I'd always struggled with. Objects as small as a conch shell or as massive as distant mountains became miraculously alive, as charcoal sticks, conté crayons, or pastel shading indicated light and form. The first session flew by as my hand guided pen, pencil, and other tools across my drawing pad. It felt like a gift from heaven.

With Adelaide and her sardonic chain-smoking companion, Babs, I rediscovered the jocular give and take I'd so enjoyed while barnstorming New England with Harry and Forman. After only my third session, the two invited me for coffee at the Nook. No sooner had I sat down than Babs fixed me with a skeptical gaze and demanded, "Now, you didn't come to this godforsaken village just to take Addie's workshop, did you?"

"Pay no attention," Adelaide shot back. "She thinks Woodstock's the ass end of the world."

"It is!" Babs insisted. "The place is infested with Sunday painters from April till the frost is on the pumpkin."

"Present company excepted," said Adelaide apologetically.

As I waved it off, Babs rolled her eyes and repeated her question.

I smiled. With much still to talk about after my final session with Dr. Thomas a week earlier, and feeling comfortable with these women, I decided to share a little. Beginning with Payne Whitney, I went on to reveal that David and Dan were in a private school, and I was also disarmingly frank about the beginning of my relationship with Harold. But I couldn't bring myself to talk about the heartbreaking events that followed. "Guess I'm still trying to figure why things didn't turn out between us," I admitted.

"Did you love him?" Adelaide asked gently.

I lit a cigarette and considered for a few moments.

"If anyone had asked me that six months ago, I'd probably have said I made a huge mistake. Now, I'm not so sure. For quite a while, I've been puzzled about how I could have married a man whose life had actually been a huge collection of falsehoods."

"Sounds to me like he was insane," huffed Babs.

"Insane or a genius," countered Adelaide.

"Genius?" challenged Babs.

"Maybe both," said Adelaide. "Or maybe I should have said, 'the potential for genius.' You often find that in people whose minds run around like caged mice. You know, they've got creative ability in one thing or another, but then they go off the deep end: Van Gogh, Kafka, Mary Shelly, Virginia Woolf . . ."

"Bum analogy!" retorted Babs. "Those were all smart people."

"I think you're right, Adelaide," I cut in, going on to recount Harold's inventive skill with anything mechanical and his ability to make up stories on the spur of the moment.

"Mostly packs of lies, right?" interjected Babs.

Adelaide sighed. Clearly, when it came to judging others, she and Babs tended to become prickly with one another.

"I don't know," said Adelaide, thinking. "Why is it that some people compulsively fib, spin entire worlds out of whole cloth?"

"Because they're mad," Babs answered.

"Too simplistic," retorted Adelaide. "I think of that quote by Santayana, you know, the philosopher. 'If you prefer illusion to reality, it's only because all decent realities have eluded you and left you in the lurch.'"

Babs huffed again. But in relation to Harold, I could see the truth in it.

◆◆◆◆◆

After I left the Nook, a Woodstock panorama caught my attention: hunters in their red caps and checked jackets moving into town for the weekend to be up and out for the chase when the deer season opened on Monday; the young girl from the boarding house and her parents walking by as their poodle trotted ahead, sniffing the ground; and a young boy I'd seen earlier in the Nook, whose father had cuffed his head for some innocuous remark. I'd called to the man, "That doesn't seem appropriate, sir." To which he'd replied, "Mind your own damn business!" Now the boy was running through and deliberately scattering a huge pile of leaves like the one I'd seen the old man raking up hours before. I smiled at his obvious pleasure.

Thoughts about children kept surfacing, with David and Dan uppermost in my mind. Mostly a concern for their future, a secure future I'd have to plan to make happen. *How can I guarantee it? What direction should I take? If I fail to create that security, what then? What kind of men will they turn out to be? Men as hurt and insecure as Harold?*

Then Adelaide's quote came to mind: *If you prefer illusion to reality, it's only because all decent realities have eluded you and left you in the lurch.*

Is that Harold's story? I wondered. All the months we'd been together, he'd been tight-lipped about his childhood, revealing only, "It waren't so good. Ol' man took a belt t' me quite a bit." And, "I run off when I was no mor'n sixteen, when he beat me 'bout the head with the handle of a pitchfork." I'd sensed his vulnerability; the hidden need to present himself to me as a strong, capable husband. So I hadn't pressed. But there was much I still had to learn.

Back in my room, my thoughts continued. By 2 a.m. on the night of Harold's arrest, Alvah had arrived from New York. Within minutes, we'd bundled Danny and David into the car and started on the 125-mile drive back to Manhattan.

◆◆◆◆◆

After leaving both boys asleep under the watchful eye of Alvah's new wife, Helen Clare, Alvah and I were on the road again—to the Doylestown jail this time, where Harold had been locked up. Each of us was apprehensive when we got there. After a brief questioning by two detectives, I was absolved of any involvement in the crime and permitted to visit Harold.

"And we'll want to speak with you too," one of the detectives said to Alvah, who immediately flinched.

As another detective unlocked the cellblock door, he announced,

"You should know, Mrs. Frisbie, that your husband's confessed to the killing."

After nearly collapsing, I somehow managed to hold myself together, to remain as strong as I could in the face of whatever might lie ahead. Harold broke into tears the moment he saw me. And as I tried to offer comforting words, I noticed how disheveled he was, and that he had a cut lip and a black eye.

"Did they beat you?" I asked.

"Sure. They al'ays do."

"My God. What kind of police are these?" I whispered through clenched teeth. Then, more gently after I regained my composure, "But I have to ask: Why on earth did you go off with a gun?"

Harold immediately began sobbing. Through it all, he managed to let go with a rambling (and to him believable) story.

"I did it for you, Mom. On account'a the bills we owed, that letter from a lawyer. Thought they was gonna take you off t' jail an' all . . . an' for the boys, I thought—"

"Why didn't you tell me how worried you were?" I cut in. "We could have talked about it, and—"

Before I could go on, he buried his face in his hands and continued to cry.

Shattered by the visit, and with Harold still trying to swallow his sobs, I returned to the waiting room expecting to be able to lean on Alvah for support, but found him nervous and upset.

"They gave me a terrible time," he blurted out angrily as soon as we were outside the building. "Just terrible. They asked about the gun, and I really fucked up. 'What gun?' I answered, and this one cop jumped on that, implied I was involved in the killing, and kept after me. For a while, I honestly thought I'd be locked up along with Harold."

The night Alvah came to get the boys and me, he'd asked about the gun. I'd told him the detectives hadn't bothered to search for it, and as far as I knew it was still upstairs in a shoebox. He'd apparently retrieved it, noted it had been cleaned, and decided to take it to his brother Everett's apartment in New York. To pretend otherwise would have been just plain foolhardy, but I like to think he was trying to protect the boys and me.

"Boy, is Everett going to be pissed when the cops turn up for it," Alvah fretted.

"Well, neither of you had anything to do with this," I said, trying to ease his worry.

"Terrible business," he replied. "Terrible business."

"I spoke with Harold," I began, "and—"

"Oh, right," Alvah interrupted. "How's the boy? How's he doing?"

"Not good," I sighed.

"Hmm," he said. "Not surprising," as he took my arm and led me quickly toward his car.

◆◆◆◆◆

That day in the Doylestown jail was still fresh in memory as I sat looking out the window. I recalled feeling numb, frozen, and with no clue about what to do, whom to ask for advice, or what terrors the future might hold. The memory turned to concern for my boys, a frightening shiver ran through me, and I had a sudden urge to call them. Mrs. Birdwhistle let me use the phone.

Minutes after I placed the call, a small voice said, "Hi, Mom. When can we come home?"

After assuring Davy I was trying hard to make sure we'd all be together by Christmas, I went on to ask how he was getting along.

"Okay, I guess."

"Are you having any problems?"

"Stop listening!" he complained to someone nearby. Then, "I don't think so."

We went back and forth, with me asking questions and Davy protesting that Dan kept trying to grab the phone until he finally said, "Here, you talk to her."

Dan came on, whispering.

"Say that once more, sweetie. I can barely make out what you're saying."

"We're in Mr. Musgrove's office," he whispered again, but a bit louder. "It's where the telephone is." Clearly, Mr. Musgrove was nearby.

"All right," I said, "I'll ask the questions. Are you and David getting along okay?"

An awkward pause then, "Okay, I suppose."

"Are you just lonesome and want to come home?"

"Yeah, soon," replied Dan.

"Is something serious going on?"

Another pause, then, "Uh, not really . . ." Then he added, "I heard you tell Davy we're gonna come home by Christmas."

"That's my plan," I answered. "Do you think you can stick it out until then?"

"I guess we have to."

"You know, if there's anything you—"

The operator's voice came on to announce, "Your three minutes are up."

"Okay, just a second . . . but Danny, don't forget, sweetheart, if you need to talk with anyone about anything, I think that George would be happy to—"

"Sorry, time's up, ma'am," came the operator again, and the call was disconnected.

"I didn't even have time to say goodbye!"

"Sorry about that. Rules, you know. But if you'd like me to connect you again—"

I thanked her and hung up.

◆◆◆◆◆

Reliving the visit to Harold and the business about Alvah and the gun, then being able to share but a few words with my boys left me so emotionally drained that I didn't feel like joining the other guests for dinner. Instead, I was in bed by eight, and soon fell into a troubled dream crammed with fractured feelings, impressions, and sounds from the recent and distant past:

David and Dan were in a strange house, waiting for me; a house piled high with shabby furniture inside a maze of rooms that I felt an urgency to get to so I could help them arrange everything. *No need to phone,* I thought. Though I was desperate to get in touch with the boys, it seemed okay because they knew I'd be along soon.

After waking briefly then drifting off again, I found myself sitting in a railroad car as it rocketed past stations, each with a sign registering a place I'd lived: Oyster Bay, Franconia, Henry Street, Brooklyn, the old stone farmhouse in Pennsylvania. I needed to get off at one of the stations, but which one?

And the train never stopped.

Then I found myself climbing a long, winding staircase to Alvah and Helen Clare's New York apartment. I came into the front room, collapsed on their sofa, and began to sob. Alvah cried out, "Oh for God's sake, Mary!"

"What about the boys?" I asked. "What's going to happen to them?"

Then again, his "Oh for God's sake, Mary!" repeating and repeating, like a distant echo. He seemed to be hurrying to escape, to be fading into a shimmering distance as though my presence annoyed him. I called out through my sobs, "I'm so grateful to you, Alvah, for the boys; for David and for Dan, that we brought them into the world."

Abruptly, with a *poof* and a cloud of smoke, Alvah was gone. Finally, the bizarre dream faded like the last scene in a movie, and I fell into a deep sleep.

43.

Five a.m. The lamp was still on. I lay under the covers, cozy and warm for another fifteen minutes, then pushed up to a sitting position and reached for my notebook, ready to write what I'd been too tired to tackle the previous evening:

Pennsylvania memory, 1941

The year of hell. One year among many. By December, it was over. Or had it just begun? So much was over; my mother had died in Glencoe hospital, and the boys and I were in Danbury. There was July 1940, the strange marriage and the "glass breaking" fear. Then there was October 12 and the washtub with hot water to bathe Harold's injured foot. The arrest. The jail visit. Alvah's panic at being questioned. Isaac Josephs, the lawyer, a wonderful man who gave me a shot of whisky a few times during that long and frightening night before Harold's day in court. Then the hearing, and on and on through the summer into November of 1941. And on to Danbury, and there was Mackie, David's oh so loyal Cocker Spaniel, and there were my dear children, my sons, one just turned nine, one not yet seven. *Oh God, how in the world did they . . . How did I . . . ?*

I stopped writing. As so often in the past when I found myself seeking greater clarity, I began to feel a presence. I knew who it was.

"Dad?"

I didn't really need to ask. There was no answer, and I didn't expect one. That he was there and would be listening was enough. Hadn't he always been there when I needed to make sense of the road ahead, helping me steer around life's potholes? Now, continuing to make sense of the past and looking for a direction for my years ahead, I needed a listener. And while Dr. Thomas had given me a jumpstart and Adelaide was clearly sympathetic (even Babs's cynicism made me think), my beloved father always had an especially understanding ear.

And so I began, talking in a whisper:

"The whole episode with Harold and the gun and the killing was a fiasco, Dad. He'd set out to hitchhike to a store he'd known as a kid, a store where the owner kept his money in a cashbox. After losing his nerve as several cars passed by, this Oscar Burroughs driving a new maroon Oldsmobile spotted him and pulled over. 'Always like to stop and give fellows a ride,' he said."

Now, my tears were flowing. Somehow, verbalizing brought everything back much too vividly. *Maybe write the rest of it down,* I thought, *just the highlights. Otherwise, I'll be blubbering all night long.* I picked up my pencil.

This guy Burroughs asked Harold where he worked.

> "There ain't no work," Harold replied.
>
> Burroughs apparently became testy, implied that Harold was a loafer, and said something like, "Bullshit! There's work for any mother's son that wants it."
>
> It seems this triggered Harold's decision. He pulled out the gun and demanded the guy pull over. But as soon as he did, Burroughs grabbed for the gun. They struggled, both tumbled out onto the roadway, and the gun went off. Several times, it seems. Quickly realizing what had happened, and with Burroughs bleeding, Harold decided to take him to a hospital. But as he tried to lift him into the car, he found that Burroughs was dead.
>
> It was all so horrible, Dad.

Even writing that much had me feeling wrung out like a wet dishrag. I got up, lit a cigarette, and stood by the window. Morning mist was giving way to a light rain. A leaking gutter allowed steady drips to splash onto the window ledge.

"It feels as if the sky is weeping too, Dad," I whispered. "You should see me, an endless flood of tears running down my face."

I stubbed out the cigarette and continued:

> Harold wasn't stupid, Dad. Actually, with most practical things he was quite clever. But here, I suppose he panicked. He left clues a ten-year-old could figure out. Two women saw him riding with Burroughs. Workmen laying blacktop saw the Olds turn off onto a forest road. Later, he hid the body under a small bridge,

then stopped for gas. The attendant recognized him. And since he'd also shot himself in the foot when the gun went off, he saw a doctor to have it treated; and gave the doctor his correct name, for God's sake! Well, it didn't take long for detectives to show up at our door the night we came back from the ride in that Olds he told me was his brother's.

The local press had a field day. Burroughs employed forty men, and for a time, his dairy closed down. There was a lot of hostility, with everyone blaming Harold for the men losing their jobs in the midst of the hard times folks were having anyhow. Detective magazines wrote lurid stories about Harold, building up the killing as the crime of the century, with state troopers practically breaking down our door with their guns drawn. A total fabrication.

As the detectives grilled him, Harold made up a story about someone else doing the killing, and a couple other bizarre concoctions. They'd also found Harold's shoe with a bullet hole through it in our bedroom closet. And when Alvah told the detectives he'd found the gun in an old cardboard box, and taken it to his brother's New York apartment for safe-keeping, Harold finally broke down sobbing and confessed everything to a kindly sheriff from up where he'd lived as a boy and who'd come down to visit him in the Doylestown jail.

But would you believe, on the day before he was

arrested, Dad, he'd done one other thing: he stopped in Doylestown to pay the minister who married us the three dollars he'd promised.

Traumatic as it felt to continue, these were the events leading to my eventual breakdown and near suicide. If I wasn't able to relate them to this always-empathetic listener, I figured, when would I ever complete the journey? My patient, ever-attentive father would understand:

There was no jury trial, Dad. Having already confessed, Harold pled guilty. So it was simply a hearing. The way it worked in Pennsylvania, a judge was appointed to listen to arguments and decide the punishment: life in prison, or death.

Death, I thought. *Almost two years later, and the word still makes me tremble.* Several long, quiet moments passed before I whispered, "Bear with me, Dad. I wish I didn't have to go through it again, but . . ."

The newspapers didn't help. Headlines screamed "hitchhike killer," and in their interviews, people around there said Harold was "a bad egg" and "a vicious ex-con." Those who came to the hearing, plus the usual courtroom regulars . . . you know the kind, folks tantalized by sensationalism . . . packed every session. We had almost no one in our corner, Dad . . . well, a tiny clutch of Alvah's New York friends, our neighbors, Burt and Marion, and our attorney, of course, Isaac Josephs. A good man, but he could only tell me what I already knew: that while he'd try to build a case, he could tell by looking at the spectators' faces that almost each one reflected a strong desire for revenge, for Pennsylvania law to be upheld—that if a man went out with a gun, it was assumed he intended to use it. So with Harold's guilty plea, he held out little hope for anything but life in prison. Possibly worse.

The prosecution's case was well laid out: the witnesses who'd seen Harold driving around, tedious testimony about the gun and bullets from a ballistics expert, the doctor who Harold visited to have his injured foot tended to, and finally, a bunch of grisly photos of the body—which, fortunately, I wasn't close enough to see clearly.

"Shot full of holes, he was," said the photographer who took them.

"Still with me, Dad? Of course you are." I raised a hand to my shoulder. I could almost feel him beside me, listening.

Naturally, the prosecution's portrait of Harold was much like that in the pulpy detective magazines. Emphasizing him as a hardened criminal, they highlighted crimes he'd committed that had landed him twice in prison, his effort to cover up the murder, and the lies he told detectives after his arrest.

Without exploring what was behind all that, Dad,

one might assume justice demanded a just punishment. But when Harold took the stand, under Joseph's questioning a much different picture emerged, one that had me barely able to hold back my tears.

Harold had two sisters and a brother. All were boarded out to strangers for three years until their mother remarried to a man who was really brutal, and who Harold didn't learn wasn't his natural father until he was twenty-one.

God, the things some kids go through, Dad. . . . He got beaten with a rubber hose or steel rod for such things as coming home late from school or accidentally spilling a glass of milk. He ran away from home three times, but was always caught and brought back . . . for more beatings.

One night, the stepfather forbade him to go to a Christmas party. But Harold sneaked out and went off with another boy, who suggested they burn down the local schoolhouse. Harold refused, but the other boy went back and did it, while Harold, who was thirteen at the time, kept watch. Well, the other boy lied to the local sheriff, saying Harold was responsible. Harold was arrested. (The stepfather said they should have killed him instead of sending him to jail.) Harold was sent to reform school. In his testimony about the Burroughs killing, he told the court that for breaking the reform school rules, all the kids were whipped with willow branches soaked in vinegar. One time, it left him with blood running down his legs.

Next, he was sent to jail for six months for stealing a jug of cider from the cellar of a farmer he worked for, and ended up serving five years for joy riding in a brother-in-law's car after the brother-in-law reported the car stolen—even though he'd phoned the man to tell him he'd bring the car back the next morning.

There's so much more, Dad, all in the same vein. Some of it I knew about, because once in a while when we were together (though not often), he'd say a few words about his former life. And I never pressed him, damn it!

He said he looked for work, but what chance does an ex-con have? So he ended up living with the Salvation Army in Philadelphia. On relief.

In February 1940, he eventually landed a job on a farm near Doylestown, and was working there when we married on July 22. As fall came on, he was no longer needed and was thrown out of work.

My tears having abated, I felt better about talking now.

"I remember so clearly, Dad, how Josephs gently guided Harold through this whole story. It was about two hours long. Then the state's attorney began an even longer cross-examination, pressing him for details that by now I knew all about.

"'Didn't you even have a hint you'd get into serious trouble with this holdup?'

"'Yeah, I knew I was doin' wrong. But I had this happy home, first time in my life, and I was in fear it would get broke up. You see, these bills was pilin' up and a letter come from a lawyer to my wife, and I was scared she'd get thrown in jail, and—'

"'So this is what led you to kill a man.'

"'I didn't plan on shootin' Mr. Burroughs. I was hopin' just t' take his car and drive to this store I knowed about, and—'

"'So you thought that robbing a store would solve your problems, is that it?'

"'Well, I was willin' t' make the sacrifice, because, you see, there was not only all these bills, but the milk man threatened to cut off the milk for the children if he didn't get some money.'

"'And why did you deceive your wife?' the state's attorney demanded. 'Lied to her, as a matter of fact, about the house you owned, about Burroughs's car belonging to your brother. And about your entire criminal past.'

"Harold's reply was a simple, forlorn apology: 'I did it t' ease her mind.'

"If only he'd not kept so much hidden. If he'd just opened up to me when we first got to know one another. . . . Oh, I don't know. . . . I always had a feeling there were things left unsaid. Maybe I should have pressed him, probed for more about his background. Probably, I just didn't want to rock the boat.

"Oh, Dad, you have no idea what a day that was. Just like now, I was crying. Even though I'd asked Harold about all this when I'd visited him in jail, I guess I felt terribly hurt at that moment. Even angry. It was all I could to do restrain myself from jumping up and shouting, 'Why the hell didn't you talk to me?' I could tell when Josephs looked at me that he'd read my thoughts.

"After Harold's last reply, and hoping an explanation of my life with him might carry some weight, Josephs called me to the stand. I did the best I could, telling the court how Harold and I met, how he had David and Dan eating out of his hand within a couple hours; how he entertained them with all kinds of amazing stories . . . some pretty damn outlandish, I admit, though I didn't say that on the stand . . . the boys helping him on the hay wagon, tagging along whenever he'd set off harrowing or sowing seeds, David helping him build those models of the Mayflower, the secret tunnels he built for them in the hay. And how he helped me around the house, fixing things that were broken, and taking care of the boys when I had to run errands. I talked about his basic decency and cooperation in everything we did while we were a couple, and how we struggled to try to keep the home together even though the times were hard.

"I testified for . . . well, it must have been an hour. And the state's attorney didn't ask me a single question after.

"Finally, Josephs called the doctor who had treated Harold's shattered foot. Describing him as 'the unfortunate product of an abject home environment in the early growing years,' and that, 'while physically mature, he has the mentality of a child ten or twelve years old,' the doctor concluded with, 'I feel that at heart he is honest, but the good qualities have not been developed.'

"Cross examining, the state's attorney, noting the doctor's remarks about Harold's lowered mental abilities, then asked if he believed he could distinguish right from wrong. 'He probably could,' admitted the doctor.

"I remember looking around the courtroom, Dad, trying to figure out if there was any increased sympathy for Harold. To my surprise, several spectators, women in particular, had handkerchiefs out and were wiping their eyes. I guess at that point I still held out a little hope.

"But the state's attorney soon extinguished my optimism when he concluded, 'No more brutal crime has ever been committed in this country. And if any individual deserves the death penalty, it is surely Harold Frisbie . . .'

"And yet, one newspaper report's final paragraph ended with a compliment. 'The spirit of the woman standing by a man facing a possible death penalty,' he wrote, 'gripped the spectators in the hot, stuffy courtroom.'

"Even the special prosecutor shook hands with me and expressed his sympathy as the session ended. But it made no difference. In spite of all that, the judge's decision was as expected: death by electrocution."

Almost two years since this all began. My tears were welling up, and soon I could no longer feel Dad's presence.

◆◆◆◆◆

What had I learned? While the events surrounding the murder had shocked me, Harold's litany of childhood abuse helped me develop a deeper sense of his thinking process and of what formed it. And of how those convoluted thoughts, combined with how he'd felt it was his job as a husband and father to rescue our little family from financial disaster, had let him become capable of killing another human being.

For a while, the thought stuck in my mind like a never-stopping merry-go-round. But I knew second-guessing would get me nowhere; water over the dam. Time to move on, make a determined effort to shuck off what couldn't be fixed.

Still, something troubled me: Harold's childhood. *Is that the crux of all this?* I asked myself. Struck by the thought, I picked up my pencil again:

> Maybe that's the key. And for me, the clue to what might lie ahead. If the too-often-haphazard and chaotic way in which our world produces people like Harold, men and women who have enormous possibilities yet bottle everything up inside, who create fantasy worlds in order to buck themselves up and convince themselves they're "someone," then why can't it create healthy individuals instead? Children who stand at least half a chance of growing into warm, sensitive, and caring human beings?
>
> Maybe that's where I come in.

I recalled telling Dan and David something about that when answering their questions about Harold during the Monopoly game at Musgrove School. They seemed to understand how sometimes people could invent stories in order to make themselves look better in the eyes of others.

Hadn't I examined my own life enough, my own growing years, to be able to draw from that an understanding of how I might play a role in helping at least a few others toward a healthy head start? A few children, that is. Because really it all begins in childhood. If children come out of that with happy experiences instead of the miserable lives that trigger the type of confusions that form a person like Harold . . . well, then they have a chance.

"I've made a start," I declared aloud. "Developed a bit more insight into where I could be of some use. Beyond that . . ."

Enough! After all the dredged-up emotion, remaining alone in my room felt too isolating. Not what I needed right now. I could come back to processing my memories later. Now, I had an overwhelming need for fresh air and a desire to be among people, where I could eavesdrop on conversations and feel the warmth of laughing, jostling humanity.

I was getting a bit hungry. And I knew just the place.

44.

"Hold on now . . . you're telling me he *killed* a man?"

"For Christ's sake, Babs!" muttered Adelaide, glancing furtively around. Though the Nook was packed, no one in the café had reacted to her partner's loud and callous gaffe.

I stared at Babs for a moment, then nodded.

"When was this?" demanded Babs.

"Almost two years ago . . . in Pennsylvania."

"How terrible," said Adelaide in a barely audible whisper. "But . . . well, you hadn't mentioned this . . ."

Perhaps I should have, but at our last get-together, it hadn't seemed appropriate. After all, I'd only recently met them. But today, after an exchange of greetings, Babs had begun to press me about what brought on the depression leading to my stay at Payne Whitney, and added, "Yeah, I realize I'm nosy, but that's me: Popeye the Sailor Man. 'I yam what I yam.'"

I had to smile. Adelaide looked as though she wanted to crawl under a rock.

Well, why not? Why shouldn't I just let it out? It had been rolling around in my head for so long that once more wasn't going to make a difference. And on meeting these two, I'd quickly felt openness, as if I'd known them forever.

With that, I briefly told them the whole story, everything from Harold turning up in a stolen car to his arrest and on up through the hearing and its tragic outcome.

There was a long silence. Until Babs blurted out, "So, he got the chair, huh?"

I stared at her, nonplussed.

"You are so God damn *insensitive!*" Adelaide growled.

"Criminy," Babs mumbled. Her chin dropped to her chest, and she shook her head slowly. Finally, she looked up at me. "Okay, I'm sorry, I apologize. Guess I'm just too much like a bull in a bakery sometimes."

"China shop," I said, trying to ease her discomfort.

"Huh?"

"Bull in a china shop. That's the usual expression." Then I laid a hand on one of hers and added, "Yes, that's what happened. He was executed in November 1941."

How deeply should I get into this? I'd read the transcript of the hearing over and over, had run it through my head like an endlessly repeating phonograph record. While I didn't want to keep dwelling on it, both women seemed increasingly sympathetic, so I steeled myself and let it all out. "It was a long process," I began. "Almost a year after the hearing. First, Harold's lawyer filed a notice of appeal. That delayed carrying out the sentence. But months later and less than a week after submitting his brief, the Pennsylvania Supreme Court, three old men they were, upheld the verdict . . ."

"Wouldn't ya know," snorted Babs.

"Actually, one inclined toward leniency. Life in prison was enough, he said. But he was outvoted. And one good thing did come out of it: for the first time in Pennsylvania, a plea for mercy based on diminished capacity was allowed. It set a precedent."

While Adelaide and Babs sat quietly, waiting for me to continue, I paused and stared off into space. Moments later, I was back with them.

"Alvah, my former husband, wrote a petition to the governor, and had it signed by thirty-five or forty names, many prominent people, mostly in the arts. I was even able to see the governor myself, but he claimed that his hands were tied and said he was sorry. Then after two more appeals were denied, a new execution date was set. And that was it. We had nowhere else to go."

After a long silence, Adelaide asked, "How did he hold up? Harold, I mean?"

I dabbed at my eyes. "At first, it was terribly hard for him. He cried a lot at the hearing, and after, when I visited him in the local jail; feeling, I guess, that he'd let the boys and me down. But later I think he became pretty much resigned to what would happen. I tried to keep up his spirits, of course, started a kind of correspondence course, teaching him to write. Soon after he was arrested, when he was in the county jail, he thought I'd leave, desert him, but I reassured him I loved him and had no intention of going anywhere. I sent him a little money for things he needed—soap, cigarettes; things like that. But he didn't spend it on himself. He saved it, and at Christmas a package arrived. When the boys and I opened it, we found . . ." I managed to utter the last words through a sudden flood of tears . . . "a box of handkerchiefs for me, and toy trucks for David and Dan."

Babs and Adelaide didn't need to probe further. Their eyes said it all, each harboring their own thoughts as customers' chatter registered dimly in the background. Moments later, Babs looked at her watch, rose from the booth, and softly said, "We've got the workshop in fifteen minutes. I'll pay the bill, then go get things ready."

"I'm not scheduled this afternoon," I said. "But count on me tomorrow."

Adelaide nodded, then quietly asked, "One more question. Your boys—how did you . . . I mean, what did you—"

"What did I tell them? Well, not much. In fact, what happened was quite unexpected. When I returned home after my last visit with Harold . . . When I knew he was . . . gone . . ."

I could feel my tears welling. Then, as so often happens to us all, I experienced a sudden memory flash. Taking a deep breath, I continued: "I asked the boys to come upstairs to my room. As I sat on the edge of the bed with little David on one side, Dan had hung back, standing in the doorway.

"'I have something sad to tell you both,' I began.

"'I know,' said Dan.

"I looked up, surprised, and asked, 'What?'

"'It's about Harold, isn't it? He's dead, isn't he?'

"I was stunned. 'How did you know?' I blurted out.

"'I don't know,' Danny replied. 'I just know. Did he die in the army?'

"I stared at him for several moments, then nodded slowly, my tears flowing. Dan rushed to me then, and I gathered both boys in my arms."

Now, as my tears overflowed once more, I found Adelaide enveloping me in a long and caring hug. "Not so surprising," she whispered. "Some children are just very perceptive."

Yes, maybe not so surprising, as I think about it now; after all, when the detectives first took Harold away, I told the boys he'd gone into the army.

It had, of course, been a lie, about Harold dying in the army. I'd reasoned that at their ages, the truth might be too difficult to absorb; they would know in time. As another part of his effort to seek clemency for Harold, Alvah wrote a semi-fictionalized novel about the case: *Bread and a Stone*. Someday, I hoped, my boys would be ready to read it.

The afternoon was cool but pleasant. Instead of retreating to my room, I found a bench at the edge of the Green and sat thinking. I took out my notebook and began slowly turning pages until I found a series of sketches I'd created at Payne Whitney; sketches created after one particular session during which Dr. Thomas had suggested it might be helpful to recapture some of my feelings by drawing images. "Just as an exercise," he'd added.

With eyes closed, I'd written, above the drawing of a man (Harold) soaking his wounded foot in a washtub. I sat at a table in the background, facing away, both hands covering my ears.

Another sketch: a cardboard box coffin holding Dan's twin. The box labeled, *Dead Baby (male)*. Above it I had written, *Landgrove, Vermont, 1932.*

A self-portrait holding a dishtowel. Behind me, a stairway leading to the boy's room and a sketch of them in bed. Below, the words, *Dread of night one October in 1940. Brittle me; felt made of glass.*

Another sketch, created not long after Harold's arrest. *Novem-*

ber, December, January, February, March 1940 / 1941 is written in next to another self-portrait: head down, clutching a handbag as I walk along New York's bleak Barrow Street near the apartment building where the boys and I lived for several months before moving to Danbury. Below this, I'd added, *All the rest of my life; to take the overnight trip, talk to him through the glass. The boys will grow up, marry, and leave home. Then what? I feel a hundred tonight and wonder how I will ever make it.*

In her later years my mother vividly recalled the trauma of 1941 in her drawings

Man crying
Who?
Harold in Dock.

Mary created this drawing with her eyes closed.

I sighed and shook my head at the thought. "But that never happened, did it?" I whispered. "Should I feel guilty at being relieved?"

A drawing of Harold in his prison clothes, of me in a topcoat; we're embracing in front of a wire cage. Under, I'd written, *Come out now and say goodbye to your wife. . . . But by then, I knew he had gone. Knew he was dead. As dead as the crazy woman kept in the attic room in the sheriff's house back home in Michigan, as dead as Danny's long overdue twin brother.*

And as dead, even, as I had felt for brief moments in my own life.

Finally, a sketch of myself sitting on a small sofa, one son on each knee, tears streaming down all our faces, the night I told them, 'He is dead,' and we sobbed together.

Harsh memories, recorded in a tableau of bleak drawings.

I looked up, away from them, my eyes blank, fixed on nothing in particular; the surrounding trees, perhaps, the falling leaves.

Then, suddenly burying my face in my hands, I began to sob. How long I sat there I have no idea.

"Wat'cha cryin' for, lady?" a voice interrupted.

A young boy stood by the bench; the same boy I'd seen the previous day in the Nook, the boy who had been roughly smacked by his father. I dabbed at my cheeks and tried to smile away the tears. "Oh," I said, "Well, I was thinking about a sad time.... Do you ever cry when you're sad?"

"Sometimes," he replied. "By myself, mostly. My father don't like it when I cry."

I nodded slowly and looked at the boy for several moments. Finally I asked, "What's your name?"

"Donald."

"Donald! That's almost the same name as my older boy, Daniel; do your mom and dad call you Don?

He shook his head. "Just Donald."

"My Dan is eleven now," I went on. "How old are you?"

"Eight.""

"Eight's a good age. Do you have any brothers or sisters?"

"I got a little sister, Nelly. She's five." Then Donald screwed up his face and asked, "How come you yelled at my father? In the restaurant, I mean."

"I didn't yell at him. I just didn't think it was very nice of him to hit you in the face, and that's what I told him."

"It don't hurt much. But if I do things he don't like, that's when I get it."

"I don't believe in hitting children."

Donald thought about this for a moment, then volunteered, "I ain't gonna hit my kids when I grow up."

I smiled at that, then said, "I have a hunch you're going to be a very good fath—"

"Donald!" commanded a loud voice from the edge of the Green. "Hop to it. Your mother wants to go shopping!"

I looked up to see a new model Chevrolet parked along the street, the boy's father standing by it. Donald's mother sat inside. A tiny girl peeked out from a rear window.

"I gotta go," said Donald, starting to run toward the car. Then he stopped, turned back briefly, and called, "I hope you feel better."

As I watched him open a rear door and climb in, I heard the father demand, "What were you doin', talkin' to that bitch?"

As the Chevy drove off, I sighed. But then began to think: *Children; they don't have it easy. So many never get a chance, become defeated before they're half grown then struggle on, trying to make sense of a mixed-up world most of them never really understand.*

I looked around at the idyllic little town, the mostly white frame houses, picket fences, manicured lawns increasingly blanketed with leaves. Except for one. The old man, rake and leaf bag in hand, had emerged from behind his home ready to attack the latest accumulation. I watched him for several minutes as he went about his task, raking leaves into piles, pausing now and then to stretch, seeking relief for an aching back, then stuffing the leaves into his bag.

Here's a purposeful human being, I thought, *a man who, despite his years, needs to feel useful. What other reason for living is there than to feel of use, to serve a purpose? And to perhaps help others feel the same way?*

All I'd gone through these past two years had been pointing in one direction. I no longer felt a need to wonder what it was. Fogs of the past had been lifting, and the road ahead was increasingly clear. I knew the kind of future I was determined to carve out for David, Dan, and myself.

You're Mary Burnett, shouted my inner voice. *You've survived an anxious, frustrated mother, decades of struggle, three unfulfilled marriages, and the heartbreak of seeing a husband put to death. No turning back. You've got the strength, and you're ready to move on to create a life of purpose and use.*

Firmly resolved, I rose from the bench and started across the Green back toward the rooming house.

PART IV:
NEW DAWN

“When your mind is full of failures,
As through dark nights you grope,
Have faith that dawn is on its way,
That you will wake to a better day,
So open your door to the sunrise,
And step over the threshold to hope.”
—Jeanne Johnson[6]

6 From her poem, “The Wee Small Hours”

45.

Prompted by my contact with Donald, I continued to focus on thoughts about children. Random and miscellaneous as they so often were, as the Trailways bus rolled south out of Woodstock this crisp fall morning, I was recording these in my notebook:

> Do I know of anything more precious, more human on earth than the marvelous little exchanges with girls and boys who trust you—before the rough, hard days of battling the world have toughened their skin and spirits? The moments are rare, I grant, but they are golden, moments to be treasured.
>
> I'm feeling closer now to children than I ever hoped to be. I recall the gilt-lettered, violet-bordered piece of heavy watercolor paper I once laboriously worked over, labeling it, *This is my symphony*; My dear God, at what age; thirteen, fourteen, fifteen? It's as though I knew then of what I was basically made, without the slightest comprehension of the joy, the pain, the struggle that goes into concocting your own symphony. What did I know of a "symphony"? What do I know today?
>
> Hmm . . . don't sell yourself short, Mary; perhaps

> you've learned more than you thought you had. This is my life, and I am me, and parts of it keep rearranging themselves. There is beauty here.

Adelaide and Babs had seen me off at the depot, with hugs and wishes of Godspeed for the next leg on my life's journey. Though the time with them had been brief, their probing conversations opened new avenues to explore. Then too, afternoons in the art studio provided new insight for drawing, suggesting exercises I could do on my own, as well as inspiring thoughts about how I might pass on what I'd learned in future work with children.

I'd already phoned Laura to let her know I'd be returning to Danbury. "But first," I reported, "I'm heading down to Poughkeepsie."

"What's in Poughkeepsie?"

"Vassar College. They have an outstanding program in early childhood education. When I phoned yesterday, they said that if my academic records from Michigan are up to snuff, I can enter their MA program."

A pause, then Laura asked, "Do you really need that, Mary? I mean, if you want to teach, you should simply be able to do it, shouldn't you? Going back to school at your age, and with two young boys, seems like biting off an awful lot. And that little playgroup you ran in Danbury, well . . ."

Patience, I reminded myself. "It would only be for a year. Part-time. And it might qualify me as a teacher, maybe even as assistant director in some preschool."

After a long silence, I asked, "Laura?"

"I'm here." And after another hesitation, "Look, if this is something you really want, well . . . Verne and I will stand the tuition."

Good old Laura, I thought as I expressed my gratitude, then went on to point out that, with the Roosevelt administration's emphasis on support for young children, "especially those with mothers working in war industries," anyone now entering the field was encouraged to apply for state and federal grants being offered through colleges. And I'd certainly do so.

As it happened, Vassar was at the top of the list.

Recalling the conversation as the bus sped toward Kingston, where I'd change for Poughkeepsie, I began fantasizing about the kind of preschool I'd run if I ever got a chance. *Better get it down on paper,* I decided. *While it's fresh in the mind.*

> Dirt and water, plenty of those, so kids can create that inevitable concoction called mud. From their own moist beginning, every child starts to struggle for the right to explore and enjoy the earth, to make use of it for their own purpose, to create and recreate new worlds, new forms, to use it for all kinds of imitative play in an attempt to relate themselves to the grownup world of "doers."
>
> Admonitions to "Get out of that mud!" or "Get away from the water; do you want to catch your death of cold?" won't be allowed. Children who play under those kinds of restrictions may learn early on to be crafty, to slip away for messy play before some stern adult swoops down and discovers their secret hideout. Or they might learn that "cleanliness is a virtue." Most people have met

> a child who doesn't dare get a spot of mud on themselves without worrying. The kid has already learned that dirt is among the "bad" things of the world, and rushes to get "sweet and clean" again. I won't have it.

I dwelt on that for a time, then added:

> And I suppose there'll be as much need to teach parents as there will be to teach the kids themselves; likely even more.

I gazed out at the rolling hills bordering the Hudson. Passing through a small village, I noticed a wrecking yard crammed with rusting autos.

> An old car would be nice. Kids would love to climb in and turn the wheel, shift gears, beep the horn. We'll have to remove any sharp or jagged metal, of course; make it safe. And a boat. I'll bet there are plenty of old boats nobody wants. We'll get one and embed it in a big mound of dirt and plant long grass around it, so it looks like it's riding the crest of a wave.
>
> What else? Let's see . . .
>
> Harold created a "secret fort" for the boys out of hay bales in the Pennsylvania barn, so why not?
>
> Blocks! Lots of blocks to build with. But not just those small play blocks; big ones, giant blocks that the children can pile up like steps or arrange into forts or walls. We'll cut hand-holes in them so they're easy to carry.

Paint. Buckets of paint; red, blue, green, black, white, purple, magenta, chocolate brown, more colors than are in a rainbow. And reams of newsprint to paint on; easels, and a huge supply of brushes of all sizes. Kids love to mess with paint.

We'll have a supply of flour, and I'll mix it with water and food dyes so it will be a sort of cheap clay the kids can mold into whatever they want. And a board with locks and keys, with shoelaces to tie and untie, with switches and latches, lots of everyday things that fascinate children, things they'll need to learn about as they grow. I can probably build a couple by myself, like the one I made in the Danbury preschool.

A gentle rain had begun to fall as the bus rolled into Kingston. Maple and Ash along the streets revealed more colors than a few days earlier. *Another few weeks,* I thought, *and they'll all be naked.* Many yards were covered with fallen red and rust and yellow leaves. Wet leaves. In one yard, someone (children, perhaps?) had piled them into large mounds. *Not much rustle as yet, but soon the wind will be blowing.*

The sight brought back memories of growing up in Saint Johns. I recalled building a large "bird's nest" of leaves—leaves for the carpet, leaves for the nest itself, up to my chest—then sitting in it alone and feeling cozy.

So many warm feelings of childhood emerged: my brothers and I, scuffing through the drying leaves as kids; Dan, as a toddler, kicking them around outside our rundown house in Vermont; he and David doing the same in Connecticut, in Pennsylvania. Both boys, along with Dan's friend Kenji, with long sticks for rifles, racing across the snow-covered vacant lot next to our home in Danbury, then throwing themselves into a drift in order to ward off a fanatical attack by imaginary Nazis; this, just days after FDR announced we were at war.

Hi, David. Hi, Dan. What are you up to right now?

Just thinking about them brought to mind those dark thunderclouds in some of their letters; I knew these signaled unhappiness, but what the specifics were, what was going on, I had only a vague idea.

46.

Trees around Musgrove School were alive with autumn colors, and Arbuckle's dumb cronies were complaining that it was getting too cold in the cave to continue their zombie imitations. Even though they kept daring us younger boys to go inside, word was spreading that the whole thing was a moneymaking hoax, and their revenue was falling off.

For a while, George's advice to just keep on pooh-poohing the idea of zombies, "which their ain't none of, anyhow," worked. Doing so, he suggested, would leave them frustrated. But the gang kept on ragging Henry and me anyhow, with taunts about us being cowards, and passing notes in the dining hall like one that pictured Henry with his pants pulled down to show a Nazi swastika on his butt.

A few nights after that drawing had been passed around, I was awakened by a kind of scraping and bumping from somewhere. I got up, jostled Henry awake, and whispered, "There's this noise," I said. "From downstairs, I think."

He got up, and we went to the door, opened it a crack, and peeked out. The noise continued. We crept to the edge of the stairwell and looked down. Gordon Arbuckle's chunky stooge, Charlie, was on the lower landing, lugging a heavy railroad tie. And Arbuckle himself, along with Morris, was starting up the stairs. Henry and I quickly scurried back into our room and shut the door.

"What are we gonna do?" I whispered.

Now someone was turning our door handle.

"Just yell bloody murder," Henry replied. "Somebody's sure to hear."

Before we had a chance to, we heard, "You boys up here for doin' what?" It was George's deep voice.

Then immediately, another voice: "Hold on, Sambo, you don't wanna spoil our little game, do you?"

Cautiously, Henry opened the door.

In the corridor, George, wielding a long push broom, was blocking Gordon Arbuckle and Morris with it. Charlie, sweating under the heavy railroad tie, had just arrived on the landing.

"All we're gonna do," said Morris, "is grab those freaks and—"

"Which freaks is that?" demanded George.

Ignoring a flurry of racist insults, George, using his push broom as a wedge, began to force the trio back toward the stairs. In a panic, Charlie let the railroad tie drop to the floor and half stumbled back down the steps.

"You fellas got one choice," warned George. "Go back on downstairs now, real quick like, but quiet. Get rid o' that hunk o' wood, an' then the three of you skedaddle back to your rooms."

"Oh, you think that's what we should do, huh?" Arbuckle shot back with a sneer.

"J'es shut your mouth and do like I say. I know about the little scheme you got goin' with your make-believe zombie cave an' all . . . charging admission! I never heard of such a thing!"

"How the hell did you . . ." Arbuckle began, but then stopped himself and stared icicles at George.

"How come I know? Ain't no secret. Whole school knows what's goin' on. All the boys. That's how come you ain't getting no business; I told everybody . . ."

"You damn well told everyone?" shouted Arbuckle.

"'Cept your auntie and uncle . . . Least not yet."

Gordon just kept staring.

George gave no ground.

Finally, with a jerk of his head for Morris to follow, Arbuckle pushed past George, and the two clomped off for the stairs.

"One more thing," George called out. "I ever hear you hasslin' one more boy; just one, you understand? Your folks gonna hear about it."

"Fuck you," Arbuckle barked over his shoulder.

George stood quietly for several moments, glaring after the retreating schemers.

By now, every door was open, and curious faces were peeking out. George looked around. "Show's over, boys," he announced. "Time y'all was asleep."

As the doors closed and George headed back along the hall, we heard footsteps below. Couldn't be Arbuckle and his pal, we reasoned; they'd have reached the ground floor by now. George leaned over the banister and looked down. I took a few steps and looked too. In the lower corridor stood Dayy, looking up. He smiled. George winked, then gave him two thumbs up and a broad grin. Then he turned, spotted me, and grinned.

Within minutes Henry and I were back in bed, and I was already half-asleep and into a dream about going home.

◆◆◆◆◆

It would be a few years before I told Mom about the incident between George and the Arbuckle gang. On the other hand, she must have suspected something, because a brief note to her late father I discovered in one of her journals while writing this book seemed to hint at how Davy and I handled ourselves when we were still kids:

> They'd be your pride and joy, Dad. Dan's an outgoing kid. Takes after his father in some ways, I think, has quite an imagination . . . But he's also a bit of a loner; kind of lives inside his own head a lot. Maybe too much; I can't quite tell yet. And David, dear Davy, quite a fellow he is, sort of a tough guy exterior but vulnerable on the inside. Strong for his age. Independent. They stick up for each other, too, and I like that.

Considering all Mom had to deal with in her own life, I've been amazed at how sensitive she also was to us and to nearly everyone else she encountered. But what her feelings about my brother and me mostly bring to mind in relation to the almost yearlong ordeal we endured at Musgrove was the successful culmination of what finally transpired between me and Davy and the Arbuckle gang.

Credit my dear brother and his smarts for being brave enough to stick up for me. (And for cluing George in about what was going on.) I'm not sure I'd have had the perception to do the same. Probably because, as Mom recognized, I was living inside my own head too much.

47.

My interview for the Early Childhood Education program at Vassar went well. As they were impressed with my early background in teaching and the fact that I'd set up my own nursery school in Danbury, I was quickly enrolled. Moreover, Vassar's grants-in-aid application, the welcoming director had assured me, would only be a formality; financing to cover tuition was guaranteed. "Older women returning to the field with previous experience among young children are especially encouraged," I was told.

To top it off, the director let me know, "We've been advised there'll be an opening soon in one of the Poughkeepsie schools to take over from a woman who currently heads their program for children of working mothers. I have a hunch you'd be a prime candidate."

Since courses were about to start and a commute from Danbury was impossible, I had rented two tiny rooms and kitchenette on the third floor of a Poughkeepsie rooming house. So, with everything packed into Laura's car, we were off to set up the place. In my free time, I planned to look for a home for myself and the boys, who would soon be released from "captivity" (as I saw it) at Musgrove. In spite of Laura's continuing effort to convince me they should see the term through until the following spring, I'd promised they'd be home by Christmas.

And long before I'd earned my MA at Vassar, I had definite news for them.

Tuesday night, November 23, 1942

Dear Dan,

I just came home from work and found your dear letter here. It did make me so happy. I am going to mail this tonight in the hope that you will have it for Thanksgiving.

I suppose you and David will talk about the pilgrims and Indians and the giving of thanks for the harvest . . . and eat! Me, I will probably work all day. Yes, I have a job now teaching in a nursery school. But I will be thinking of you both.

I'm glad you wrote to Pop. I had a letter from him tonight, too, and he tells me about some nice things he has mailed here for Christmas. I went shopping myself on Saturday night. What fun.

To think of it. Only four weeks from now, you will both be home for good. Of course, Aunt Laura and I will drive up to get you. Here's a little picture I drew of a Christmas tree, with you and David decorating it. Won't it be jolly, though?

Dan, I'm afraid we won't be able to have your two friends in for several days because of room here. This apartment is very small. But perhaps they can come in for a visit one day during their vacation. You decide what's best. Here's a little drawing of you thinking.

This is tin can week in Poughkeepsie. We have opened and flattened about a hundred cans in the nursery. If you were here, I'd have you jump on them to flatten them, like in the little drawing just below.

Write again when you have time. Love to you, boopus. I like you very much too, you know! —Mom

P.S. We will buy the Scout suit!

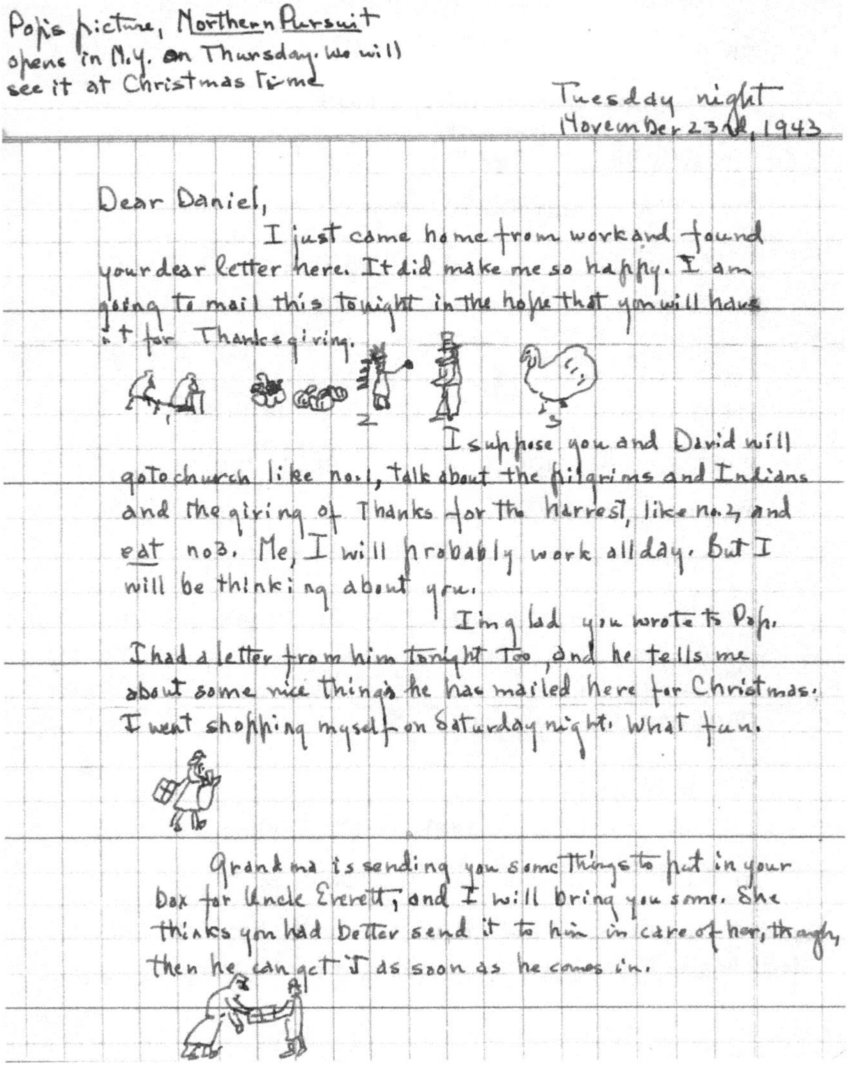

Pop's picture, Northern Pursuit opens in N.Y. on Thursday. We will see it at Christmas time

Tuesday night
November 23rd, 1943

Dear Daniel,

I just came home from work and found your dear letter here. It did make me so happy. I am going to mail this tonight in the hope that you will have it for Thanksgiving.

1 2 3

I suppose you and David will go to church like no. 1, talk about the Pilgrims and Indians and the giving of Thanks for the harvest, like no. 2, and eat no. 3. Me, I will probably work all day. But I will be thinking about you.

I'm glad you wrote to Pop. I had a letter from him tonight too, and he tells me about some nice things he has mailed here for Christmas. I went shopping myself on Saturday night. What fun.

Grandma is sending you some things to put in your box for Uncle Everett, and I will bring you some. She thinks you had better send it to him in care of her, though, then he can get it as soon as he comes in.

To Think of it. Only four weeks from now you will have a Christmas vacation.

Won't it be jolly, though.

Dan, I'm afraid we won't be able to have two boys in on Christmas day, because of room here. It won't be very simple. But perhaps they can come in for a day. You decide what's best.  ← Dan thinking.

Honey boy, I wish I could come earlier on Sunday, But there isn't an earlier bus. However we'll make the most of the few hours we have. O.K.? I'll be seeing you Sunday morning, with the Hems I hope.

This is tin can week here in Poughkeepsie. We have opened and flattened about a hundred cans in the nursery. If you were here I'd have you jump on them to flatten them

Write again.

Love to you boopus. I like you very much too, you know.

Mom

We will buy the scout suit, Dan.
You'll be glad to know your Mom is getting a raise in salary.

> *How different such a simple act as climbing stairs can be,* I thought while making my way up to the two tiny rooms after my first working week found me comparing the vast difference between now and then. "Now" means coming home each day from a job helping shape the lives of preschool children; a job I find exhausting, but also exhilarating. "Then" being the weeks dominated by the "end-of-the-rope" feeling that seized me when I'd climbed to my Danbury bedroom, only to wait for the rope to break. Then, I could only surrender. Payne Whitney became the lifeline, and now I could smile inwardly and look forward to tomorrow with buoyant anticipation and the same upbeat confidence I'd once eventually acquired while teaching the country school in Michigan. The same sense of purpose I'd felt while working so hard to solicit food for the seamen in Brooklyn during their strike, the freedom and joy of helping create puppets and traveling with Harry.

Though heading a nursery program at one of Poughkeepsie's schools signaled the beginning of a positive and satisfying future, when combined with prepping the apartment for Dan and David's arrival, enrolling them in a new school, seeking a permanent home for us, and attending courses toward an MA, by the time I climbed the stairs each day, my forty-five-year-old bones were definitely aching.

Still, a hot bath and a pot of coffee on the stove soon found me ready for a full evening of study. And since there were no student papers to grade, weekends were my own. So in addition to tackling a raft of chores, much time was left to think about children, especially David and Dan, and to allow a flood of memories to wash over me.

As so often, blank notebook pages were there to embrace my reflections:

> I think of the little baby, the little dead baby; Dan's twin. I never saw him; they wouldn't let me; the child I never cried for.
>
> Alvah and I living in the Vermont hills. Struggling to exist; the joy, the laughter, the furious lovemaking. And sadly, the lack of any really deep mutual understanding.
>
> Waking this morning to look out my window at Poughkeepsie rooftops, I see not Poughkeepsie, but all of a sudden, the hills of Vermont on a bright October morning of 1933. My a-little-over-a-year-old son, crawling on the floor, pulls himself to his feet by grasping a kitchen chair (barely a month before the time he'll take off across the living room to walk straight, erect, in his short blue knitted pants and white slip-over shirt, into his father's "office," where he was not allowed to touch anything and where his father went to write and couldn't write). So I looked out that October morning over the Vermont hills and knew that I could hold the scene in memory for as long as I live.
>
> I remember leaving that lovely green mountain

state. In thought, I walked once more through the empty rooms. Saw the sun of a late August afternoon fall across the bare floor of my young sons' bedroom. Knew that their beds, their clothes, their toys were in the van. Knew they waited outdoors for the friend's car that would take them and me, their mother, to a train and on to another empty house. In Brooklyn this time. *Will it also be peopled with the kind of honest, hard-working folks that we've come to love here? I know it will.* I stooped down to gently pat the floor on which Davy and Dan learned to creep, to stand, to walk, to run. *Now we must go and not look back.*

Another afternoon: in Brooklyn now, 1937. Hitler was on the radio, and Dan was five. For some reason (curiosity?) he stuck one of my hairpins into the set. The radio sparked, he yowled in pain, and the hairpin shape burned into three of his fingers.

Why do I think of this now? A child's vulnerability? Innocence? Their cluelessness? David . . . That Danbury day I had such a terrible headache, and he brought me a glass of water and an aspirin; his sticking up for Dan at Musgrove School.

Matt raced through my thoughts, decent and caring and consumptive Matt. I was Mrs. Matthew Parker then, and he sweated all day, trudging the streets of Chicago, and couldn't sell his vacuum cleaners. And I stayed for three years and was never in love.

Forman. Marvelous, creative, inspired Forman, who wrote me poems and wanted to love me but couldn't love me. The way he describes me in the book he wrote in 1933, the one recognizing his homosexuality and where he calls me "a cameo done in some strange and disturbing medium. The curved throat, the strong chin, the full expressive lips, the Roman nose." (*I think of it as big! Alvah called me "eagle beak."*) ". . . the low forehead, the sleek lacquer of black hair pulled smoothly over her head to a knot low in the neck—she was like the portrait on a Messina coin, or a bas relief from a Roman theater."

How could I not be flattered? It was the same description he made up on the spot that night in the little Italian restaurant in the Village.

Brooklyn once more. The seamen's strike. David and Dan, hearing chatter from our committee meeting in the living room, crept along the upstairs corridor to spy on us through the railing near the top of the stairs. "Back to bed, boys; sleepy time."

Alvah was in Spain, fighting the good fight, helping to try to save the world from fascism. It was a noble effort. *Too bad the marriage didn't seem as noble to him. Or was it too bad? I don't know anymore.* We were on relief part of the time, and Dan and David sold comics on the corner, and the Puerto Rican boy, Frankie, played with them almost every day, and came with us to the Prospect Park Zoo.

I remember a rainy day, feeling trapped inside when I really wanted to be out and about, and trying to adjust myself to the idea of the rain, and then of Harold alone in an eight-by-ten cell for an entire year (maybe a little longer), of what must happen to the mind ("psychopathic," I wrote of him), but a mind either born with a vast imagination or forced from circumstances to create a whole new world for himself. And from then on, this thought alone would give me pause when I felt some slight frustration at a turn of circumstances, or even a turn of the weather. Or when I think of all the grownups that never had the kind of start in life children need and deserve.

The night in Danbury when I'd come home to tell Dan and David that he had died; the lie I told about how it happened.

I think about other children. The older boys at Musgrove School, the bullies. What circumstances turned them into people who feel a need to lord it over others? What kind of parents? And the three kids in the Nook at Woodstock who fiddled with the paper Halloween cat and pumpkin in the restaurant before their lunch was served. "Don't touch," said their mother. Of course they touched again, while a nervous father paid the check and watched.

And Donald, the boy who got slapped.

David and Dan will be home for Christmas; and my

meandering mind skips back to a Christmas long, long ago. Harry and I were still young enough to thrill at the excitement of every detail that helped speed the time toward the climax of the big day. We pasted chains of red and green tissue paper and draped and re-draped them across the windows and the doorways, finished pasting small calendars on the cards we had made for presents, cheerfully ran errands upstairs and down or back and forth to the grocery store for five or more pounds of brown sugar, carefully scraped the snow off our rubbers on the mat outside before we came into the hall, hung up our coats and hats, and even pinned our mittens on the line near the stove in the kitchen if they were wet. The excitement mounted day by day. If we thought about it at all, there was only one uncertain element about the climax. It would rise to the moment when Dad said, "For your mother." That would be his special gift for her from him.

When he had given her the bottle of perfume he'd bought at Hunt's drug store on his way home Christmas Eve after he'd finally closed his dry-goods shop, what had happened? Out came, "Thank you Dad," and then she pouted the rest of the day. One year he presented her with a Persian lamb cape for church and dress up. "You know you shouldn't have done it. It's too expensive," she said. It went back to the store next day. When he gave her five dollars, he "shouldn't have done it."

And then there was that marvelous afternoon when . . .

I stopped writing in mid-sentence. I had to, could feel Dad's presence and began speaking to him, almost in a whisper. . . .

"You remember that Christmas, don't you, Dad? The one where you gave Mother a caracul cape? The look on your face said it all after she claimed you were foolish to have spent the money. Harry and Verne and Leo and I used to talk about it, you know. The marriage, that is. We often wondered why you put up with her. On second thought, I guess you didn't. After all, you eventually moved out.

"Ah well, spilt milk. Time to plunge ahead, right?

"I guess you know that Laura and I will be driving out to bring the boys home in just a few weeks. They're terribly excited, of course, Christmas and all, Alvah's presents, a little celebration we'll have in this fairly cramped space. Even so, I wish you could be here. We'd make room. And you'd be so proud of these two grandkids you've never known. They're smart boys, growing and changing in front of my eyes, gradually conquering their fears—with a bit of help from their mom, I'm happy to report. If limits are set, kids quickly get a sense of those boundaries. They catch on, make better decisions, figure out stuff more easily, and should have a less difficult time in life . . . whoops there I go, being the pedagogue. Sorry, Dad.

"I haven't told them yet, it'll be a surprise, but Alvah has offered to pay their way to California this next summer for a visit. They'll be thrilled; Hollywood, movie stars, the beaches. . . . Did I tell you their father's writing films for one of the big studios?

"I hope you'll think what I'm about to tell you is a good plan: I won't let David and Dan know about it just yet, but once my credentials are more solidly established as a teacher, I'm thinking about moving the three of us out there permanently. It shouldn't be a complete shock. After all, they've been shifted around probably a dozen times since they were born; Vermont, Connecticut, Brooklyn, Pennsylvania, now Connecticut again, and soon here to Poughkeepsie. Not a great start for kids, but I'm hoping a move to California might bring a greater feeling of permanence to all our lives. And we've got family there; Alvah of course—they talk about him all the time—and getting to know him better would do them good. At least, I hope it would.

"Harry and Forman have been urging me to make the move for quite a while. And now that their marionette theater looks like it's becoming one of *the* places to be seen by the 'cultured *clawses*' (as Harry calls them) and the movie crowd, it might be fun to help out by dressing some of the puppets like I did years back when we were on the road. I'd really enjoy that. If I have time, of course."

Oh, stop equivocating, Mary. You'll make time.

"You know, Dad, I feel wonderfully privileged. What a good feeling it is to soak in a hot tub, get the body back together after a hard day, and be flooded with a gentle love for the past, for the parents I chose. Especially you. And yes, even Mother. I've been thinking about her a good deal, wondering if, quite possibly, like me, she was torn by a conflict of emotions her entire life but without knowing how to tackle them? Did her occasional dramatic 'talents' spill over to relieve her own misery? Her lost possibilities? I remember opening a bureau drawer in her room before one Christmas and finding doll clothes she must have kept since childhood, a beautiful black velvet coat, blue silk lined with ermine at the collar, a pink and white striped bathrobe, delicate underwear, all lace and ribbons. I'm sure she made them all. Perhaps she had wanted to make costumes or get into fashion design? How often our childhood dreams become frustrated.

"Most of all, my dear sons are my treasure. Without them, it too often seemed there'd be little reason for my being here today. They've been what's let me pull myself together, and with that understanding, I feel inside the same joy before the dawn as on that 'Charlie Britton' morning of long ago when the eighth-grade graduation class was going to Round Lake on a picnic for the day, and he and I shared a strawberry pop, and we rowed and blushed and rowed some more. Oh how blessed have I been. . . ."

◆◆◆◆◆

I sat back in the chair, thinking. Dad seemed to have gone. But he'd always be there whenever I had an idea to bounce off him, thoughts or experiences to share. That I could count on.

I focused again on the coming weeks; collecting the boys, their Christmas celebration, the overwhelming joy we'd all feel at being together once more. And after the presents were unwrapped and the dinner I'd make had stuffed them to the gills, I'd tuck them in bed and perhaps read a little. Maybe a chapter of *David Copperfield*, or something from *The Wind in the Willows*; crazy Mr. Toad was always a favorite.

After that, I'd probably retreat to my bed with a cup of coffee and, as I do now, locate a blank page in my trusted friend and whisper,

Hello, battered old notebook. We've been around the block a few times, haven't we? Around a thousand blocks. Dare we look ahead? I suppose trying to predict the future is kind of like skating on thin ice, isn't it?

Oh well, guess I've always been one to stick my neck out. And if I've learned anything, it's that this life tends to throw up more surprises than there are golden daffodils in Wordsworth's crowded field, so why, dear friend, should you and I not speculate a little?

The next years will be productive years, busy years, because through your own efforts and your own experiences of the past, and your own basically hopeful, cheerful nature, you will feel comfortable with life and with most of the people you meet; though you will of course not like them all.

None of your three marriages has been to a man you loved in a deep sense, because you were never able to like yourself in a deep sense before.

Perhaps the time will come when you are free to choose and to attract a man who is also free to choose, who has learned to like himself, because his purpose for being here has taken him through many painful periods before his time of self-realization comes.

Your children will be men. Good fortune may bring grandchildren. You will no longer need to worry about your children, and you will be free to choose.

When this period comes, you can then move with considerable confidence toward a relationship with such a man—and much joy, and much mutual understanding and learning and growth can come from this relationship. For your basic nature is to love and be loved. Had you told me this when I was very young . . .

Hold on, Mary. Are you being reasonable? What if the speculation's a pipe dream? After all, you've let your mind meander down the garden path more than once in your now forty-five years. What's your fallback?

Fortunately, I've always had one. Just before leaving Payne Whitney, I'd let my imagination run free and sketched a small picture of it.

I picked up a much earlier notebook and found the page I was seeking. In the midst of bright blue waves, whipped into almost tooth-like swells by an unseen wind, I'd drawn the figure of a woman. Barefoot, hair cut short above her shoulders, and wearing a long smock-like coat, she stands on a small, circular, and grassy island, sprinkled with yellow flowers.

Below the image I had written:

> Today, tonight, I know there is a little island from long ago. It has snatched me back to its shore more than once.
>
> The island, the little island? Was there once a "magic island"?
>
> Does one create, of sunshine, grasses, and flowers, one's own magic island? Possibly yes. And does the island undergo all kinds of weather, seasons changing from summer to the tears and downpours of late fall? Then into winter, sometimes? The bare trees, stark and black against a magenta February dawn?
>
> I do not own a cottage or a summerhouse
> There is no mountain retreat for times of stress.
> No seaside shack for refurbishing the flesh and soul and mind.

No cave to explore for answers, no nothing outside of me that I have ever found—though often wished for. But somewhere long ago, in a verdant backyard of childhood, when the rains of fall arrived, the sometimes bitterness of winter, the occasional cruelties of spring, and summer sloughs, I clung to the little island. I could almost hold it in my hand, like a jewel, a golden something without a name. I have no name for it besides the magic island.

Sometimes months go by (have in the past, let's say) and I mislay the little jewel, not believing I will ever need to hold it in my hands again, to know it's mine, for I created it, and once created it is forever.

Yes, I guess each of us has the power to create such an island. You create yours; I'll create mine. Somehow the little island will go with me, with or without all those I love. Wherever I go, I'll bring mine. And you must bring yours too.

◆◆◆◆◆

Today, Tonight I know, Ther is an
island- from long ago; it has snatched me
back to its shore more Than one time...

Oh! There is beauty here
Love—hearts that ache
Searching vainly
and alone
among the ruins of fallen houses
and dead loves
for beauty
life is here, and I have been away.[7]

7 This was my mother's last poem in her journals.

48.

Wednesday, March 31, 1982

My mother, Mary Burnett, concluded her life's eighty-three-year-long journey on this date.

Drawing from her diaries and never-before published writing, I've tried to paint a portrait of the life and times of one remarkable woman; a woman who, despite an often-confusing childhood, endured the trials and heartbreaks she encountered by accepting what the mirror of experience taught her. Pulling herself up by her own bootstraps, she dwelt on the past only to understand herself more deeply, to better anticipate a bright future for her sons, and to help others. Especially children.

In this, she succeeded admirably.

Dedicating her later working life to preschool education, she served as director of two nursery school programs: the first in Poughkeepsie, New York, then sixteen years as director of a parents' cooperative nursery school in Santa Monica, California. For two of those Santa Monica years, until managing both jobs became burdensome, she also directed the preschool program for the city of Santa Monica.

Highly respected in her field in Southern California, she was offered the position of assistant director of the preschool program for the entire state, but she declined. Directing the parents' cooperative school while continuing to shepherd my brother and me through our growing years seemed more than enough.

Mary Burnett shortly before her retirement as director of the Santa Monica, California Parents Cooperative Nursery School

At sixty-seven, Mom retired, but only from the workaday nursery school routine. For the next fifteen years, she was a neighborhood grandma to dozens of children, and a confidante and informal advisor to their parents and to a legion of friends. She was a source of support to her nephew, who needed help with his four kids when their mother was going through a personal crisis. And she frequently took two-hour bus rides to Hollywood to spend days snipping cloth and sewing costumes for brother Harry Burnett's puppets. When I decided to give up a well-paying truck driving job to apprentice on *Tom and Jerry* cartoons at MGM (at minimum wage), Mom somehow came up with an extra fifteen dollars a week to help my growing family survive.

Along with working with young children, my mother probably found her greatest satisfaction creating marionettes alongside her adored brother Harry

She read endless books and took painting classes and writing courses.

She made two nostalgic trips east, one to old haunts in Greenwich Village and Danbury, then on to Woodstock, a town with fond memories. For a time, she thought of settling in that stimulating colony of music and art.

My mother's mind was a bubbling stream, drawn from a broad river of memory and experience. She noted people, nature, feelings—everything from "the blue top button of my blue sweater sparkling in the light from the tall wicker lamp;" to "the pigeon cuddling, shivering in the corner of a shelf outside the door of Harry's workshop;" to "the small creatures who shared a Woodstock path with me as I went for an autumn walk."

Her broad connection with life ranged from studying the paintings of Paul Klee, to hours spent drawing a "poetic onion," to nights of cutthroat pinochle at Harry's house; from seeing *Cabaret* with her cousin (and once-hoped-for life partner Forman Brown) to watching Michigan football on TV. She took the process of growing old with a large grain of philosophical salt, relating it not so much to herself as to humankind in general.

Even at seventy, she still entertained thoughts about finding a new companion.

If the notion was romantic, this was because Mom *was* a romantic. But she'd also made peace with herself. She'd burned her bridges and reconstructed her life, and she was content with what she had created. If a man came along, that would have delighted her; if not, that would have been all right too. She had a strong sense of her deepest needs, of when to let go of the past and move on.

The heritage she left for so many, and especially for my brother and me, was imaginative and powerful; one that helped us grow to lead essentially happy and productive lives, and, each in our own way, to pass on much of what she gifted to others. Amazingly, she didn't really tell us how to do it—just offered an occasional hint or a cogent thought. David puts it best: "She didn't need to say much; her example was more significant than any commentary."

March 31, 1982

A LETTER TO MY MOTHER, WRITTEN ON THE DAY SHE CONCLUDED HER LIFE'S JOURNEY

Dear Mom,

I feel completely empty but have already begun to think about you and about your life. So, I'm at the typewriter to record what I remember.

So many images: like when I was six, racing down the block on a "push-o"—a homemade forerunner of skateboards. Remember? You were watching from the window, your heart in your throat as the neighborhood kids and I dodged in and out between cars. And how, when I finally came in and climbed on a chair to watch my friends still scooting around, I tumbled off and banged my head on the floor. As you reached for a washcloth to sponge off the blood, you sighed, shook your head, then laughed at the incongruity of me having survived Brooklyn's unpredictable and sweltering summertime streets, only to crack my head open in our living room.

I think of how hard you fought to keep the nursery school you directed in Poughkeepsie from closing because New York State wouldn't grant the funds to keep it open after the war. How, on your last morning there, when you went in to collect your personal papers, you caught a glimpse of the mayor and a clutch of businessmen—who'd come to inspect the place for its conversion to an office building—anxiously scurrying into the children's bathroom rather than confront you. And how (no surprise), you'd chuckled at the absurdity, even though you had lost your teaching job and the means to provide childcare for working mothers.

I remember you coming to my and David's rescue time and again with support, offering advice and small sums of money. I remember the loving, grandmotherly care you lavished on Rose's and my three kids—especially your care for our mentally challenged daughter, Lisa. We were undergoing financial difficulties during those years and, finding ourselves unable to care for her at home full time, Rose and I were forced to rely on state-supported institutional care for Lisa. Your kindness in having Lisa at your apartment for weekends when she returned for a visit meant so much to us and helped to relieve some of the pressure we felt.

But you expressed this love not only for me and mine but also for almost every child and adult you met, listening patiently to their everyday troubles and concerns—how you were always so genuinely interested in everyone as an individual.

I think of when David and I were little kids, and we'd rub your feet when you'd come home from work, dog tired; of you doing the same for us, or scratching my head when I couldn't sleep, or giving me or David an alcohol rub when we had a fever.

So many memories.

I think of your stories from the years in Vermont, before and after David and I were born, when you and our father scrabbled by on potatoes and not a hell of a lot more—yet how in later years you frequently recalled your great enjoyment of the mountain greenery surrounding our little family and spending time with our rustic, kindly, dirt-poor, moonshine-brewing neighbors.

I think of your own mom, my grandmother Rosa, who hung up the phone on me when I once pretended to be Mickey Mouse. "That sure wasn't nice of her," you said.

Of the men you met who briefly played substitute fathers to David and me: Charlie Petersen in Brooklyn; and Harold Frisbie in Pennsylvania, who you married—out of loneliness, I suspect—and the tragic events that followed, events I didn't even know about until I was in my teens.

Chinese restaurants too! Where you'd take us for a special treat—where it was always chop suey or chow mein.

The three of us went to Coney Island too, remember? David and I still chuckle over our scary ride on the parachute jump.

You had a long and interesting life, Mom. Sometimes terribly sad but also richly rewarding. Even following the long, dark days after you lost Harold, you had the unique ability to climb out of that bleak hole and relate enthusiastically to the world and its people, and to live in the moment without dwelling long on what might have been. You always seemed to find a way to make sense of the craziness around you and make time for absolutely everyone who came into your life.

"Oh, I don't know . . ." I can hear you saying.

Maybe you never found enough time for *you*. I know how hard you worked to understand yourself, and it seems to me you mostly succeeded. You grew to be happy just being who you were. Bottom line, your life was a success, not only on your own terms but also in the eyes of so many others. It's a life that deserves to be celebrated.

How to do that?

Well, maybe someday I'll use this typewriter to write a book about you. You've written throughout your life—journals, diaries, and notebooks full of stories inspired by your diverse and intriguing experiences. (The crappy ones, too, as you've told me . . . I'm grinning.)

If I do write such a book, I'll try damn hard to tell your story the way you would yourself, with candor and honesty, with the tell-it-like-it-is attitude I've so often seen you bring to your dealings with people, adults and kids alike—a straightforwardness tempered by compassion and understanding, and just the right amount of judgment you felt they were ready to accept.

I'd probably craft it something like a novel, because I suppose that's how, having spent much of my later adult years as a writer, I see the story of your life: in chapters. And I'd begin such a book at a black and stormy period in your life, Mom. Maybe the blackest. But it would go on to tell a story that moves beyond those dismal days, tracing your long and carefully considered journey through time as you searched for the goal that seemed to elude you until your early forties: "To do something in this world, to be of some use."

It was a goal you ultimately achieved—in spades!

Witnessing the struggle you went through to reach that goal would, I hope, offer an understanding of the amazing person you always were, and maybe even encourage others along their equally difficult journeys. Yes, it's a book I have to write.

I need to close now, before my tears soak the typewriter ribbon.

Goodbye, dear Mom. I love you. Rest easy . . .

Dan

November 30, 2020

P.S.

While sitting at my computer writing (yep, the cranky typewriter is long gone), I sometimes imagine you perched on a fluffy cloud somewhere in the Great Beyond.

You're probably meditating on the world, it's people and all their problems. And about your own life and all you made of it while you were here. But then I think: no, you're taking it easy now, settling into the good long rest you so richly deserve; then you pause a moment, look around, and out comes one of the same kind of thoughts I found one day while browsing through your private notebooks—the type of idea you expressed in assessing your own life—and one that I'm sure you felt might well serve for anyone:

So now it's time to pack the memories, the madness, the wounds of childhood and youth; time to put them all away, I think, and search, rather, for the sights and sounds from birth that form into a beauty, a riot of color, at times; at others, the calm and soothing blue of certain sky.

And remember: Don't ever take yourself too seriously, for if you do, the world and all its people and all its beauties will elude you.

—Mary Burnett

Acknowledgments

Grateful thanks to Lucia Capacchione for her glowing foreword; to my friends Mary Jackson, Elaine Smitham, Mary Reinholtz, Sara Friedlander, Lisa Jensen, Rebecca Schiller, Sarah Ragsdale, Fred McCormick, and a few others who regrettably didn't add their names to the replies I received—each of whom read early drafts of the manuscript—please know that your comments and suggestions were most helpful; and to my dear sister, Eva Wilson, for also reading early drafts and offering advice; to my project manager, Grace Ball, and her colleagues at Brandylane Publishers, who recognized when saying less often meant saying more. And finally, to Howard McCann, who generously scanned all the photos and other graphic materials.

About the Author

DAN BESSIE was born in rural Vermont, where his parents eked out a hardscrabble existence during the Great Depression. His early years were also spent in New York, Pennsylvania, Connecticut, and finally, Southern California. Following high school, Dan became a shipboard steward in the merchant marine, a longshoreman, and an automobile assembler. Dan worked at various factory jobs to support his wife and children until 1956 when he realized his childhood dream—to become a cartoonist.

Following an apprenticeship at MGM Studios working on *Tom & Jerry*, Dan enjoyed a more than forty-year career in the industry, animating TV commercials and Saturday morning children's programs, like *The Marvel Superheroes*, *Spiderman*, and *Linus the Lionhearted.* When Dan transitioned to live action, he directed a series of patient advice films for doctors' offices. Between 1970 and 1975, he ran his own studio, producing films (including several award winners) for schools and libraries, and co-produced the feature *Executive Action* (starring Burt Lancaster) that dramatized the assassination of JFK.

Dan relocated to Santa Cruz, California, in 1978, and until 1995, he continued to write and direct educational and TV films, including the highly successful *Peter and the Wolf*, featuring Ray Bolger (Scarecrow in *The Wizard of Oz*). Between 1986 and 1987, Dan wrote and directed *Hard Traveling*, a feature film that recalled an incident in his mother's life. By 2006, Dan had authored three published titles and illustrated books written by his former partner, Helen Garvy. The same year, Dan and his wife Jeanne Johnson moved to southwestern France, where they both continue to write and Dan creates cartoons.